FRANCISCAN STUDIES

FRANCISCAN STUDIES

A series of monographs published under the auspices of the Franciscan, Conventual, and Capuchin Fathers of the United States and Canada.

Publication Office, 54 Park Place, New York, N. Y.

Correspondence in regard to contributions should be sent to Editorial Office, Capuchin College, Brookland, Washington, D. C.

ST. BONAVENTURE

The Seraphic Doctor

FRANCISCAN STUDIES

No. 6 SEPTEMBER, 1927

FRANCISCAN MYSTICISM

A critical examination of the Mystical Theology of the Seraphic Doctor, with special reference to the sources of his doctrines

(Essay Crowned by Oxford University)

By

DUNSTAN DOBBINS, O. M. Cap., B. Litt. *(Oxon)*

IN SANCTITATE ET DOCTRINA

New York
Joseph F. Wagner, Inc.

NIHIL OBSTAT
HENRY B. LAUDENBACH,
Censor Librorum

IMPRIMATUR
✠ GUILLELMUS TURNER,
Epus. Buffalensis

Buffalo, N. Y., August 12, 1927

PREFACE

THAT Oxford with its hoary traditions of scholarship should foster literature, history and the classics, is only what is to be expected of her. But to find her encouraging the study of mysticism, and Catholic mysticism at that, is as surprising as it is hopeful in these days, when the much-vaunted 'modern research' has with such apparent triumph ousted the mystics and replaced them by psycho-analysts.

Yet that is what the acceptance of the following Thesis as a fit subject for a Research Degree and its subsequent triumphant 'crowning' really imply. Oxford wisely recognizes that the day of the mystics is *not* over, and by her approval of a further examination of one of the theological wells of the thirteenth century she seems to be anxious to recover some of the sources of her mediaeval greatness. For in those far distant days, Oxford owed most of her fame throughout Europe to those grand Masters of theology and science, her alumni, whose names are commonplace amongst the real scholars of to-day.

Adam Marsh, Roger Bacon, Duns Scotus, Richard Middleton, William Occam, were illustrious sons of Oxford, of whom Oxford to-day is still proud. These men were not only the contemporaries but also the brethren of the great St. Bonaventure, whose Mystical Theology is examined in the following pages. Thus is there an old link between Oxford and St. Bonaventure, and doubtless it was this old memory which prompted the proper authorities to welcome such a Thesis as the present one, offered by a later son of St. Francis.

The subject is indeed a fascinating one: fascinating even to the very modern minds of our work-a-day scientists. For whilst they are perpetually busy upon the scientific examination of material problems, ever and again are they, seemingly, forced to turn aside and discuss the less material problem of God and the soul. For our comfort, several great men of science have already confessed to the existence of God; others have even gone so far as to admit an after-life, and have suggested that there may be in man some power other than that supplied by flesh and blood and the 'grey matter' of his brains. Others have become so 'spiritual' that the plain Christian is bewildered.

But there remain a few teachers in Israel, who speak with the voice of authority on these tremendous questions. St. Augustine,

St. Gregory, St. Bonaventure, still hold the field for Christianity. Their broad and sane principles of Mystical Theology are not merely the sign-posts for saints, but, one may say, the very supports of all true spiritual life. For if holiness be one of the marks of the truly Christian man, then must the principles of holiness be fundamental to the Christian life and the whole of Mystical Theology may be said to be concerned with nothing more nor less than this—the art of holiness.

The main principles of an art — we speak analogously — are fixed and stable, but just as in painting there are various schools of art, so too amongst the Masters and, one may say, the Mistresses, of mystical theology are there various divergencies of method which form a very interesting study for the attentive student. How fascinating such a study may be, becomes apparent when we come to reckon the number of books recently put forth on the subject of mysticism. Not all have been written in the spirit of critical research, and extravagances have abounded, especially where the lamp of faith has not attended.

How refreshing then to recur to one or more of those clear springs, whence flow to us the pure waters of holy knowledge and sound doctrine! The writings of St. Bonaventure which are here examined present us with one such spring, wherefrom we may safely draw.

Fr. Alfred Barry, O. M. Cap.

CONTENTS

AUTHOR'S NOTE

THE following Thesis is the result of post-graduate studies pursued in the University of Oxford during the years 1922-25. It was submitted at the end of that period for the Research Degree, *Bachelor of Letters.* Since the examination, the writer has frequently been asked to publish in book form, and the requests have come from members of the University itself, as well as from a number of scholars interested in things Franciscan.

Many reasons, however, have contributed to the delay. University methods of Research demand the quotation of original works. The results attained are not usually suitable for popular perusal, though they may and do furnish the basis of more popular works.

It is felt that this is true of the present treatise with its multiplicity of Latin quotations. But it is to be questioned whether, published with a translation of these Latin quotations, it would find a wider circle of readers. Indeed, the writer was assured by his Examiners in the University, who were kind enough to recommend its publication, that to attempt a translation would not merely entail a great deal of useless labour, but would also do positive damage to the treatise in the eyes of those who are likely to be drawn to a study of St. Bonaventure's Mystical Theology. For, it was argued, Mystical Theology, in spite of the phenomenal amount of literature that has been produced on that subject during these last few years, is still, on its scientific side at any rate, a subject which only fully-equipped students will approach. To such, the Latin quotations will offer no difficulty. The majority will probably prefer to examine the contributions of the Seraphic Doctor to Mystical Theology in their original form. Be this as it may, the writer himself ventures to think that the scientific study of Mystical Theology should not be attempted until towards the completion of normal courses of Philosophy and Theology, both Dogmatic and Moral. For it is all too often forgotten that the great Mystics have written their works, aided by that special illumination which is part of the reward of their life of stern asceticism. Christian Philosophy and Theology will enable us to enter into their thought and to appreciate rightly their 'difficult sayings.' Hence, no doubt, St. Teresa's preference for a Confessor who was a well-trained theologian. But it will always remain true that, to be in entire sympathy with the thoughts and feelings of a mystic, one must be a mystic oneself. And that, as St. Bonaventure insists in the following pages, means that one must first be an ascetic.

Another reason bids the writer pause before offering translations of the quotations. It is this. Excerpts from an author, if they are well chosen, frequently lead to the direct examination of the major works of the author himself. This has been clearly shown of late years in the case of Bonaventure's great contemporary and friend, St. Thomas Aquinas. Books abound in which St. Thomas is directly quoted in the original Latin. Such books are largely responsible for the present wide reading of the *Summa*. It is matter for rejoicing that the *Summa* grows more popular every day, but it is matter for regret that the works of the Seraphic Doctor, excellently edited by the scholarly Fathers at Quarrachi, are still too seldom opened.

Where Franciscan students are concerned, this is surely a lamentable fact. The Constitutions of the Capuchins commend the study of St. Bonaventure. Nothing has yet been defined which would commend the relegation of his works to unused bookshelves. On the contrary, all Franciscan tradition seems to call for a keener interest in his teaching. For St. Bonaventure gives us a theology which, in its powerful and appealing synthesis of Dogma and Devotion, is eminently suited to the Sons of St. Francis: a theology too, which we should do well to popularize in these days when it is so frequently declared that Creeds and personal religion are mutually antagonistic. The Seraphic Doctor shows so clearly that Dogma is the only sound basis of personal devotion: that Creeds are in truth the very life and breath of true religion, which is the service of God. Bonaventure's rôle in the realm of Catholic teaching is akin to the rôle of that eminent Oxford scholar, Cardinal Newman. It needs no proficiency in mental gymnastics to follow the Franciscan theologian as he writes of the great Christian mysteries. But it does require love. "Nolo Te cognoscere nisi ut Te diligam" prayed St. Bonaventure. He received the knowledge himself and he can still impart it. But with the knowledge comes a greater love of God, and a more deeply-felt yearning after the better things of life.

This work then is sent forth in the earnest hope that Bonaventurian Theology, that rich inheritance of the Franciscan Order, will not be neglected in the present enthusiastic movement towards the illustrious figures of the past. If only the following pages serve to draw a few more students to the *Opera Omnia Sancti Bonaventuræ,* they will have justified the present publication.

The writer's expression of gratitude is due to the Very Rev. Fr. Cuthbert, O. M. Cap., M. A. (Oxon), whose *Life of St. Francis* is now known wherever the *Poverello* is known and loved. At his suggestion the work was first undertaken, and under his kindly direction it was completed for the purpose of examination. Also he is indebted to the Most Rev. Fr. Symphorien, who, before his death, frequently sent valuable help from Rome where he was acting as Definitor-General of the Capuchin Friars Minor. His indebtedness to Professor C. C. J. Webb, Oriel Professor of Christian Philosophy in the University of Oxford, is likewise gratefully acknowledged. In his capacity as University Supervisor, he did much to eliminate from these pages many of those literary defects which may even yet be present. He it was too, who initiated the writer into the difficult art of critical research. The writer's thanks are now offered to another, who does not wish his name to be mentioned, who, in his brotherly devotion, spent many laborious days verifying references and assuring a faithful presentation of the teaching of the Fathers and the Seraphic Doctor. Finally, to the FRANCISCAN STUDIES, whose editor, the Very Rev. Fr. Felix M. Kirsch, O. M. Cap., first suggested the publication of the following Thesis in book form.

FR. DUNSTAN DOBBINS, O. M. CAP.

FRANCISCAN MYSTICISM

A CRITICAL EXAMINATION OF THE MYSTICAL THEOLOGY OF THE SERAPHIC DOCTOR, WITH SPECIAL REFERENCE TO THE SOURCES OF HIS DOCTRINES

DUNSTAN DOBBINS, O. M. CAP., B. LITT. *(Oxon)*

CHAPTER I.

Purpose of this Essay. — Brief sketch of Bonaventure's Life. — His contribution to mystical thought chosen as special subject of research because of the interest manifested in Mysticism in general, and the acknowledgment that Bonaventure is a great mystical writer. — This acknowledgment existing side by side with comparative neglect of his mystical teachng, and the belief that his works contain but rare references to Mysticism.—The diversity of opinion accounted for.—The works from which his doctrines have been gathered.—Reason why his Dogmatic and other writings relevant in our study.—The criterion adopted in selecting his mystical ideas.—Limits in the attempt to trace the sources of these ideas.—Reasons given for declaring him to be primarily indebted to Sacred Scripture and certain Patristic writers.—Defence of his claim to have continued the spiritual traditions set up by St. Francis of Assisi.—Bonaventure's teaching possesses the essentials of Franciscanism in spite of his legalism, and his tendency to the Monasticism repudiated by the 'Poverello.'—The question of possible Joachistic influence upon his thought discussed.—Declaration of method adopted in the development of Essay.

THE present treatise represents an attempt to examine the works of St. Bonaventure, with the primary purpose of discovering his ideas on Mystical Theology, and, within certain limits, the main sources of those ideas. Since his teaching is found scattered throughout several of his works, we have tried to synthetize it, and it is hoped that both in the synthesis itself and in the indication of the sources to which he seems to have been indebted, the principal characteristics of his doctrine will reveal themselves. The remarks added by way of conclusion to the various sections are merely intended to emphasize such characteristics, and, where possible, to point out individuality of thought or expression.

The life of Bonaventure, or, to give him the title consecrated by centuries of use, the 'Seraphic Doctor,'[1] has been written again

---

1. He was also known as 'Doctor Devotus.' 'Doctor Mellifluus;' see Analecta Franciscana, ed ad. Claras Aquas, MDCCCLXXXV, T. I, pp. 258-261.

and again. So too, his place in the history of Theological and Philosophical thought, his position within the Order of Friars Minor, the attitude he adopted towards the various problems which made themselves felt during his Generalate, have frequently formed the subject matter of critical research. It would be difficult to add anything new to what has already been written. Since we wish to concentrate upon his Mystical Theology, we have not attempted to do so.

With regard to the details of his life there is an extraordinary diversity of opinion: a diversity which will continue, as the Quarrachi Editors of his works have declared, until the biography written by Frater Aegidius Zamorra has been recovered.[2] It seems to be generally accepted that Bonaventure was born in the year 1221 at Bagnorea,[3] near Viterbo. According to local tradition, his parents were Giovanni di Fidanza and Maria Ritella. Of his early youth, little is known beyond the incident narrated in his own *Legenda Sancti Francisci,* namely, that whilst still a child he was preserved from death by the intercession of St. Francis of Assisi.[4] It is also to a prophetic utterance of the 'Poverello' on this occasion, 'O buona ventura,' that pious tradition has traced his name within the Franciscan Order.

The nature of the studies he pursued before he received the habit is clouded in uncertainty.[5] Equally uncertain is the date of his entrance into the Order. Wadding,[6] and Père Van Ortroy of the Bollandists,[7] are united in favour of the year 1243, whilst Sbaralea [8] and the Quarrachi Editors [9] have formulated weighty arguments to prove that it was in 1238. To us, this seems to be the more probable date. Bonaventure calls Alexander of Hales, who died in the year 1245,

2. See Opera Omnia, T. X, p. 39.

3. See Salimbene, Catalogus Generalium, in Monumenta Germaniae Historica, T. XXXII, p. 664.

4. 'Ad huius tam venerabilis viri vitam omni imitatione dignissimam describendam indignum et insufficientem me sentiens, id nullatenus attentassem, nisi me Fratrum fervens incitasset affectus, generalis quoque Capituli concors induxisset instantia, et ea quam ad sanctum Patrem habere teneor devotio compulisset, utpote qui per ipsius invocationem et merita in puerili aetate, sicut recenti memoria teneo, a mortis faucibus erutus, si praeconia laudis eius tacuero, timeo sceleris argui ut ingratus.' Op. cit., T. VIII, p. 505.

5. Clop, however, basing his assertions upon the numerous quotations found throughout the works of Bonaventure, declares that he was very well grounded in the liberal arts, Grammar, Rhetoric, Dialectic, Arithmetic, Geometry, Music and Astronomy. See his Saint Bonaventure, Paris, 1922, pp. 4-15.

6. See his Annales Minorum, Romae, MDCCXXXII, T. III, pp. 83 sqq.

7. See Analecta Bollandiana, Bruxellis, 1903, T. XXII, p. 362.

8. See Supplementum et Castigatio ad Scriptores Trium Ordinum S. Francisci, Romae, MDCCCVI, p. 169.

9. See Opera Omnia, T. X. pp. 40-41.

'patrem et magistrum'[10] and according to Franciscus de Fabriano, he was 'licentiatus sub Magistro Alexandro, primo Magistro Ordinis.'[11] Now, even at that period of the history of the Order, every new candidate for admission had to undergo a certain time of probation, and even though we limit that time, in the case of Bonaventure, to a few months, it is difficult to reconcile this last statement of Fabriano with the date assigned by Wadding and Van Ortroy to his entrance into the Friars Minor. There are many reasons why we are inclined to favour a more prolonged connexion between Alexander and Bonaventure. The 'Doctor Irrefragibilis' as Salimbene testifies, had time to determine the personal worth of his pupil: 'Tanta bone indolis honestate pollebat (Bonaventura), ut magnus ille magister frater Alexander diceret aliquando de ipso, quod in eo videbatur Adam non peccasse.'[12] In addition to this, he seems to have taken his pupil through the whole course at Paris, for Bonaventure, when he delivered in due time his own Commentaries on the Sentences, asserted more than once, that he was continuing the teaching received from Alexander.[13] It is admitted that these points prove nothing conclusively, but they indicate a longer acquaintance than Wadding's or Van Ortroy's date can account for.

Whether he entered in 1238 or 1243, it is certain that he was speedily sent to the University of Paris, to study at the Franciscan Friary. There he came under the influence of others besides Alexander of Hales: John of Parma and the Dominican Hugo a S. Charo for example.[14] The best authorities declare that he began to teach privately, that is, under the guidance of a Master Regent, in the year 1245. Three years later, at the command of the Minister General, John of Parma, he began to lecture publicly. He continued to do this till the year 1257, during this time producing much of the literature upon which our study of his Mystical Theology is based.

It was during this time, too, that the quarrels between, the University authorities and the Mendicant Orders arose. The Friars, both Dominican and Franciscan, appealed to the Pope, Innocent IV,[15] whose successor, Alexander IV, attempted to reconcile the opposing parties by promulgating the

---

10. II. S., D. XXIII, a. II, q. III, ad finem, T. II, p. 547.
11. Cited by Sbaralea, Supplementum, p. 143.
12. Catalogus Generalium, in Mon. German. Histor., p. 664.
13. See II S. Praelocutio, T. II, pp. 2-3.
14. See De fontibus Commentarii S. Bonaventurae in Ecclesiastem, art. in Archivum Franciscanum Historicum, Quarrachi, T. X, pp. 257-270.
15. See Denifle, Chartularium Universitatis Parisiensis, Parisiis, MDCCCLXXXIX, T. I, p. 247.

Bull, *Quasi Lignum Vitæ.*[16] On the contrary, his Bull only served to intensify the quarrel. From a mere attack upon the general policy of the Friars, and their refusal to fit in with the time-honoured customs of the University, it changed into a direct onslaught upon their mode of life. Bonaventure had at one time satisfied himself, rather weakly perhaps, that the quarrels were due to jealousy on the part of the secular clergy,[17] but the entrance of Guillaume de Saint-Amour into the lists made him concentrate his whole attention upon establishing the Evangelical origin of the Mendicant ideal. Guillaume, in his *Tractatus de periculis novissimorum temporum,*[18] tried to prove that mendicancy threatened the very existence of true morality and religion. Bonaventure's *Quæstiones Disputatæ de Perfectione Evangelica*[19] aimed at destroying the arguments of the *Tractatus,* by showing that, far from being so many hypocrisies, the various practices of the Friars had been adopted in a sincere effort to imitate Christ.

Unfortunately for the Friars, the Introduction to the *Evangelium Aeternum* written by Gerard de Borgo San Donnino,[20] the staunch Joachite, gave Guillaume and his followers an opportunity which they immediately seized. To the other charges they added that of open heresy. We mention the quarrel here, because it is very often from works written during it that we have drawn much of Bonaventure's ascetical teaching. He was eager to defend the Poverty which Francis had made the corner-stone of his Order; consequently, we find in them a rigidity which is not so apparent elsewhere. The *Tractatus* was eventually condemned by Alexander IV, on the fifth of October, 1256,[21] and later on, in the same year, the Pope promulgated certain decrees which he compelled the University Authorities to obey. The quarrel had delayed the reception of Bonaventure and Thomas Aquinas into the ranks of the 'Magistri.' Their reception was to be delayed no longer.[22] The Pope, however, was not obeyed at once, for it was

16. See Bullarium Romanorum Pontificum, Romae, MDCCXL, T. III, pp. 353 sqq., also Denifle, Chartularium, pp. 279 sqq.

17. See his Determinationes Quaestionum, pars I, quaestio XXVII, T. VIII, p. 355.

18. Contained in Opera Omnia M. Gulielmi a S. Amore, Constantii, 1632.

19. Opera Sti Bonav. T. V, pp. 117 sqq.

20. See Denifle, Chartularium, T. I, p .297. For further information concerning Gerard's book, see infra.

21. See Denifle, Chartularium, T. I. p. 333.

22. 'Secundo, quod fratres Predicatores et Minores Parisiis degentes, magistros et auditores eorum et specialiter ac nominatim fratres Thomam de Aquino de Ordine Predicatorum et Bonaventuram de Ordine Minorum doctores theologie ex tunc quantum in eis esset in societatem scholasticam et ad Universitatem Parisiensem reciperent, et expresse doctores ipsos reciperent ut magistros.' Ibid. p. 339.

not till the following year, October 23rd, 1257, after the promulgation of another Bull, that the University complied with his command.[23]

From this concession, Bonaventure derived very litttle benefit, for in the meantime, he had been called upon to govern the whole Order, in succession to the saintly John of Parma. On the third of June, 1273, he was created Cardinal and Bishop of Albano by Gregory X, in whose election he had played no small part. He did not, however, relinquish his Generalate, until the close of the Chapter which he had convened at Lyons at Pentecost, 1274. On May the seventh, in the same year, the Council of Lyons was opened, and Bonaventure's services were much in demand. After preaching an eloquent sermon on the principal end of the Council, the reunion of the Eastern and Western Churches, he fell ill, and died. This was on the fifteenth of July, 1274. He was canonized on the fourteenth of April, 1482, and in 1587, his name was placed on the list of the Doctors of the Church.[24]

These had been years of labour for the Franciscan General. During his term of office, he had worked incessantly for the benefit of his Order, striving with all his power to make it a well-organized society. With sound organization in view, he had held six General Chapters, that of Narbonne, in 1260, being the most important, and the best proof of his ability in this direction.[25] On the outbreak of the old feud between the University of Paris and the Mendicants, he had resumed his rôle of apologist, composing his *Apologia Pauperum*[26] in reply to the newly-worded accusations. He had checked the growth of Joachimism within the Order: but of this, we must treat in another place. The study of his life reveals him as a man of many abilities. He was more than the dogmatic Theologian, more than the writer of devotional literature; he was one of those rare personalities who combine in themselves lofty ideals with regard to an organized society, and a practical knowledge of the weaknesses of its individual members.[27]

Several facts have inspired the selection of his contribution to Mystical Theology as the subject of special research. In the first place, there is the general interest in Mysticism witnessed during

23. Ibid. p. 366.
24. See Opera Omnia, T. X. pp. 67-71.
25. See Ibid., T. VIII, pp. 449 sqq.
26. Ibid., pp. 233 sqq.
27. All the materials for his life and work will be found in the Dissertationes de Scriptis et Vita S. Bonaventurae, Opera Omnia, T. X. A more complete account is given by L. Lemmens, S. Bonaventura, Milano, 1921. Less critical is the account of E. Clop, Saint Bonaventure, cited above.

the last few years. Secondly, there is the frequency with which Bonaventure's name is mentioned as a great mystical writer of the thirteenth century, without any, or with but little, attempt to give a detailed account of his doctrine. Again, there is the all too common belief, that from the fusion of Scholasticism and Mysticism we can scarcely hope to obtain a living and powerful spiritual teaching.

It is felt that the general interest should extend to Bonaventure's contribution to mystical thought. Interest in the subject there undoubtedly is, and it is so widespread, that in itself, it would furnish the competent critic with sufficient material for a work of great historical, psychological and religious value. Attempts are repeatedly being made to trace the development of Mysticism: to exhibit its powerful influence in human life and thought. Within the Church, endeavours are being made to synthetize the subject in much the same way as Dogmatic and Moral Theology have been synthetized. New editions of the writings judged mystical by common consent appear in abundance; lesser known mediaeval works are gradually being made accessible to the general public. The mystical experience itself is approached from every possible point of view, and there is no evidence for the belief that this great interest is on the wane.[28]

Again and again, Bonaventure's name is mentioned in the enormous amount of literature which stands as proof of the widespread interest in Mysticism. But, as was said, anything approaching a detailed account of his mystical doctrine is rarely given. In critical treatises, his name is all too often connected with works, which, in deference to most recent research, we must cease to associate with him directly. The position he holds is indeed peculiar. On the one hand, there are many, evidently acquainted to some extent with his genuine works, who enthusiastically acknowledge his claim to be regarded as one of the great lights of Western Mysticism. Pope Leo XIII, is responsible for the assertion that in the common opinion of the most learned he is 'facile princeps' in the realm of Mystical Theology.[29] He is referred to as having attempted to establish a school of Mystical Theology,[30] and those who have examined his works for various purposes seem to be

28. It is curious that when non-Catholic writers approach the subject they nearly always look to the Catholic Saint as the highest type.

29. See Acta Ordinis Minorum, ad an. 1890, Romae, p. 177. 'Is, (Bonaventura) postquam maxime arduas speculationis summitates conscendit, de mystica theologia tanta perfectione disseruit, ut de ea communi hominum peritissimorum suffragio habeatur facile princeps.'

30. Mandonnet, Siger de Brabant et l'Averroisme Latin au XIIIme siècle, Fribourg, 1899, p. CXIII. 'Thomas engage son école et son Ordre

agreed that he was preëminently a great Christian mystic.[31] He is quoted as a great figure in the attempt to unite the contemplation of the mystic with the dialectics of the Schoolman,[32] and practically every critical treatise on our own English mystical writings connects them with his name.[33] It must be admitted, too, that works written principally on the spirituality of Continental writers seldom fail to assign an important place to him.[34] In this manner, information of a valuable nature is frequently given. It is also given by the few minor works and articles which have been written with Bonaventure's mystical theology as the central subject of interest.[35]

On the other hand, side by side with this general acknowledgment that Bonaventure finds a place among the greater Mystical Theologians of his century, there is the direct assertion that, though an ecstatic himself, he has no place in his intellectual system for the subject with which we are concerned: that his works contain but rare references to Mysticism.[36] This opinion is traceable, no doubt, to the very indefinite understanding of what is meant by Mysticism, which, like Socialism, seems to admit of an unlimited number of interpretations, as well as to the fact that the Seraphic Doctor did not leave any work which we may

---

dans un puissant intellectualisme philosophique et théologique, tandisque Bonaventure vise à établir une école de théologie mystique en maintenant autant que possible la théologie augustinienne antérieure.'

31. See for example, Jourdain, C., La Philosophie de Saint Thomas D'Aquin, Paris, 1858, T. II, pp. 56 sqq. Hauréau, B. Histoire de la Philosophie, Paris, 1880, Seconde partie, T. II, pp. 5 sqq.; Picavet, F. La place de Roger Bacon parmi les Philosophes du XIIIe siècle, art. in Roger Bacon Essays, ed. by A. G. Little, Oxford, 1914, p. 70.

32. Vaughan, Hours with the Mystics, B. V. c. 2, p. 154. This writer is not trustworthy.

33. Thus, Deanesly, M. The Incendium Amoris of Richard Rolle of Hampole, Manchester, 1915, pp. 58-9; Horstman, C., Richard Rolle of Hampole, London 1895, vol. I, p. XIII; Underhill, E., The Scale of Perfection by Walter Hilton, London, 1923, p. XIX; idem, in the Introduction to The Fire of Love and the Mending of Life, trans. by F. Comper, London, 1914, p.23.

34. See Bremond, H. Histoire Littéraire du Sentiment Religieux en France, Paris 1916, T. II, pp. 137 sqq. Pourrat, La Spiritualité Chrétienne, Paris 1921, T. II, pp. 261-277; Saudreau, La Vie D'Union à Dieu, Paris, 1921, pp. 187 sqq.

35. As far as possible we have obtained all these, and some have proved very useful. We mention the most accessible: Richard, J. Le Mysticisme spéculatif de saint Bonaventure, Heidleberg,1869. This little work is not properly referenced. Many quotations come from works now judged to be spurious. Peralta, V. El pensamiento de S. Buenaventura sobre la contemplacion mistica, art. in Estudios Franciscanos, 1912, T. VIII, pp. 426-442. Longpré, P. E. La Théologie mystique de saint Bonaventure, art. in Archivum Franciscanum Historicum, T. XIV, 1921, pp. 36-108. This is a brief synthesis, without reference to sources, but otherwise very valuable. Tempesti, C. L. Mistica teologia secondo lo spirito e le sentenze di S. Bonaventura, Venezia, 1748. Unfortunately, this is rendered practically useless, since it is based almost entirely upon the many devotional works falsely attributed to the Seraphic Doctor.

36. Chapman, art. Roman Catholic Mysticism in the Encyclop. of Religion and Ethics, ed. by Hastings, vol. 9, p. 95, holds this view. His opinion is endorsed by Butler, in his Benedictine Monachism, London, 1919, p. 115.

quote as a sum of his mystical teaching.[37] If Mysticism have as its end the fullest possible communing of the soul with God in this life; if the mystical experience be regarded as the highest development of the love of God; if, moreover, the science of Mystical Theology be understood to comprehend all those principles of a directive or explicative nature, which are intimately connected with that experience, it must surely be confessed that, scattered though they are, Bonaventure has definite ideas on the subject. Tradition seems to be right when it regards him as a Prince among Mystical Theologians. He recognizes the validity of the experience described by the most saintly among men; he determines the means to be used to attain to that desired experience; he has defined views as to what takes place during the phenomenon which he calls 'ecstasis,' and he is well aware of the particular dangers to which the mystics are exposed.

It is a little disappointing that all his teaching is couched in purely objective language. The nearest approach to information concerning personal religious experience is his confession that he was guided in his own inner life by certain spiritual counsels, which he formed into the *Epistola continens viginti quinque Memorialia*.[38] True, from his works both as Theologian and as organizer of his Order, we may judge his personality, but on the whole, the man has disappeared behind the work.[39] He is not an outstanding figure like St. Francis of Assisi. We are forced by the very nature of the case to treat our subject in very much the same way it is treated in the *Opera*. If Bonaventure views the mystical experience as a possibility in the Christian life, it is with the characteristically objective attitude of the Scholastic.

The works from which his doctrines have been gathered are numerous.[40] There are the Commentaries on the Sentences of

---

37. The Mystica Theologia often attributed to him, and contained in the Vatican Edition of his works, is now proved spurious. See Opera Sti. Bonaventurae, Romae, MDLXXXVIII, T. VII, pp. 699 sqq. Examination of the genuine De Triplici Via, shows that this can hardly be called, in a strict sense, a perfect compendium of all that is best in Christian Mysticism. See infra, chap. III.

38. 'Haec autem, carissime, non ideo tibi scripsi, quia te crederem talibus indigere, sed quia haec eadem collegeram pro me ipso, cernensque meae constantiae parvitatem, cogitavi ea tibi tanquam coadiutori fideli communicare.' Op. cit. T. VIII, p. 498.

39. Gilson, La Philosophie de Saint Bonaventure, Paris, 1924, p. 9. 'Pour saint Bonaventure, plus encore peut-être que pour saint Thomas d'Aquin, on peut dire que l'homme disparait derrière l'oeuvre.'

40. Throughout this work unless otherwise noted, the most recent edition of Bonaventure's writings has been used: Doctoris Seraphici S. Bonaventurae S. R. E. Episcopi Cardinalis Opera Omnia, 10 vols. Ad Claras Aquas (Quarrachi), 1882-1902. This edition has been continually praised by competent critics. See Pelzer, A. Revue néo-scolastique, 1903, p. 98; Gilson, É. La Philosophie de Saint Bonaventure, pp. 40-41.

Peter Lombard, the principal source of his Theological ideas. Herein, Theology is presented as being preëminently one science; there is no sharply drawn distinction between Dogmatic, Moral, Ascetic and Mystical Theology, such as is met with in modern manuals. His method of approaching the great Christian truths makes these major works relevant in a study of his mystical teaching. For him, the *Scientia Divina* is primarily a practical science: 'Pro fine habet tum contemplationem, tum ut boni fiamus, et quidem principalius, ut boni fiamus.'[41] He reveals the direct application of this principle when he continues: 'Nam cognitio hæc iuvat fidem, et fides sic est in intellectu, ut, quantum est de sui ratione, nata sit movere affectum. Et hoc patet. Nam hæc cognitio, quod Christus pro nobis mortuus est, et consimiles, nisi sit homo peccator et durus, movet ad amorem; non sic ista: quod diameter est asymeter costæ.'[42] But a slight acquaintance with his works is needed, to discover that, to Bonaventure, the Church, her dogmas and her ordinances, are all directed towards one end: the arousing of Divine Love, and the desire of attaining to mystic communion with God. All knowledge, even of the most exalted mysteries of faith, the Incarnation and the Blessed Trinity, is vain, he would argue, unless it serves to increase within the soul a more intense love of God: unless it is acquired with a view to perfecting the spiritual life. Consequently, his Mysticism repudiates intellectualism, though it by no means repudiates intellect. No matter to what heights of speculation in the realm of Theological truth his intellect may soar, he remains ever the 'Doctor Devotus,' the 'Doctor Seraphicus,' eager to discover the practical application of the Christian Mysteries.

In the Commentaries and other theological works, the science of Theology is set forth, as proceeding from the Revelation contained in Sacred Scripture and Tradition, safeguarded and explained by the Church throughout the ages. It becomes a coördinated system of revealed truths, with their manifold consequences: a system whose precepts and counsels are founded upon, and inseparable from, such revealed truths. It is the one science that treats in apparently speculative language of the mysteries of faith, and which shews how, by the steadfast practice of Christian virtue, and by the obedience to the impulses of the Holy Ghost, the soul may attain to something more than a mere belief in these revealed mysteries. Bonaventure the

41. I. S. Proem. q. III. T. I. p. 13.
42. Ibid.

Theologian, the Master of the Schools, is revealed in his major works, as the soul striving after Christian perfection, and making all forms of knowledge stepping-stones thereto: as one who would help others to attain to a like end. His dogmatic works are obviously the result of his obedience to two instincts; we might legitimately call them the mystical instincts. The one is a desire to know, as far as is possible to the human mind when aided by grace, the great truths emanating from the Father of Lights; the other is a craving to be united, again as far as is allowed in this mortal life, to the Supreme and Infinite Good, by the bonds of pure, indissoluble friendship. In the following, which may rightly be called his Theological works, the intellect guides, and its discoveries are not despised; but love strives to penetrate still further. It stretches forth in all purity to the God still hidden in the depths of His Being, from the finite intellect.

Dogmatic Works.

1. *Commentarii in quattuor libros Sententiarum Petri Lombardi.*
2. *Quæstiones disputatæ de Scientia Christi, de Mysterio SS. Trinitatis.*
3. *Breviloquium.*
4. *Itinerarium mentis in Deum.*
5. *Opusculum de reductione artium ad Theologiam.*
6. *Collationes in Hexaëmeron.*
7. *Collationes de septem donis Spiritus Sancti.*
8. *Collationes de decem præceptis.*
9. *Sermones selecti de rebus theologicis.*[43]

From the above works too, his Philosophy must be gathered. Next in importance are his

Scriptural Commentaries:

1. *Commentarius in Librum Ecclesiastes.*
2. *Commentarius in Librum Sapientiæ.*
3. *Commentarius in Evangelium Lucæ.*
4. *Collationes in Evangelium Joannis.*

These Scriptural works all become, with the above mentioned theological treatises, relevant in our study, since Sacred Scripture, as we hope to show, is the principal source of his Mystical Theology.

---

43. These are in various volumes of the Quarrachi Edition. Whenever they are quoted, the number of the volume is always noted.

His works pertaining to the Order, defending its interests, or explaining its mode of life, are likewise relevant, as they contain to a large extent his ascetical doctrine; and for him Asceticism is the indispensable preliminary to Mysticism.

WORKS PERTAINING TO THE ORDER.

1. *De Perfectione Evangelica.*
2. *Apologia Pauperum.*
3. *Epistola de tribus quæstionibus.*
4. *Determinationes quæstionum.*
5. *Quare Fratres Minores prædicent et confessiones audiant.*
6. *Epistola de sandaliis Apostolorum.*
7. *Expositio super Regulam Fratrum Minorum.*
8. *Sermo super Regulam Fratrum Minorum.*
9. *Constitutiones Generales Narbonenses.*
10. *Epistolæ Officiales.*
11. *Regula Novitiorum.*
12. *Epistola continens XXV memorialia.*
13. *Epistola de imitatione Christi.*
14. *Legenda S. Francisci.*
15. *Legenda minor S. Francisci.*

To these we must add his sermons, which, although they lack the fire and the striking illustrations of a St. Anthony of Padua, or a Berthold of Regensburg, to mention only two of the many popular Franciscan preachers of his generation, contain a rich spiritual doctrine. Nothwithstanding his many labours in other spheres, his activity in the pulpit was great. His audiences were diverse, and included the Roman Curia, the assembled Chapters of the various Religious Orders, the Universities of Italy and France, and the less learned laity of the large cities of these two countries. His most recent Editors have grouped these sermons under the following headings:[44]

1. *Sermones de Tempore.*
2. *Sermones de Sanctis.*
3. *Sermones de B. Virgine Maria.*
4. *Sermones de Diversis.*

However, it is naturally to the *Opuscula*, gathered together under the title *Mystica*, that we should look with especial care, to discover his ideas on Mystical Theology. The following have been proved authentic:

44. Cf. Lecoy de la Marche, A. La Chaire Française, Paris. 1868, pp. 133 sqq.

1. *De Triplici Via, alias Incendium Amoris.*
2. *Soliloquium de quattuor mentalibus exercitiis.*
3. *Lignum Vitæ.*
4. *De Quinque Festivitatibus pueri Jesu.*
5. *Tractatus de præparatione ad Missam.*
6. *De Perfectione Vitæ ad Sorores.*
7. *De Regimine Animæ.*
8. *De Sex Alis Seraphim.*
9. *Officium de Passione Domini.*
10. *Vitis Mystica.*[45]

To us, it seems that the title *Mystica* has not been chosen too happily. They are not all genuinely mystical works, unless we use the term in a very wide sense. Nevertheless, like the Theological, Scriptural, and other writings, they do contain ideas of great importance. It would be better, it seems, to retain the title 'mystical,' when applied to a definite work, for that which deals expressly with the secret communing of the soul with God. As it is, a few of the above would never be regarded as mystical in these days. The *De Præparatione ad Missam,* is written for priests, and contains counsels for the devout celebration of Mass; the *De Sex Alis Seraphim* is intended for the guidance of those placed in authority as superiors of religious communities; the *Officium de Passione Domini,* is but a collection of psalms and prayers, drawn up according to the pattern of the Roman Breviary. The other works are far more helpful, and have in view a fuller development of personal religion.

To make this treatise as representative as possible, we have tried to use all Bonaventure's writings. But the urgent question is: For what precisely are we to seek in the literature produced by his pen? There is perhaps no subject which has been defined so often and so diversely as Mysticism.[46] Doubtless, to a few,

45. For a right understanding of these Opuscula, it is necessary to bear in mind what he himself has to say regarding his literary method. The method of expounding a doctrine, he declares, differs according to the class of readers addressed. There are the 'intelligentes' and the 'sensuales.' He makes his meaning clear in his Commentary on St. Luke: 'Iterum (beatitudines) in Mattaeo proponuntur pluraliter et in tertia persona, quia loquitur ad intelligentes; in Luca particulariter et in secunda persona, quia loquitur ad sensuales. Ex his colligi possunt rationes aliarum diversitatum; quia pro diversitate audientium, diversimodus est sermo Doctorum, secundum illud Apostoli: (Coloss. iv, 6). Sermo vester semper sit in gratia sale conditus.' Op. cit., cap. VI, n. 63, T. VII, p. 152. Bonaventure manifestly addresses his De Triplici Via, to the 'intelligentes' who are able, with ease, to call to mind the concrete cases included in the extension of the general ideas. His Soliloquium, and De Perfectione Vitae ad Sorores, are written for the benefit of the 'sensuales,' who must be addressed directly, and instructed in details.

46. See the imposing list of definitions gathered by W. R. Inge, Christian Mysticism, London, 1899, Appendix A. pp. 335-348.

the doctrine which has been gathered together here may seem to have no claim to be regarded as definitely mystical. To call Mysticism the Love of God, as some have done,[47] is to express the truth, but it is too wide a definition. Bonaventure's teaching, centring in the possibilities of this love of God, will certainly be included among doctrines judged truly mystical on such a basis. But with what treatment will it meet at the hands of those who only see in Mysticism the opposite of rationalism: the result of the despair of the intellect which has begun to doubt the power of reason, and to dream of direct communion with God: the blind faith which will acknowledge no medium between God and man, either in the sensible universe or in reason: the substitution of effortless contemplation in the place of all endeavour, intellectual and moral? Mysticism has been made to mean all these things and much more; in popular esteem it has even degenerated to the extent of being classed with the patter of the magician.

Now, whilst we despair of offering a definition which will meet with universal acceptance, we must in some manner, establish Bonaventure's claim to have treated of that which may in truth be called Mystical Theology. Amid all the confusion which surrounds the subject, it does seem possible to discover points upon which the best accredited authorities are agreed. This can only be done by the elimination of the purely accidental. In the descriptions of the individual mystics who have tried to translate their experiences and their whole conception of human life into language, even as in the case of those who have attempted, like the Victorines, and Bonaventure, to sketch an objective path to God, there are, and must be, various psychological characteristics which should in no way be identified with the essence of Mysticism. Thus, if, in St. Francis of Assisi, the spiritual Father of Bonaventure, we discover an extraordinary power of finding traces of God in nature, and an intense love of created things, born of the recognition that in His Power they find their origin, and in His Providence their sustenance, we should hesitate before identifying these characteristics, however attractive they may be, with the essence of mystical religion. There have been others who have been mystics, but to whom created things were but so many stumbling blocks. Again, if certain mystics, in a disgust with

47. See the following:—Id. Studies of English Mystics, London, 1906, p. 37; see also Joly, The Psychology of the Saints, London, 1898, p. 38; Tyrrell, The Faith of the Millions, (First Series) London, 1901, pp. 261 sqq. These represent Mysticism as the love of God. This proposition is true, but it is not convertible; for not all love of God is Mysticism, though, as Bonaventure teaches, all love of God contains the rudiments of Mysticism.

the puerilities of a degenerate Dogmatism, or in a depression due to a failure to satisfy their soul's cravings by plunging into a world of speculative thought, have turned away from these things, there are many reasons why we cannot say that herein we have discovered the basis of Mysticism. There have been others, whose Mysticism we may not lightly reject, to whom intellectual speculation, systematized dogma, Scholasticism itself, with its maze of division and subdivision, have been as the very breath of life. St. Thomas Aquinas is no less a mystic because of the energy he expended in composing his *Summa*.[48]

To us it seems that the more correct attitude to be adopted in approaching the problem, is to separate whatever is obviously due to diversity of temperament from the fundamental claim made by the best accredited mystics. That claim, expressed in the widest manner possible, is to an experience of a union with God of a more exalted nature than that enjoyed by the majority of men. The methods by which they have attained to this end have differed in various details, but it is from some form of union with God, known only to those who have experienced it, as Bonaventure declares, and hidden in its nature from those who have not experienced it, that they derive their strength. To establish our claim to have discovered in the writings of the Seraphic Doctor a teaching which may be called mystical in the true sense of the word, we must trace in them the recognition of such a union: we must discover what place it occupies in the whole spiritual life, as well as his directive principles. He has not left us what might be called a strict definition of Mystical Theology. That frequently ascribed to him, though expressive of his own thought, is not his: 'Mystica Theologia est animi extensio in Deum per amoris desiderium.'[49] But he has sufficiently emphasized his idea, that Mystical Theology centres in the vital act of union between God and the soul, effected by grace, and increasing in intensity according to the threefold order of Purgation, Illumination and Perfection, or Union. The primary task of the present work, is to set forth his various ideas on this union, and all relating to it.

We have, however, attempted to go still further, and to trace the origin of his ideas. This must needs be within certain well

48. See The Mysticism of St. Thomas Aquinas, by V. McNabb, O. P., Oxford, 1924.

49. Cited by W. R. Inge, Christian Mysticism, Appendix A, p. 335. It is taken from the spurious work, Mystica Theologia mentioned above. See Vatican Edition of his Opera, T. VII, p. 699. For declarations concerning the spurious character of this work, see Quarrachi Edition, T. X, p. 24.

defined limits. It would have been possible to go to sources other than Scriptural and Patristic teaching: to Platonism and Neo-Platonism for example. There can be little doubt that such influence should be recognized. But, apart altogether from the gigantic proportions such a task would assume, it does not seem absolutely necessary to do this. Bonaventure's knowledge of non-Christian literature, is, for the greater part, indirect. It is mainly through St. Augustine that he is acquainted with Platonism and Neo-Platonism. If such sources are neglected here, it is not because we have adopted the attitude of those who think it absurd, that the writers of the thirteenth or fourteenth centuries should be indebted in any way to non-Christian thought. Bonaventure's debt to Plato or to Plotinus is none the less real because of its indirectness. He has been guided by those who, in turn, drew largely upon the expressed ideas of these two great thinkers, who, in their own way, made the supreme happiness of man to consist in union with the Uncreated Godhead.[50] Bonaventure's first source is Sacred Scripture, which is so intimately bound up with the expression of his ideas on the spiritual life, that it finds its due place in the attempted synthesis. He expressly declares that the first duty of the Theologian is to consult the Scriptures,[51] in this, demonstrating St. Francis' love for this source of spiritual wisdom.[52] His faithfulness to this principle is evidenced by the copious use he makes of the Bible. Texts are joined together to form whole passages; they are made to bear upon every conceivable subject, and the facility with which he quotes, demonstrates

---

50. The following is interesting as showing his attitude not only towards Plato, but also towards Aristotle: 'Indubitanter tamen verum est, secundum quod dicit Philosophus, cognitionem generari in nobis via sensus, memoriae et experientiae, ex quibus colligitur universale in nobis, quod est principium artis et scientiae. Unde quia Plato totam cognitionem certitudinalem convertit ad mundum intelligibilem sive idealem, ideo merito reprehensus fuit ab Aristotele; non quia male diceret, ideas esse et aeternas rationes, cum eum in hoc laudet Augustinus; sed quia, despecto mundo sensibili, totam certitudinem cognitionis reducere voluit ad illas ideas; et hoc ponendo, licet videretur stabilire viam sapientiae, quae procedit secundum rationes aeternas, destruebat tamen viam scientiae, quae procedit secundum rationes creatas; quam viam Aristoteles e contrario stabiliebat, illa superiore neglecta. Et ideo videtur, quod inter philosophos datus sit Platoni sermo sapientiae, Aristoteli vero sermo scientiae. Ille enim principaliter aspiciebat ad superiora, hic vero principaliter ad inferiora.'
Christus unus omnium magister, n. 18, T. V, p. 572.

51. 'Sunt ergo quattuor genera scripturarum, circa quae oportet ordinate exerceri. Primi libri sunt sacrae Scripturae. Qui ergo vult discere quaerat scientiam in fonte, scilicet in sacra Scriptura. Studere debet Christi discipulus in sacra Scriptura, sicut pueri primo addiscunt a, b, c, d, etc.' Coll. in Hex., col. XIX, nn. 6-7, T. V, p. 421.

52. See Celano, Legenda Secunda, cap. LXXI, p. 249 (Ed. P. Eduardus Alenconiensis, Romae, 1906).

not only the width and depth of his scriptural studies, but also his truly Franciscan love for Holy Writ.[53]

It is at times quite erroneously taught that Bonaventure has no use for Scripture, except in its mystical sense.[54] His commentaries disprove this entirely. Throughout these, he continually dwells upon the literal sense of Scripture, and makes no attempt to give a mystical interpretation of every single text. We do not think he ever violates the principle he enunciates in his *Breviloquium:* 'Qui litteram sacræ Scripturæ spernit ad spirituales eius intelligentias nunquam assurget. Attendat autem expositor, quod non ubique requirenda est allegoria, nec omnia sunt mystice exponenda.'[55] It remains true that he has a well balanced predilection for the mystical interpretation of Scripture: well balanced, because his allegories never become authoritative and dogmatic. He had witnessed the evil consequences of making the meaning of Scripture subservient to a present need; the havoc wrought in the Order by the Joachite Friars with their fanciful interpretations would suffice to make him guarded in this respect.[56]

An interesting point to be noted here is his use of the Synoptic Gospels. Appeal is not infrequently made to the Johannine group of writings, as if in these alone can be found the more inward spirituality of the mystics. On the contrary, as one of the best authorities on the subject of Mysticism and its sources has remarked, even the Synoptic Gospels embody the fundamental principles of the Mystical life.[57] It is to them that Bonaventure turns to illustrate the mystical possibilities awaiting a sincere attempt to imitate Christ.[58] Assuming as it does so important a place in Bonaventure's view, it is only natural that we should regard Scripture as the primary source of his Mystical Theology.[59]

The second source of his doctrine is the enormous amount of literature bequeathed to the Church by the Fathers. Their writings, Bonaventure argues, help us to understand Holy Writ.[60]

---

53. See Breviloquium, Prologus, T. V, pp. 201-8.
54. Thus P. Cornely, S. J., Historicae et criticae Introductionis in V. T. libros sacros compendium, Parisiis, 1909, p. 162.
55. Op. cit., T. V, p. 207.
56. One exception is noted at the end of the present chapter. It is in connection with his interpretation of the vision of St. John recorded in Apocalypse V. 7 .2.
57. Baron Von Hügel, The Mystical Element of Religion, vol. I, pp. 31-2. Quoted infra.
58. See infra, chap. III.
59. Whenever we have quoted the Scriptures in English, we have used the Douay Version.
60. 'Ad hanc intelligentiam (S. Scripturae) non potest homo pervenire per se, nisi per illos quibus Deus revelavit, scilicet per originalia Sanctorum, ut Augustini, Hieronymi et aliorum.'
Coll. in Hexaëm., col. XIX, n. 10, T. V, p. 421.

They give valuable testimony to the great spiritual traditions which have remained within the Church, and for him their use becomes an objective act of faith in the Divine origin of these traditions. His respect is for the Fathers as a body; he is convinced that all cannot err on any particular point.[61] But individuals may do so. Consequently, Bonaventure's reverence never degenerates into a blind credulity. Even his beloved Augustine is not credited with infallibility.[62] Of course, he has quoted the writings of others besides those whom we shall mention.[63] In declaring that he is indebted principally to Pseudo-Dionysius,[64] Augustine, Gregory, Anselm, Bernard, and to those two scholars of the Abbey of St. Victor, Hugo, and Richard, we have been guided, not only by the frequency with which he quotes all these, but also by his expressed predilection for their writings. They have not all influenced him in the same way. We feel convinced that, in spite of the difference of outlook upon various subjects manifested in their works, it is largely from them that Bonaventure has derived his ideas. Augustine's principal contribution to his thought is the vast dogmatic background of religious life. Augustine it is who unites in himself the best qualities of Plato and Aristotle.[65] Through the influence of Gregory and Bernard, he has become eager to find the practical bearings of all dogmatic truth. Pseudo-Dionysius and Richard have led him to the heights of contemplation. He writes: 'Tota sacra Scriptura hæc tria docet, scilicet Christi æternam generationem et incarnationem,

61. 'Firmitas fidei est ex testificantium concordia plena, quae est in tribus: in eloquiis Scripturarum, in decretis Conciliorum, in documentis Sanctorum.' Coll. in Hexaëm., col IX, n. 19, T. V, p. 375.

62. He differs from him on various points; see II. S. D. XVII, A. I, q. III, T. II, p. 417; ibid., D. XIII, a. 1, q. 1. p. 312.

63. A full account of all the writings used by Bonaventure will be found in the Quarrachi Edition of his works, T. X, pp. 265 sqq.

64. The literature concerning Pseudo-Dionysius and his works is enormous. He was in all probability a Syrian monk, of about the year A. D. 500, who chose to issue his profound treatises under the name of Dionysius the Areopagite, (Acts, XVII, 34) thus gaining for them a quasi-apostolic authority. Their authenticity seems to be undoubted by Bonaventure, who gives to 'Beatus Dionysius' the reverence given by many previous writers. John Scotus Eriugena translated the works of this elusive character into Latin, at the instance of Charles the Bald, and was himself profoundly influenced by his thought. Careful comparison of Bonaventure's quotations from the Dionysiaca, with the Latin Versions of Eriugena and others, proves sufficiently that it was through the medium of this translation that the Seraphic Doctor became acquainted with the works. Eriugena's translation will be found printed in Migne, P. L., T. CXXII, cols. 1030 sqq. J. de Ghellinck, S. J., in his Le Mouvement Théologique du XIIe siècle, Paris, 1914, p. 70, declares moreover, that this was the version used by Hugo of St. Victor, for his Commentary, and by St. Thomas Aquinas, etc.

65. 'Uterque autem sermo, scilicet sapientiae et scientiae, per spiritum sanctum datus est Augustino, tanquam praecipuo expositori totius Scripturae, satis excellenter, sicut ex scriptis eius apparet.' Christus unus omnium magister, n. 19, T. V, p. 572. Cf. S. Bonaventura Doctor Seraphicus Discipulorum S. Augustini Alter Princeps, P. Dominicus Facin, Venetiis, 1904.

vivendi ordinem, et Dei et animæ unionem. Primum respicit fidem, secundum mores, tertium finem utriusque. Circa primum insudare debet studium doctorum, circa secundum studium prædicatorum, circa tertium studium contemplativorum. Primum maxime docet Augustinus, secundum maxime docet Gregorius, tertium vero docet Dionysius. Anselmus sequitur Augustinum, Bernardus sequitur Gregorium, Richardus sequitur Dionysium, quia Anselmus in ratiocinatione, Bernardus in prædicatione, Richardus in contemplatione. Hugo vero omnia hæc.'[66] There are several reasons, however, why we cannot concentrate entirely upon the last mentioned: reasons which will manifest themselves in the examination of Bonaventure's ideas.

It will be noticed that all these, with the single exception of Pseudo-Dionysius, with whom he was acquainted only through the medium of a Latin translation, are Western writers. With the Greek Fathers he does not seem very familiar. St. John Chrysostom and St. John Damascene are frequently quoted, as their works had recently been made accessible to him.[67] To the other Greek Fathers, references are decidedly fewer in number. We very much doubt whether he was able to go directly to any Greek source, for we can find no real evidence for his knowledge of the language. One author professes to have been sufficiently persuaded that Bonaventure knew Greek.[68] But his persuasion seems to be traced to the numerous quotations from the Greek Philosophers which he has found throughout Bonaventure's *Opera*. These prove nothing. Aristotle[69] had already been used as extensively by Alexander of Hales; with Plato and Plotinus he could become acquainted through St. Augustine. It is a minor detail, but we do not think that any importance should be attached to his quotations of the Greek Philosophers.

We have also claimed throughout this Essay, that Bonaventure has been directly influenced by the spiritual traditions initiated by St. Francis of Assisi. This is probably one of the most difficult points to establish. The two seem so diametrically opposed. Francis is the saint to whom, it is frequently asserted, all legislation is repugnant; he stands for a freer spiritual tradition

66. De Reductione art. ad Theol., n. 5, T. V, p. 321.

67. See J. de Ghellinck, op. cit., pp. 245 sqq; compare Haskins, C. H., Studies in the History of Mediaeval Science, Harvard Univ. Press, Cambridge, 1924, pp. 206 sqq.

68. Clop, Saint Bonaventure, pp. 6-7.

69. For the works of Aristotle known to the Scholastics, and for the translations extant at the time of Bonaventure, see Jourdain, C., Recherches sur les anciennes traductions latines d'Aristote, Paris, 1843, pp. 21 sqq. Also Haskins, C. H., op. cit., pp. 223 sqq.

than that which could possibly be known to Bonaventure, who is above all things a legalist. Francis, without being illiterate—his magnificent *Canticle of the Sun,* and his knowledge of the poetry of his day, make it impossible for us to associate illiteracy with him—had not the scientific training of the Schools;[70] Bonaventure is the Master of the University of Paris, and wholeheartedly adopts the scientific methods of his day. Francis cries out for the perfect observance of his Rule, 'simpliciter et sine glossa;'[71] and he will leave it to the individual conscience to dictate to what extent it is binding. Bonaventure calmly interprets the Rule, and determines its degrees of obligation.[72] Francis steadfastly repudiates Monasticism;[73] Bonaventure undeniably monasticises his Order to no small extent. Francis refuses to see the worldly wisdom of large and well appointed houses for the Friars;[74] Bonaventure, in deference to such worldly wisdom, forcibly defends them.[75]

Before declaring that the spirituality of the two must needs differ because of these and similar contrasted characteristics, it is as well to remember the state into which the Franciscan Order had fallen, at the time when Bonaventure was called upon to rule over it. In the first place, it had increased to an almost incredible degree; difficulties which could hardly have been visualized by the 'Poverello' were continually making themselves felt most acutely. Far from declaring that Bonaventure's methods of meeting the problems were decidedly unfranciscan, we are inclined to think that he dealt with them with the spirit of Francis himself. The increase of the Friars had brought to the Order many who could in no way be compared with the devout men who surrounded the 'Poverello' during his lifetime, and whose power among the people was due to their constant communings with God. The main end of the Order was still the preaching to the people. What prayer and devotion did for many of the first Friars, could, for a later generation, only be supplied by study. It was a recognition of the fact that there can be but few Fran-

---

70. For further evidence on this point, see Felder, Histoire des Études dans l'Ordre de saint François, Paris, 1908, pp. 66 sqq.
71. See his Testament, ed. Sabatier, in Speculum Perfectionis, Paris, 1898, p. 313.
72. Expositio super Regulam F. F. Minorum, T. VIII, pp. 391 sqq.; also Constitutiones Generales Narbonenses, ibid. pp. 449 sqq.
73. See infra.
74. See the account of the manner in which he regarded the building of a large house for the Friars by the people of Assisi, in Speculum Perfectionis, cap. VII, ed. Sabatier, p. 17.
75. See Determinationes Quaestionum, Pars II, Quaestio XV, T. VIII, p. 567: 'His de causis magis diligimus magnos conventus quam parvos, videlicet, quia maior disciplina potest ibi servari,' etc.

cises, but few like to his companion Brother Leo, that urged Bonaventure in his promotion of scientific training. Apart from this, St. Francis had never intended his followers to be ignorant men; he merely forbade them to make study their primary end.[76] Study of whatever kind was to be made subservient to prayer, but not entirely excluded. Bonaventure's promotion of studies within the Order did not militate against the desire of its Founder. Francis wanted his Friars to be effective preachers. For the majority of men, effective preaching could only follow upon the scientific study of Theology.[77] Theology, in turn, depends for its right understanding upon many subsidiary sciences. These must all be included, argues Bonaventure, in the mental equipment of the true Friar who is to fulfil his vocation within the Church. His *Reductio artium ad Theologiam,* a little work whose title is sufficiently indicative of its contents, admirably illustrates his reasons for urging his Friars forward in the quest for knowledge.

Granting the validity of his arguments, is it not likely that his own scholastic attainments would remove him to a sphere in which he could not fully appreciate the simple spirit of Francis? The answer to this objection will be found in his works. That which made Francis the powerful Saint he was, was his love: love which led him to dedicate himself and all else to God. Bonaventure has not done otherwise. It is the spiritual inheritance received from Francis, which makes him write: 'Non est perfecta cognitio sine dilectione,'[78] and again, 'Curiosus autem devotionem non habet. Unde multi sunt tales, qui vacui sunt laude et devotione, etsi habeant splendores scientiarum. Faciunt enim casas

76. We are well aware that we have touched upon a much debated point. Certainly Bonaventure did not formally disregard his Founder's wishes. His sincere belief seems to have been that Francis wanted his Friars to study, though to study with devotion. Thus, he writes in his Legenda Sti. Francisci, cap. XI, n. I, T. VIII, p. 535: 'Quaerentibus aliquando Fratribus, utrum sibi placeret, quod litterati iam recepti ad Ordinem intenderent studio sacrae Scripturae, respondit: Mihi quidem placet, dum tamen exemplo Christi, qui magis orasse legitur quam legisse, orationis studium non omittant nec tantum studeant, ut sciant, qualiter debeant loqui, sed ut audita faciant, et cum fecerint, aliis facienda proponant.' See also his Epist. de tribus quaestionibus, n. 10, T. VIII, p. 334. Modern writers, using the material at hand, have widely differed. Jörgensen, St. Francis of Assisi, trans. by T. O'Conor Sloane, London, 1912, pp. 226-235, represents him as distrusting, but not wholly condemning scientific study; Sabatier in his Vie de Saint François d'Assise, Paris, 1894, pp. 318 sqq., thinks Francis viewed it as the worst enemy of his Order; F. Cuthbert, St. Francis of Assisi, London, 1921, pp. 346 sqq., emphasizes his plain disregard of learning for its own sake, and considers that he only valued knowledge in its relation to character and action. Felder, Histoire des Études dans l'Ordre de Saint François, pp. 72 sqq., makes Francis positively encourage studies.

77. 'Sanctus Franciscus, ex quo volebat Fratres suos in praedicatione et studio per consequens exerceri.' Expositio super Reg. cap. III, n. 2, T. VIII, p. 407.

vesparum, quæ non habent favum mellis, sicut apes, quæ mellificant.'[79] Such sentiments as these are expressed continually in his works. We do not declare categorically that St. Francis expressly wished to have eminent Theologians in his Order; but we feel it perfectly safe to say that had he wished them to add to its prestige in the eyes of the world, he would have desired them after the pattern of Bonaventure. When we find Bonaventure, both in theory and in practice, combining the highest intellectual attainments with the steadfast purpose of making all endeavour, intellectual and other, subservient to the spirit of prayer, to the love of God, we are unable to discover any barrier to his inheritance of the true Franciscan spirit.

Nor could his Scholasticism, too often represented as an enemy of mystical religion, prevent his full appreciation of that same spirit. After all, Scholasticism is only a mode of expression. When he is said to have attempted, with Hugo and Richard of St. Victor, to unite Mysticism and Scholasticism, there seems to be the implication that they are poles asunder: or at least that they do not usually exist side by side. It is perfectly true that Scholasticism, the outcome of the rational tendencies of the times, gravitated in the direction of the intellectualism which the author of *Christian Mysticism* has rightly judged to be the enemy of mystical religion.[80] Also, it seems to be an indisputable fact, that it frequently ran the risk of degenerating into a system altogether divorced from concrete human life. All this is acknowledged. But the generally recognized sanctity of men like Albertus Magnus, Alexander of Hales, Thomas Aquinas, and the earlier writers of both Mendicant Orders, is sufficient proof that scholasticism is not the very antithesis of Mysticism. What was best in Scholasticism was inspired by mystical devotion. We may, and do, very often regret the form in which some of Bonaventure's finest spiritual conceptions appear, but because of his phraseology, we can hardly, in justice, declare that he has missed anything of the inner spirituality of St. Francis of Assisi. In fact, the scholastic method continued to be that of many succeeding generations of mystical writers.

---

78. I. S. D. X., a. I, q. II, ad 1mum T. I, p. 197.

79. Coll. in Hex., col. I, n. 8, T. V, p. 330. The same ideas are expressed in the following places: Itinerarium, prologus, T. V, p. 296; Soliloquium, cap. II, n. 5, T. VIII, p. 46; Sermo V de Dom. II post Pascha, T. IX, p. 304. This last is very beautiful and worthy of full quotation: 'Vae illis! qui toto tempore vitae suae student in logica, physica vel in decretis, et nihil saporis in ista scientia inveniunt; si in ligno crucis Christi studerent, scientiam salutarem ibi invenirent.'

80. W. R. Inge, Studies of English Mystics, p.32.

Those who have treated of Bonaventure and his relationship to the true Franciscan ideal, have emphasized his attitude towards studies. To us it appears that if there had been any element preventing his inheritance of the spirit of the 'Poverello,' it would have been an unnecessary legalism, an unnecessary reversion to Monastic principles. These appear to be more opposed to Franciscanism than anything else. For Francis's message to his Friars, was that they should give themselves up willingly to the service of God and their fellow men; it was after the careful examination of the well formulated Rules of the older Monastic Orders, that he drew up his own Rule of life.[81] He fully appreciated the value of other Orders, but the dominant characteristic of the spirituality which he wished to embody in the Community of Friars was that of freedom. So long as he had those around him who could use that freedom as it was meant to be used, he could find little to regret in the consequences of his principle.

When Bonaventure entered the Order, and when he became General, the situation had very much changed. His legalism, and his tendency to Monasticism, were both the result of unfortunate circumstances. They were necessary, if the Order was to be saved; they were necessary if any element in the Franciscan ideal was to be conserved. As General of the Order, he had his finger on the very pulse of Franciscan life in his day, and he saw that the existence of the Order as a society, based upon the vow of absolute poverty, was threatened from without by economic conditions, and from within, by the never-ending quarrels among the Friars themselves, as to what was, and what was not, according to the mind of Francis. Added to this, there were the lamentable abuses of so-called Franciscan liberty, of which he was the witness. Only legislation of the most subtle form, centring in the vow of poverty, and having a direct bearing upon the obligations of the Friars in their many spheres of activity, could meet the problems of the hour, and quiet the consciences of those who

81. Celano, Legenda Prima, cap. XIII, ed. Alencon, p. 34, narrates how Francis went to Rome to obtain Papal confirmation of his Rule of Life, and was charitably received by a certain Joannes de Sancto Paulo, who evidently enjoyed a certain amount of influence in the Roman Curia. He continues: 'Verum, quia homo erat providus et discretus, coepit eum de multis interrogare, et ut ad vitam monsticam seu heremiticam diverteret suadebat. At sanctus Franciscus suasionem eius humiliter, prout poterat, recusabat, non persuasa despiciendo, sed alia pie affectando altiori desiderio ferebatur.' See also his answer to certain Friars at the Chapter of Mats: 'Fratres mei, fratres mei, Dominus vocavit me per viam simplicitatis et humilitatis et hanc viam ostendit mihi in veritate pro me et pro illis qui volunt mihi credere et imitari. Et ideo volo quod non nominetis mihi aliquam regulam neque sancti Benedicti, neque sancti Augustini, neque sancti Bernardi, neque aliquam viam et formam vivendi praeter illam quae mihi a Domino est ostensa misericorditer et donata.' Spec. Perfectionis, cap. 68, ed. Sabatier, p. 132.

were disturbed. Francis's simple Gospel Rule must fit in with the needs of an organized body. With these convictions, Bonaventure proceeded to effect a reconciliation. Corporate and individual poverty, the specific element in the Franciscan ideal, was safeguarded by the well defined doctrine of use. The Friars were not to be owners of property. This was vested in the Holy See. Only the simple use of all things, houses, lands, and libraries, was allowed them.[82]

On the other hand, his tendency to Monasticism was the result of an endeavour to check the many abuses within the Order itself. He found it impossible to grant to so large a body of men the same liberty of action enjoyed by Saint Francis and his first companions. He does not gloss over the faults he finds existent when he assumes the Generalate, but he emphasizes their serious nature in the first letter he had to write on assuming his new office. The greed and laziness of many of the Friars, their familiarities which gave rise to so many scandals, their eagerness to obtain legacies, their constant unnecessary wanderings to and fro, all these are abuses which he denounced in vigorous language.[83] But he does this without the bemoanings of the 'Spirituals,' who are sweeping in their denunciations, and whose writings are characterized by an almost inhuman perfectionism. Bonaventure realizes the gravity of the evils he denounces, but can make the hopeful assertion: 'Plurimi reperiuntur, qui non sunt culpabiles in aliquo prædictorum.'[84] The writings of the 'Spirituals,' which are responsible for many mistaken conceptions of Bonaventure's influence on the Order, contain nothing so well balanced as this.[85]

In the face of such dispiriting conditions, Bonaventure's only course lay in recalling the whole Order to a stricter internal and external discipline: to a discipline ruling lives more monastic than those of the Friars were intended to be. Liberties hitherto enjoyed and found capable of so many abuses were withdrawn;

---

82. See Constitutiones Narbonenses, Rub. III, T. VIII, p. 452; Apologia Pauperum, cap. XII, ibid., p. 323.

83. 'Sane perquirenti mihi causas, cur splendor nostri Ordinis quodam modo obfuscatur, Ordo exterius inficitur, et nitor conscientiarum interius defoedatur; occurrit negotiorum multiplicitas, qua pecunia, nostri Ordinis paupertati super omnia inimica, avide petitur . . . Occurrit quorundam Fratrum otiositas. . . Occurrit exagatio plurimorum. . . Occurrit importuna petitio. Multiplicatio familiaritatum. . . improvida commissio officiorum. . . sepulturarum et testamentorum avida quaedam invasio. . . mutatio locorum frequens et sumptuosa,' etc., etc. Epistolae Officiales, ep. I, n. 2, T. VIII, pp. 468-9.

84. Ibid.

85. See the Arbor Vitae Crucifixe Jesu of Ubertino da Casale, ed. Venetiis, 1485. To Ubertino da Casale, Bonaventure is only a cowardly compromiser. Lib. V, cap. V, f. 427.

obligations with regard to the recital of the Divine Office in choir were carefully worded so as to admit of no wilful misunderstanding; new customs were introduced to rule the normal day spent within the Friaries; journeys which hitherto had required only the permission of local superiors were to be undertaken only after referring the matter to those in a more central position of authority.[86]

It cannot be doubted that his spirituality is thereby monasticised to a certain extent, but we think that it remains fundamentally Franciscan. Bonaventure must be credited with an attempt to save what could be saved of the Franciscan ideal, in times of distress. When possible, he makes a deliberate effort to safeguard the essential elements of Franciscanism. With St. Francis he shares a deep reverence for Holy Writ, and encourages its study among the Friars.[87] As for Francis, so for him, the Figure of Christ is the centre of devotion. With St. Francis, he shared an abomination for idleness parading under the cloak of contemplation, and a zeal that the Brethren should work for their sustenance.[88] Finally, with Francis, he exhibits a love of Nature and all created things, because of their association with Christ, the Lord of the World. These are but few of the reasons why we have insisted upon connecting his spiritual ideas with the traditions associated with the 'Poverello.' Had his Monasticism been due to anything but the deplorable conditions he found, we might have been otherwise persuaded.

Lest there should be any misunderstanding due to our dwelling upon this point, a word must be added. It is fully recognized that Monasticism will produce and has produced Saints: Saints whose service to Religion and Humanity is appreciated by every historian.[89] But we are concerned with types of spirituality, and the monastic type differs very much from the Franciscan. A St. Bernard and a St. Francis, both mystics, both powerful in their own way, could be contrasted in many details. The one insists

86. See Constitutiones Narbonenses, passim, T. VIII, pp. 449 sqq.

87. Indeed, for Bonaventure, Scientia Sacrae Scripturae and Scientia Theologiae are synonymous. See his Breviloquium, Prologus, T. V, pp. 201 sqq.

88. Laziness is the vice of which he seems to make most frequent mention. See Legenda Sti. Francisci, cap. V, T. VIII, pp. 517-8, where he denounces it, with especial reference to the good example given in this dierction by St. Francis of Assisi. Compare Epistolae Officiales, ep. I, cited supra. For further information concerning Francis' vigorous actions against laziness, see Celano, Legenda Secunda, cap. CXVIII, ed. Alencon, p. 289.

89. See Montalembert, C. F. Les Moines d'Occident, Paris, 1860; Hannay, J., Spirit and Origin of Christian Monasticism, London, 1903; Lecky, W., History of European Morals, London, 1911.

upon an absolute seclusion from the world of men, and to guarantee that seclusion for future generations he provides his monks with places well adapted in every respect to the fostering of the contemplative spirit. The other gives a practical example of how it is possible to live literally in the world, and yet to struggle against its current; he will allow his Friars no guarantee of future security. Even the peaceful possession of the places wherein they dwell is denied them. Bernard and Francis stand for two modes of approach to the fulness of the Christian life. It is undeniable that both modes can lead to the desired end.

Frequent mention has been made of the 'Spirituals,' and we know that these were in no small degree agitated by the strange doctrines emanating from that equally strange character, Joachim of Flora. It must be decided whether any of Bonaventure's mystical ideas are traceable to this source. The class of Friars known as the 'Spirituals' arose out of the struggles within the Franciscan Order, which lasted well-nigh a hundred years after the death of the 'Poverello.' These struggles raged around the Rule of St. Francis, whereby the Friars were legally bound, and his Testament, which carried with it a moral obligation.[90] The Rule declared that the life of the Friars was to be a simple observance of the Gospel of Christ, according to the three vows of Poverty, Chastity and Obedience. They were strictly enjoined not to receive coin or money, either personally or through the medium of others, and were forbidden to appropriate to themselves any place or house or any other thing. In the Testament, they were warned against the receiving of churches and dwellings built for them in a manner not befitting the poverty they had vowed. Even to save themselves from persecution, they were not to apply to the Roman Curia for letters, and all glosses upon the Rule were expressly forbidden. Francis appealed for a simple and plain observance. The contents of the Rule being such as they were, it was inevitable that many should find the restrictions expressed in the Testament irksome in the extreme. To the immediately succeeding generation of Friars, the Rule, without glosses, seemed impossible of observance. Times had changed; so too, had the spirit of those who were swelling the ranks of the followers of Francis.

---

90. The Rule, approved by Honorius III on November 29th, 1223, will be found, together with the Testament in the Opuscula S. Francisci, ed. Quarrachi, 1904. Sabatier has reprinted the Testament in his edition of the Speculum Perfectionis, pp. 309 sqq. One of the best English Translations has been given by P. Robinson, The Writings of St. Francis of Assisi; Philadelphia, 1906.

One party of Friars immediately made its influence felt. It made war, not so much upon the letter of the Rule, as upon the Testament which represented Francis's direct repudiation of the measures they were anxious to adopt. With the Testament out of the way, they could, with ease of mind and with due regularity, multiply the relaxations of the Rule according to the exigencies of the hour. Only four years after Francis's death, Gregory IX, in his Bull *Quo elongati a sæculo,*[91] replying to a number of questions submitted to him by the Minister General and his delegates, placed the desired power in their hands. The Bull quite rightly declared that the Testament did not carry with it the force of law, and it added, that the Rule itself only demanded a literal observance of the Gospel counsels expressed therein, by way either of command or of prohibition. The embarrassment of those to whom the romanticism of Francis was all in all, may well be imagined. To them, the Pope's action, and the solicitations of the more worldly-minded Friars which were responsible for the promulgation of the Bull, were the direct betrayal of the dearest wishes of their Founder.

Their embarrassment was to increase with the coming of Brother Elias in 1232 as Minister General. Under his influence, the Order lost still more of its primitive character. A vast number of the Friars settled down to a mode of life impossible to reconcile with the original Franciscan ideal. Their relaxations, their lands and possessions, their sumptuous dwellings, caused them no disquiet, however, since for every relaxation of the Rule they could point to a Papal dispensation.[92] Without going to such extremes, there were others, of whom Bonaventure was to become the leader, to whom unnecessary relaxation was repugnant. The needs of the time demanded certain glosses, but they were anxious to safeguard the spirit of their Founder. To the more zealous these were but compromisers. The 'Spirituals' claimed Francis's own authority for the direct refusal of all relaxations, and all interpretations of the Rule. Theirs was undoubtedly the distress of men who had embraced a mode of life, with their imagination fired by the Christ-like example of the 'Poverello.' In the one Order wherein they could reasonably hope to follow in his footsteps, they found their way barred by what they fiercely denounced as so many attacks

91. Printed in the edtion of the Speculum Perfectionis, by P. Sabatier, pp. 314 sqq.

92. Interesting details as to the many relaxations of the Friars are given in Eccleston's De Adventu Minorum in Angliam, ed. A. G. Little, Paris, 1909, p. 40.

upon Christ Himself. In their tribulations they betook themselves to lonely hermitages, and there gave themselves to the study of a literature which admirably corresponded with their feelings. This was the literature produced by Joachim of Flora.

Joachim, whose life and works have formed the subject-matter of detailed studies,[93] was born at Celicio near Cosenza, about the year 1132. He seems to have travelled in Palestine as a pilgrim, and in Italy as a preacher of the Gospel, before settling down as a Cistercian monk. It was as a monk, that he embodied the results of his Biblical studies in the three works: *Concordia Novi ac Veteris Testamenti, Apocalypsis Nova, et Psalterium Decem Chordarum.* In these works, the pseudo-Prophet mapped out a scheme of the world's history, which he had deduced from the Bible. Though there is a deal of confusion and obscurity in the details, and the main theme is overlaid with a bewildering complication of allegory, his fundamental idea is simple enough.

It is, that there are three Epochs in the history of the world from the Creation to the Last Judgment, during which the world is under the successive special government of the three Persons of the Blessed Trinity. Each Epoch is marked by its own characteristics, and forms a stage in the progress of the world towards the final consummation of all things. The first Epoch, from Adam to Christ, and already a thing of the past, had been under the jurisdiction of the Father; the second Epoch, beginning with Christ, was about to close at the time when Joachim wrote. It was upon his description of the third and last Epoch, about to begin, that the 'Spirituals' concentrated their attention. This was to be a new dispensation, in which disciplinary institutions would be superfluous, inasmuch as men's lives would be ruled according to the Spirit. It would be the Epoch of the Holy Ghost, since under His influence, a spiritual understanding of the Gospel would reign in place of the letter. In the spiritual regeneration of mankind, a principal part was to be played by an Order following closely in the footsteps of Christ.[94]

Ideas such as these, handed down by a man of great sanctity, came as light to the 'Spirituals' in their gloom. They themselves were the heralds of the new reign of the

---

93. See Fournier, Études sur Joachim de Flore, Paris, 1909; E. G. Gardner, Joachim of Flora, in Franciscan Essays, Aberdeen Univ. Press, 1912, pp. 50 sqq. To these two studies we are principally indebted for the few details given concerning Joachim and his works.

94. There are, however, several pasages in Joachim's works, which seem to point to two orders. See Fournier, op. cit., pp. 44-46; Gardner, op. cit., p. 61.

Holy Spirit. Their very sufferings were but proof that the war had already begun between the chief disciplinary institution, the Church, and the new spiritual awakening. Joachim's writings not only comforted them; they gave them fresh energy in the sphere wherein disciplinary activity was particularly harmful to their ideals. They fully realized that Joachim's doctrines had been expounded with much obscurity. Unless that obscurity were dispelled, they could not fully use them in their cause. Gerard of Borgo San Donnino, one of their leaders, compiled at Paris a book containing the three authentic works of Joachim, together with an introduction and glosses written by himself. To the whole, he gave the name *Evangelium Aeternum*. As a result of his work, the obscurity had indeed been dispelled to a great extent, but it was at the cost of foisting upon the pseudo-Prophet, many ideas of which he himself had been wholly ignorant.[95] Gerard's work is known to us only from the extracts made in the report of the Commission summoned at Anagni for the purpose of examining it.[96] This Commission finally condemned it. The 'Spiritual' had left notheing doubtful. He made it clear that Joachim had foretold the coming of a barefooted Order, consisting equally of clerks and lay people. This Order was to be the especial depository of the *Evangelium Aeternum*, which in his hands had become, not an unwritten spiritual understanding of the Gospel of Christ, but a written book, which was to supersede that Gospel.[97] He stated, moreover, that the 'Angel having the sign of the living God,' seen in the vision of John the Evangelist,[98] had appeared about the year 1200, and was none other than St. Francis.[99] It is certainly correct to discriminate between the teachings of Joachim himself, and those of the Franciscan enthusiasts.

The story of the manner in which Bonaventure proceeded against Gerard and another friar, named Leonard, is already familiar. Those who are disposed to rule out the possibility of his being influenced by the apocalyptic literature which was creating such havoc within the Order, rely very much upon his uncom-

95. This was recognized by the Friars apparently. Salimbene remarks that Gerard introduced many new things into his work. See Cronica F. Salimbene, ed. in Mon. German. Histor., T. XXXII, p. 455.

96. The text of the Protocol of the Commission of Anagni will be found in Archiv für Litteratur-und Kirchengeschichte des Mittelalters, I, pp. 99-142.

97. See Protocol, 91, b. ibid., pp. 101-2. Gardner, op. cit., p. 63, declares that it is this very point which separates Gerard from the authentic creed of Joachim.

98. Apocalypse, VII, 2.

99. Protocol, 91 b. loc. cit., p. 101.

promising attitude on the occasion of the trial.[100] He sentenced Gerard and Leonard to a life-long imprisonment; his saintly predecessor in the Generalate, John of Parma, was allowed, through the intervention of powerful influence, to retire with dignity to a hermitage at Greccio.[101] However, the later Ubertino da Casale was well aware of Bonaventure's action, and something he has to say in his *Arbor Vitæ,* suggests that the Seraphic Doctor was not wholly guiltless in this matter himself. Ubertino's testimony is indirect. On the authority of a certain learned doctor who had heard Bonaventure speak at a General Chapter in Paris, he declares that Bonaventure expressed with certainty his belief, that St. Francis was the Angel of the sixth seal, whom John the Evangelist had seen in his vision.[102] As we shall see, Ubertino could have found the same assertion in the *Legenda Sancti Francisci.*

It was the expression of this belief, which seems to have been one of the most cherished doctrines of the Joachists, that persuaded us to examine the *Opera* more thoroughly, for any signs of direct influence. This examination has revealed but one direct reference to the pseudo-Prophet; it is the bare statement that his book on the Trinity had been justly condemned at the Lateran Council.[103] When he was in Paris, delivering his *Collationes in Hexaëmeron,* he had an excellent opportunity of popularizing the Joachistic method of Scriptural interpretation. He was speaking at a time when the most burning question of the hour was that concerning the three Epochs. He is emphatic in his denial that any new dispensation will make void the Eternal Gospel of Christ: 'Post novum testamentum non erit aliud, nec aliquod sacramentum novæ legis subtrahi potest, quia illud testamentum æternum est.'[104] Joachim's influence, direct or indirect,

---

100. See René de Nantes, Histoire des Spirituels, pp. 198-205. Van Ortroy, Analecta Bolland., T. XVIII, pp. 205-6; see also T. XX, p. 232 .

101. For the history of the trial, see Historia Tribulationum Ordinis Minorum, ed. in Archiv für Litt., II, pp. 285 sqq.

102. 'Et ego audivi a solemni doctore istius ordinis quod frater Bonaventura tunc generalis minister et doctor solemnis praesente praefato doctore qui mihi dixit quod in capitulo parisiensi solemniter praedicavit: quod ipse erat certus et certificatus quod beatus Franciscus erat angelus sexti signaculi et quod ad litteram de ipso et ejus statu et ordine evangelista Joannes intellexit et quod in spiritu ipsum vidit quando praedicta verba protulit . . . Et hic praedictus frater Bonaventura ibidem cum maximo fervore asseruit, ut ab illo (solemni doctore) audivi si memoria me non fallit: scire se certissime per solemnes et indubitabiles revelationes factas talibus personis, quod de hoc non poterat dubitare.' Arbor Vitae. Lib. V, cap. II, f. 404.

103. 'Et ideo ignoranter Joachim reprehendit Magistrum, et quia, cum esset simplex, non est reveritus Magistrum, ideo iusto Dei iudicio damnatus fuit libellus eius in Lateranensi Concilio, et positio Magistri approbata.' I S. D. V. Dub. IV, T. I, p. 121.

104. Op. cit., col. XVI, n. 2, T. V, p. 403.

seems to manifest itself, however, in a few tentative statements concerning the signs which are to herald the end of the world. The assaults of anti-Christ, and of his fellow workers for evil, are to be combatted by the efforts of a Contemplative Order: 'Malignitatibus ipsorum iudicium Deus pauperibus tribuet, ut sint iudicantes duodecim tribus Israel; et in hac vita talibus debetur contemplatio.' [105]

Bonaventure even seems willing to identify this Order with that of St. Francis: 'Contemplatio non potest esse nisi in summa simplicitate; et summa simplicitas non potest esse nisi in maxima paupertate; et hæc est huius ordinis. Intentio beati Francisci fuit esse in summa paupertate.'[106] Elsewhere, he shows that he does not possess the same dogmatic beliefs as the 'Spirituals,' for he declares: 'Quis autem ordo iste futurus sit, vel iam sit, non est facile scire.'[107] Generally speaking too, he is far more reticent than the 'Spirituals' in his assertions concerning other future events. One of the signs of the approach of the consummation of all things will be a greater outpouring of the Holy Spirit, but not one which will result in the dethroning of the existing Gospel. Under the influence of the third Person of the Blessed Trinity, there will be a more wide-spread understanding of the Law of Christ.[108] This is not Joachism.

In the *Legenda Sancti Francisci,* he does, as was said, identify the 'Poverello' with the Angel of the sixth seal, just as Gerard of Borgo San Donnino had done. Yet he shows clearly, that Francis appeared among men, primarily in the likeness of Christ, and as a perfect example of the only perfection which will save mankind: the perfection based upon the everlasting Gospel. He says nothing which may be constructed as a belief that Francis was the herald of a new Epoch in the Joachistic sense. Francis, he affirms, is not unfittingly thought to be set forth in the true prophecy of John the Evangelist, under the similitude of the Angel ascending from the sunrising, and bearing the seal of the Living God.[109] He adds: 'Hunc Dei nuntium amabilem Christo, imitabilem nobis, et admirabilem mundo, servum Dei fuisse Franciscum,

105. Ibid., col. XX, n. 30, p. 430.
106. Ibid.
107. Col. XXII, n. 22, p. 441.
108. See Col. XVI, n. 29, p. 408; col. XX, n. 15, p. 428.
109. 'Ideoque alterius amici Sponsi, Apostoli et Evangelistae Joannis vaticinatione veridica sub similitudine Angeli ascendentis ab ortu solis signumque Dei vivi habentis astruitur non immerito designatus. Sub apertione namque sexti sigilli vidi, ait Joannes in Apocalypsi, alterum Angelum ascendentem ab ortu solis, habentem signum Dei vivi.' Op. cit., Prologus, T. VIII, p. 504.

indubitabili fide colligimus, si culmen in eo eximiæ sanctitatis advertimus, qua, inter homines vivens, imitator fuit puritatis angelicæ, qua et positus est perfectis Christi sectatoribus in exemplum.'[110] It is strange that Bonaventure, usually so careful in his statements, should write in this manner. Francis certainly never regarded himself as the fulfilment of any prophecy. Is this an entirely independent interpretation? We are inclined to think that it is not, especially in view of what he has to say with regard to the Order which is to combat the assaults of Anti-Christ.

But if there be any Joachistic element here, further reading of the *Legenda* will reveal that Bonaventure has not gone to the extremes of the 'Spirituals.' Francis, he is convinced, will bring about a spiritual awakening among men as an imitator of Christ, but not as the forerunner of any new Epoch. Even though we accept Joachistic influence to this extent, it is in a relatively unimportant detail. It may be said with perfect truth that it alters nothing in the scheme of his spiritual doctrine. The foundation of this is Our Lord Himself. His Mysticism, unlike that of Gerard and his companions, is the outcome, not of a disappointment with the existing scheme of things; it springs from a living trust in the possibilities awaiting those who will tread faithfully in the footsteps of the Saviour of the Word. For Bonaventure, Christ's Testament, and His Testament alone, is everlasting.

It is acknowledged that, except with regard to a few details having direct relation to Bonaventure himself, nothing in the above historical account is new. What has been said concerning his attitude towards the various problems confronting him as General of the Franciscan Order simply aims at correcting the idea, not infrequently expressed, that he cannot be regarded as continuing the spiritual traditions of the 'Poverello.' We hope to show that he certainly has retained all that is essential to those traditions, even though by force of circumstances his teaching lacks the picturesqueness associated with St. Francis' spirituality. The fact that the vagaries of Joachim and his Franciscan interpreters have had no deep and important influence upon his Mysticism is a sign of the well balanced mentality with which he viewed the problem of the relations between God and the human soul. We do not think that, in the following exposition of his teaching, anything will be said which will cause the critic to deny that he retains that same mentality in all his principles.

110. Ibid.

In this exposition, the Seraphic Doctor has been allowed, as far as possible, to speak for himself: this moreover, in the Latin in which he is acknowledged to have been proficient.[111] The same treatment has been given to the Patristic sources to which he was indebted. In this manner, similarity of thought seems to be made the more apparent. With regard to the division of the Essay itself, this has been made as natural as possible, and is based upon the lines adopted in many independent synthetic accounts of Mystical Theology.

111. See the appreciation of his style in Taylor, H., The Mediaeval Mind, London, 1914, vol. II, p. 210.

CHAPTER II.

Sanctifying Grace the starting-point of the spiritual life. — Grace defined.—The necessity of it.—Grace gives unity to the whole spiritual life.—Mysticism the realization of the inherent possibilities of grace.—The Gifts of the Holy Ghost.—The Theological Virtues.—'Spiritual Senses.'—The Supernatural implies human endeavour.—Division of the Spiritual life into the 'Three Ways.'—Characteristics of this division.—This the normal Patristic scheme expressed in Pseudo-Dionysian terminology. — Bonaventure's doctrine on the 'Via Purgativa.' — The 'Via Purgativa' essentially internal. — External mortification an aid to interior purification. — His moderation with regard to bodily penances.—His ascetical doctrine that of the Gospels and of the Fathers.

It is proposed to group together in this section of our Essay discussions concerning three points, which, however commonplace they may seem, must be fully understood before Bonaventure's thought can be rightly appreciated. At first sight it may appear that apart altogether from their being, in a sense, commonplace, the points in question are not correlated; but it was precisely the realization that they actually do bear upon one another, that led to the present grouping. It must also be borne in mind, that concerning each particular point, whole treatises might be written, though it is difficult to believe that research would reveal anything original in Bonaventure's doctrine.

We refer, first, to his teaching on Sanctifying Grace and its concomitants, the Theological Virtues, and the Gifts of the Holy Ghost: secondly to his conception of the threefold division of the life of Grace as a whole: thirdly to the initial stage of that same life of Grace, which, along with most spiritual writers, Bonaventure deems absolutely necessary, before any progress can be made: that is, the serious attempt with the help of grace to free the soul from sin and its evil effects. This last, he calls the 'Via Purgativa.'

Concerning the first point, it would be too great a task to attempt more than a very brief exposé. Acquaintance with the enormous amount of literature on the subject, contained in the works of Peter Lombard, Albertus Magnus, Alexander of Hales, Thomas Aquinas and Duns Scotus, to mention only a few of the better known Scholastic Theologians, will testify to the truth of the statement, that all these dealt with the subject in almost identical sense. There were differences of opinion, it is true, as to minor and purely speculative details;[1] but, for the rest, they follow one another with monotonous fidelity. To produce a synthesis of the doctrine of one, would be, allowing for the masterly treatment of Thomas Aquinas, and the added subtleties of Scotus, to produce the substantial teaching of all.

Bonaventure has covered the same ground as these theologians; he has the same doctrine to offer. In his teaching on Sanctifying Grace, however, he undoubtedly emphasises the fact that the fullest experience in the Christian life is but the culmination of the supernatural life begun in the soul by the first outpouring and reception of Grace. He makes no reference to the personality of man as possessing a mystic faculty or sense co-natural with it, which, if it be developed, will result, apart altogether from grace, in the enjoyment of the highest favours spoken of by the Mystics. If there is anything absolutely indispensable to the ultimate realization of the mystical experience, it is the primary sanctification of the soul.

Like all mediaeval theologians he defines Grace principally by its effects. Though it is really one,[2] definitions abound, probably the most comprehensive and characteristic being that contained in the *Breviloquium*: 'Ipsa (gratia) est donum, quod a Deo immediate donatur et infunditur. Etenim cum ipsa et in ipsa datur Spiritus sanctus, qui est donum increatum, optimum et perfectum, quod descendit a Patre luminum per Verbum incarnatum . . . . . Ipsa nihilominus est donum, per quod anima perficitur et efficitur sponsa Christi, filia Patris æterni et templum Spiritus sancti; quod nullo modo fit nisi ex dignativa condescensione et condescensiva dignatione Maiestatis æternæ per donum gratiæ suæ. Ipsa denique est donum, quod animam purgat, illuminat et perficit; vivificat, reformat et stabilit; elevat, assimilat et Deo iungit, ac per hoc acceptabilem facit.'[3] Whilst his works admirably illustrate that recognized characteristic of Franciscan theology in general, the insistence upon the necessity of human coöperation with the Divine work effected through grace, and expressed so fully in this

1. Thus there was the speculative question as to the distinction between the Virtues and the Gifts. Such a distinction is insisted upon by Bonaventure, see III S., D. XXXIV, p. 1, a. 1, q. 1. T. III, p. 736, but it was rejected by Duns Scotus. See III S., D. XXXIV, quaestio unic., Opera Omnia Joannis D. Scoti, Parisii apud Vivès, MDCCCXCIV, T. XV, pp. 464 sqq. He directly refutes Bonaventure in the Scholium, p. 474.

2. 'Cum gratia una sit, multiplices tamen habet divisiones secundum diversas considerationes. Habet enim gratia comparari ad suum principium a quo, habet comparari ad suum subiectum in quo, habet nihilominus comparari ad suum oppositum contra quod, habet comparari ad suum effectum, ad quem ordinatur.' II S. D. XXVII, Sub. 1. T, II, p. 669.

3. Op. cit., pars V, cap. 1. T. V, p. 252.

definition, they also emphasize the idea that it is precisely in the Divine activity, that we are to find the real starting point of all spiritual life. Without grace, even the desire of the mystical experience is wholly impossible. 'Nec desiderat (contemplationem) nisi quem ignis Spiritus sancti medullitus inflammat.'[4] In another place, comparing grace and its concomitants to wings with which the soul is endowed to return to its Creator, and the mystical experience to the heights whereon this return is accomplished, he writes: 'Sine his autem pennis, nullus potest conscendere ad montana.'[5] Perhaps he could choose no more forcible language to express the truth, that mystical contemplation, far from being the result of study or of any other form of purely natural activity, can only be the outcome of grace, than when he says, referring expressly to the delights of mystic union: 'Si autem quæras, quomodo hæc fiat, interroga gratiam, non doctrinam; desiderium, non intellectum; gemitum orationis, non studium lectionis; Sponsum, non magistrum; Deum, non hominem.'[6]

Together with this insistence upon the absolute necessity of grace as the essential starting-point of the mystical life, we find an attempt to put into bold relief the dispositive value of ordinary sanctifying grace in relation to mystical contemplation. Thus he establishes what may be called a dynamic bond between all the stages in the spiritual life, from the lowest to the highest, from the very first response to the Divine impulse, to the final states: to the 'excessus mentis' of the mystic. In this, he in some measure removes the confusion surrounding the division frequently made between the ascetic and the mystic life. We see more clearly how the ascetic, accepting the term as applicable to all who are seriously striving after Christian perfection, such a striving demanding as it does continuous correspondence with sanctifying grace, is really the potential mystic. Possessing sanctifying grace, he has within his soul, if he will but follow whither it will lead, the radical principle, which, when combined with individual effort, can produce a St. John of the Cross, or a St. Teresa.

Nor in this stressing of the dispositive value of ordinary Sanctifying Grace, is he necessarily thrown back upon that watering down of the mystical life which would make all, even those who recite the 'Our Father' with devotion, mystics in reality. A middle course is struck between this and the other extreme view, which

4. Itin., cap. VII, n. 4, T. V, p. 312.
5. Comment. in Luc., c. IX, n. 49, T. VII, p. 232.
6. Itin., c. VII, n. 6, T. V, p. 313; and cf. Soliloqu.: c. II, n. 13—n. 16, T. VIII, pp. 49-50.

makes of the mystics a class absolutely apart, and subject to a distinct economy of grace: a view largely responsible for the identifying of the mystical life with a quasi-miraculous state characterized by wondrous visions, Divine locutions and other extraordinary phenomena, more often than not affecting the body. His is a middle course, inasmuch as grace is viewed as leading the soul gradually along a path already mapped out by Divine Law. The soul begins the spiritual life by ordinary acts of prayer and mortification; but let it progress faithfully, making the development of the spiritual life its one end, not necessarily indeed to the neglect of all else, but certainly to the bringing of all other affairs into direct relationship to that end: let it do this with continuous fidelity, and it is Bonaventure's conviction that the inherent possibilities of the established order of grace will be realized. The time will come when the 'Dona Spiritus Sancti,' especially the gifts of Understanding and Wisdom, will be fully exercised on the soul's behalf by their Divine Author. This full exercise of the gifts which all possess who are in the state of grace, constitutes the normal mystic experience in his Theology, as will be seen. Thus it becomes quite clear that, though all pious men and women are not actually mystics, they are mystics potentially. If therefore, the mystics are a class apart, it is certainly not because God has willed it so, for they are the subjects of no special economy of grace, and are by no means lifted out of the established sphere of the Divine relations with mankind in general. They are mystics, simply because they are among the few who have heroically determined to make of their whole sojourn upon earth a veritable pilgrimage to God. Cost what it may, they will pass through the way of purgation; they will concentrate their whole attention upon God, their whole endeavour upon imitating the perfect Guide to the fullest Christian life, Christ Himself: all this with the indispensable aid of grace and its concomitants, which set the mystics on their road, and, according to the progress made, manifest their inherent possibilities.

Ideas such as these, emphasizing as they do the essential unity of the spiritual life, occur again and again throughout Bonaventure's dogmatic and spiritual treatises. They form the basis, for example, of the comment he makes after he has described the attractions offered to the devout soul by the mystic union: 'Qui igitur vult in Deum ascendere necesse est, ut vitata culpa deformante naturam, naturales potentias supradictas (i. e. sensus, imaginatio, ratio, intellectus, intelligentia, et apex mentis) exerceat ad gratiam reformantem, et hoc per orationem; . . . . ad sapientiam nemo venit nisi per gratiam . . . . Sicut igitur gratia fundamentum est rectitudinis voluntatis et illustrationis perspicuæ rationis; sic primo orandum est nobis, deinde sancte vivendum, tertio veritatis spectaculis intendendum et intendendo gradatim ascendendum, quousque veniatur ad montem excelsum, ubi videatur Deus deorum in Sion.'[7] Furthermore, the whole spiritual life is embraced within the threefold division of the Purgative, Illuminative, and Unitive ways, and he declares that throughout these, grace itself is the active principle: 'Ipsa est donum quod animam purgat, illuminat et perficit.'[8]

So persuaded is he of the fact that the mystic experience is but the full realization of the life of grace, that of ordinary grace he can employ certain expressions, consecrated by the use of the great descriptive mystics to the highest states of union with God. He writes: 'Gratia gratum faciens facit animam templum Dei, sponsam Christi, et filiam Patris æterni. Et quia hoc non potest esse nisi ex summa dignatione et condescensione Dei; ideo illud non potest esse per habitum aliquem naturaliter insertum, sed solum per donum divinitus gratis infusum; quod expresse apparet, si quis ponderet, quantum est esse Dei templum, Dei filium, Deo nihilominus indissolubiliter et quasi matrimonialiter per amoris et gratiæ vinculum copulatum.'[9] After all, it is merely a St. Teresa's claim to have been thus 'quasi-matrimonialiter' united to God, that persuades all who are willing to admit the validity of the mystic experience, to enrol her among the religious geniuses of the Western Church. Yet Bonaventure teaches that the union itself, consciousness of which constitutes the mystic experience, is radically effected by Grace.

Intimately connected with and accompanying grace, are the Gifts of the Holy Ghost. He has written long treatises on these;[10] their nature is discussed; weighty arguments are adduced to exhibit them as distinct from the Virtues; and at length they appear as divinely infused habits, whose purpose is to make the soul more readily responsive to supernatural impulses and to urge it on to the spiritual heroism of the saints. They are defined thus: 'Habitus expedientes recte dicuntur dona, pro eo quod dicunt quandam ulteriorem abundantiam bonitatis ad agendum,

---

7. Itin., c. 1, n. 8, T. V, p. 298. It must be noted, too, that 'sapientia' is frequently used as referring to the mystic experience.
8. Breviloq., p. V, c. 1, T. V, p. 252.
9. Ibid. p. 255; cf. II S. D. XXVIII, a. 1, T. pp. 674 sqq.
10. See Collationes de Donis Spiritus Sancti, T. V, pp. 457 sqq.

ac per hoc magis attestantur divinæ liberalitati; et propter hoc recte censentur nomine doni.'[11] These gifts, namely, Wisdom, Understanding, Counsel, Fortitude, Knowledge, Piety and Fear of God, are represented as being bestowed upon the soul in Justification, and as expediting the work of leading it to the fulness of the Christian life. This work is admirably illustrated in the *Breviloquium:* 'Ad expeditionem in contemplando dona Spiritus sancti sunt in septenario numero. Nam ad vitam hierarchicam et contemplativam necessarium est animam purgari, illuminari et perfici. Purgari autem oportet a concupiscentia, a malitia, ab ignorantia, ab infirmitate seu impotentia; primum facit timor, secundum pietas, tertium scientia, quartum fortitudo. Illuminari autem indigemus in operibus reparationis et primariæ conditionis; primum dat consilium, secundum intellectus. Perfici autem habemus per accessum ad summum, quod consistit in uno, et hoc per donum sapientiæ; et sic arcanum contemplationis a lato consummatur quasi in cubito.' [12]

To these same supernatural agencies, is attributed the removal of the spiritual obstacles, the evil habits created in the soul by sin,[13] and the quickening of the natural faculties, intellect and will especially, that they may play the part imposed upon them by the mystical quest.[14] The two gifts, Understanding and Wisdom, will be met with again, and explained more fully, since it is by recourse to them that Bonaventure illustrates his teaching on the mystical union.[15] One further remark may be made here; it is this. Bonaventure shows quite clearly that it is not the ordinary use of these gifts that constitutes the mystical experience. If this were so, the majority of Christians would be mystics, since they are operative on lower levels of the spiritual life. Rather, it is their special use, made possible by their Divine Author, at a particular stage of progress.[16]

Then there are those other concomitants of Grace: the Theological Virtues: Faith, Hope, and Charity. These too, remain with the soul throughout the whole spiritual life. Thus, he does not concede to the mystic any knowledge of God which may not rightly be termed a knowledge of faith. No doubt it is a more fruitful faith that animates him, for, without comprehending

11. III S. D. XXXIV, p. 1, a. 1, T. III, p. 738.
12. Op. cit., P. V, c. V, T. V, p. 258.
13. Ibid., p. 257.
14. Ibid.
15. Cf. Chaps. V and VI.
16. An excellent and comprehensive summary of the doctrine concerning these gifts, in their theological aspect, will be found in Dict. de Théol. Catholique, art. Dons du Saint-Esprit, T. IV, cols. 178-1781.

them, he understands more of those mysterious truths in which he professes belief; but, no matter to what extent his intellect may be described as being 'illuminated as to Divine things,' he must render the same obedience of the intellect as that demanded of the very beginner in asceticism. With characteristic unwillingness to separate faith from love, Bonaventure defines it thus: 'Fides non est aliud nisi habitus quo intellectus noster voluntarie captivatur in obsequium Christi,'[17] and he insists that it remains the principal guiding light of the soul 'in via:' 'Est enim ipsa fides omnium supernaturalium illuminationum, quamdiu peregrinamur a Domino, et fundamentum stabiliens et lucerna dirigens et ianua introducens; secundum cuius etiam mensuram necesse est mensurari sapientiam nobis divinitus datam, ne quis sapiat plus quam oportet sapere, sed ad sobrietatem, et unicuique sicut Deus divisit mensuram fidei.'[18] Whilst it is Hope, that encourages the soul in the pursuit of God, and of as full a foretaste of future blessedness as may be granted in this life, it is in Charity, the love of God, whereby He is loved as the Object of future Beatitude, that the soul finds the whole reason of its ardent longings.

It only remains to be added, to conclude this brief mention of his supernatural agencies, that in Bonaventure's Theology we not infrequently meet with the mysterious 'spiritual senses' to which many descriptive writers have recourse to make their soul-states understood more easily. Thus, they refer to a more direct communication with God, to a deeper appreciation of things Divine than that experienced in a Christian life lived on a lower level: all this in language properly applicable only to sense-experience. God is 'tasted;' He is 'touched' or 'felt;' even the sense of smell is translated to the field of spiritual experience.

To such an extent is this method of self-expression carried, so often moreover is there an absence of the warning that the writer is using purely metaphorical language,[19] that in recent treatises on the subject of Mystical Theology, the question is seriously debated: Does the soul possess intellectual spirit-

---

17. III S. D. XXIII, a. 1, q. 1, T. III, p. 471.

18. Breviloq.: Prologus, T. V, p. 201. The Scriptural references are to II Cor. 5, 6; Rom. 12, 3. Also cf. IV, S. D. III, p. 1, a. 1, q. III, T. IV; p. 201; Coll. in Hex. col. 1, n. 13, T. V, pp. 334 sqq.; col. XXIII, n. 16, p. 447.

19. St. Teresa, however does not leave us in doubt. Speaking of 'Spiritual scent' she writes: 'When reciting the Divine Office in choir without seeking to penetrate the sense, one may be seized with a delightful fervour, as if suddenly encompassed with a fragrance, powerful enough to diffuse itself through all the sense. I do not assert that there really is any (material) scent, but make use of this comparison because it somewhat resembles the manner by which the Spouse makes His Presence understood.' Interior Castle, Sixth Mansion, ch. II, 14, p. 149. (Stanbrook Ed.), 1906.

ual senses, having some resemblance to bodily senses so that in an analogous manner, and in various ways, it is able to perceive the presence of God?[20] What good may be done by insisting upon the existence of such mysterious faculties, of which most people seem entirely ignorant, it is difficult to imagine; but as Bonaventure's authority has been quoted in support of a thesis pre-supposing their reality,[21] it is as well to discover his meaning when he refers to them.

He leaves us in no doubt. 'Spiritual senses' imply nothing beyond the secret appreciation of things divine, and the name is given, curiously enough, not to new agents of spiritual activity, but rather to the terms of such activity. The ability to become the subject of spiritual appreciation is recovered with the infusion of the three Theological Virtues: 'Anima igitur credens, sperans et amans Jesum Christum . . . dum per fidem credit in Christum . . . recuperat spiritualem auditum et visum, auditum ad suscipiendum Christi sermones, visum ad considerandum illius lucis splendores. Dum autem spe suspirat ad suscipiendum Verbum inspiratum, per desiderium et affectum recuperat spiritualem olfactum. Dum caritate complectitur Verbum incarnatum, ut suscipiens ab Ipso delectationem et ut transiens in illud per ecstaticum amorem, recuperat gustum et tactum. Quibus sensibus recuperatis, dum sponsum suum videt, et audit, odoratur, gustat et amplexatur, decantare potest tanquam sponsa Canticum canticorum.'[22] Even language such as this implies for him no new soul faculties. Elsewhere,[23] he declares that he is using expressions with which he was made familiar by the works of Augustine and Richard of St. Victor.

For Augustine in an especial manner expresses his thought in such fashion. His own answer to his question: 'Quod autem amo cum te amo?' is a striking example of this transferring to the spiritual realm, the language proper to sensation. It is not the beauty of bodies, nor the fair harmony of time that he loves when he loves his God; nor yet the brightness of light, nor sweet melodies, nor the fragrant smell of flowers and ointments; nor

---

20. See Poulain, Graces of Interior Prayer, London, 1921, pp. 88-98.

21. Thus A. Hamon professedly quotes Bonaventure, but his quotation is taken from the spurious De septem Itineribus aeternitatis, (c. 1350) and adds: 'Il nous est bien difficile de comprendre ce que sont les sens spirituels dont parle le saint docteur, mais quelle bonne raison avons nous de les nier, quand les mystiques nous parlent sans cesse de voix, d'odeur, d'aliment?' He concludes: 'Il-y-a donc au témoignage des mystiques, dans cette expression, sens spirituels, autre chose qu'une métaphore: c'est une réalite dont ils se rendent compte, bien que nous ne la comprenions pas.' Art. Exstase, in Dict. de Théol. Cath., T. V, col. 1891.

22. Itin., c. IV, n. 3, T. V, p. 306.

23. III S. D. XIII, dub. 1, T. III, pp. 291-2.

manna and honey. But only by use of analogous language, finding its basis in such sense experience, can he describe his communing with God. Ruling out all these things, he hastens to add: 'Et tamen amo quamdam lucem, et quamdam vocem, et quemdam odorem, et quemdam cibum, et quemdam amplexum, cum amo Deum meum, lucem, vocem, odorem, cibum, amplexum interioris hominis mei; ubi fulget animæ meæ quod non capit locus, et ubi sonat quod non rapit tempus, et ubi olet quod non spargit flatus, et ubi sapit quod non minuit edacitas, et ubi hæret quod non divellit satietas. Hoc est quod amo, cum Deum meum amo.' [24] Similar passages might be quoted from the works of Richard of St. Victor.[25] Just as truly, however, as the spiritual senses are not new agents in Augustinian psychology, so they are not elevated in Bonaventure's scheme to this rank. Bonaventure makes this apparent when he writes: 'Sensus nominat usum alicuius potentiæ existentis in re vivente et a re vivente secundum naturam. Per hunc etiam modum in spiritualibus sensus dicit usum donorum gratuitorum, quæ quidem dona sunt eo vitalia, quo sunt gratuita. Potest igitur sensus accipi large pro quocumque usu gratiæ perfecto et evidenti . . . Alio modo sensus potest dici stricte; et sic sensus spiritualis dicitur usus gratiæ interior respectu ipsius Dei secundum proportionem ad quinque sensus.'[26] His 'spiritual senses' are manifestly the uses of grace.

It has already been said that there appears to be no immediately discoverable advantage to be gained by insisting that the 'spiritual senses' represent soul faculties. We are inclined to think that neither is there any advantage to be gained by their introduction into Mystical Theology, even when, as in Bonaventure's case, it is made so clear that they have reference merely to more intense uses of the graces sent by God. The realities they stand for may indeed be facts of experience. If we credit, as indeed we do, such witnesses as St. Augustine and St. Teresa, they are certainly facts. Their introduction, however, under such terminology, does nothing to remove the confusion already surrounding the subject, and, in view of the Seraphic Doctor's teaching of the gifts of Understanding and Wisdom, they are superfluous, and even misleading. The only good the repeated

24. Confess. Lib. X, c. VI, P. L. T. XXXII, cols. 781-3.

25. See e. g. De quattuor gradibus violentae charitatis. P. L. T. CXCVI, col. 1218. 'Saepe sub hoc statu Dominus descendit de coelis, saepe visitat sedentem in tenebris et umbra mortis . . . . Sic tamen prasentiam suam exhibet ut faciem suam minime ostendat. Dulcorem suum infundit, sed decorem suum non ostendit.' etc.

26. III S. D. XIII, a. II, q. III, dub. 1, T. III, p. 291; and cf. ibid. D. XXIV, p. 1, a. 1, q. 1, p. 737.

mention of 'sensus spirituales' can do, is to bring home the nature of mystical communion with God, and mystical appreciation of things Divine. Yet this can be done with equal force, without reference to 'senses' at all, no matter how ancient the usage may be.[27] The passage quoted from St. Augustine's *Confessions* is an example. True it is, that only the enjoyment of an experience similar to that described by the great Doctors of the Church can make us fully understand what they are referring to when they use such mysterious language, but we are not further enlightened when we are told of these 'spiritual senses.' In the minds of those already disposed to discredit the mystic claim, mention of such exalted spiritual experience, coupled with an apparently artificial terminology, might conceivably lead to the denunciation of the whole, as a purely subjective creation. What is this mysterious experience that needs artificialities to explain it? Such is the question which is often asked in a spirit of antagonism. Add to this, that not all the writers subsequent to Bonaventure had the foresight to make clear that when they referred to 'spiritual senses,' they were using only metaphorical language. From the writings of many it certainly would appear that they have in mind new and genuine agents in spiritual activity. Herein we find an example of the Scholastic tendency to carry the process of division and sub-division to such a degree that the original basis on which the division may have been made is lost sight of, and what are really mere aspects of one and the same thing, become distinct entities: a tendency so justly resented by Scotus and his disciple Occam. The so-called 'spiritual senses' are, in ultimate analysis, nothing more than aspects of grace: of grace regarded from the point of view of its reception on the part of the devout soul.

Understanding that this meaning is to be given to the 'spiritual senses' whenever they are introduced into the Bonaventurian synthesis, we are now in possession of the supernatural elements in which the Franciscan Doctor's Mystical Theology centres. Doubtless, there will be an immediate temptation in the minds of non-Catholics to dismiss the whole as a rigid and artificial system of supernaturalism, attributing all to mysterious supernatural agencies, and nothing to human endeavour. Nothing could be further removed from the truth. Grace, the Virtues and the Gifts, only represent the Divine Love which is ever working to draw back souls to Itself. Without the Divine activity which

27. Origen uses the same terminology, though he too, makes his meaning clear. See Hom.: in Levit.: Hom. 3, n. 7, P. G. T. XII, col. 432,

they represent, not only the mystical experience, but salvation, and even the very thought of salvation, is impossible. This Bonaventure declares in common with his contemporaries. But if the wealth of Augustinian and Pseudo-Dionysian Theology is concentrated in his insistence upon the need of Divine Grace, he has not gone to the extreme which would make the whole spiritual life a continuous passive reception of supernatural favours, demanding no effort on the part of the soul. There is no question of remaining entirely passive, in the expectation that God will effect the wonders of mystic union with Himself, apart altogether from human industry and effort. His ascetical doctrines bring this out plainly enough. If, in the following, we understand by 'consensus' (and it must be given this interpretation in his Theology), not merely a willingness to receive grace, but also an efficacious desire to follow whither it will lead, and to perform the tasks demanded in following it, no more concise statement regarding the necessity of human coöperation with the Divine workings on the soul could be found. He expresses his thought thus: 'Per gratiam fit matrimonium inter Deum et animam; sed lex matrimonii est, ut non fiat absque mutuo consensu: ergo videtur, nulli adulto gratia debeat dari, nisi præcedat consensus.'[28] There is no need, however, to stress the point here: it will be made clear by what he has to say regarding that arduous process of self-purgation, which must be the preliminary to every mystical life.

Understood in the above sense, Bonaventure is certainly to be classed among the supernatural mystical writers. These, as a modern student of Mysticism has pointed out, have a distinct tendency to schematization.[29] Not only do we find grace, acknowledged as objectively one, divided and subdivided, but the whole spiritual life meets with like treatment. In Bonaventure's case, the tendency leads to the familiar division into the three ways: the ways of Purgation, Illumination, and Union or Perfection. These are really stages of spiritual development, and as such, they must each receive special treatment. Here we are concerned with the place they occupy, like the supernatural agencies mentioned above, in his doctrine.

For him, the mystic way, or the ascent to God, is the gradual development of an entirely new life. It is the returning to God, through the power that comes from Him; a return, moreover, really involving all that is implied by the terms he makes use of:

---

28. II S., D. XXIX, a. II, q. II, ad. 4, T. II, p. 793; cf., ibid., pp. 694-6.
29. Inge, W. R., Christian Mysticism, p. 147, note 3.

'Necesse est igitur . . . per tres gradus ascendere, secundum triplicem viam, scilicet purgativam, quæ consistit in expulsione peccati; illuminativam, quæ consistit in imitatione Christi; unitivam, quæ consistit in susceptione Sponsi.'[30] Herein we find not only a careful delineation of each 'way,' but also an exact statement of what he considers must take place in each stage of the spiritual life. Thus each 'way' is primarily indicative of a personal soul state. At the very outset, the soul must be purified by self-discipline, and freed from all sin and its consequences. Then only is it at liberty to appreciate in any practical sense the personal duty of following Christ, by imitating His Virtues, and living, as far as possible, His life.

'Via Purgativa' is certainly, in itself, sufficiently expressive of the first process; it is reminiscent, too, of the Gospel declaration that only the clean of heart shall see God.[31] Since the practice of those virtues of which Christ is the supreme Exemplar, is viewed as gradually perfecting the soul's vision with regard to spiritual matters, 'Via Illuminativa' admirably describes the second phase. By the practise of such virtues, moreover, is a likeness to Christ effected within the soul, and when the likeness is as complete as may be in this life, God allows the enjoyment, in some way conscious, of union with Himself; a state surely best described by the term 'Via Unitiva, or 'Via Perfectiva.'

No apology therefore need be made for Bonaventure's choice of nomenclature in this respect; nor indeed for the division he has made. He can hardly be said to have originated the division. Nor is he the first to have given, as some have asserted,[32] a complete exposé of the threefold way. He emphasizes the division, it is true: it is made to embrace the whole spiritual life, but, to claim for him more than this, is to claim too much. He has given what he considers to be the best expression of the normal Patristic scheme of development.

For Saint Augustine, not in nomenclature, yet certainly in fact, has the same threefold division, especially in his *De Quantitate Animæ*.[33] We can trace it easily in the works of Saint Gregory,[34] and in Saint Bernard's mystical inter-

30. De Triplici Via, T. VIII, p. 12.
31. Matth. 5, 8.
32. Thus Pourrat, La Spiritualité Chrétienne (Le Moyen Age), T. II, p. 267.
33. Cf. Butler, C., Western Mysticism, London, 1922, p. 37.
34. See e. g. Super Canticum Cantic.: Expositio; P. L. T. LXXIX, cols. 471 sqq., also Moral: Lib. XXIV, cap. XI, T. LXXVI, cols. 300-307. Gregory here comments on Job XXXIII, 29: Haec omnia operatur Deus tribus vicibus per singulos.'

pretation of the 'three kisses of the feet, the hands and the lips of the Lord,' which, throughout the sermons on the *Canticle of Canticles,* are made to symbolize the sorrow and repentance with which the spiritual life must begin: the advancement in virtue: and finally the end of the mystic quest—union with God.[35] With less precision, may be, it is found in the writings of the Victorines. Thus, Hugo makes express mention even of the terms afterwards used by Bonaventure, in his exposition of the Pseudo-Dionysian *Heavenly Hierarchy.* This exposition, so full of enthusiastic appreciation of the *Dionysiaca,* reveals Hugo, as reading them in much the same way as the later Franciscan Theologian. Speaking of the spiritual development of devout souls, he writes: 'Primum purgantur, postea illuminantur, deinde perficiuntur. Nisi enim præcederet purgatio, non sequeretur illuminatio; et nisi esset illuminatio, non veniret consummatio.'[36] Hugo here translates to the spiritual field of the individual soul, the threefold operation of purging, illuminating and perfecting, which the author of the *Hierarchies* had attributed to angelic activity. This angelic operation disappears, and, as with Bonaventure, grace is made to perform the same work. Hugo does not, it is true, make this same terminology his own throughout his mystical works, such as the *De arca Noë mystica, De arrha animæ,* and the *De vanitate Mundi,*[37] but he recognizes that by use of the terms supplied by Pseudo-Dionysius the spiritual development may be explained.

It is to Pseudo-Dionysius that Bonaventure is indebted when he constructs his *De Triplici Via* by means of the terminology in question. As far as possible, he makes his division correspond with the mind of that master of mediaeval Mysticism, but with him, 'Purgatio,' 'Illuminatio' and 'Perfectio,' never assume the philosophical meaning originally given to them. Perhaps one example may be given, illustrating what is meant. Pseudo-Dionysius begins, as is generally acknowledged, on a very high level; his works seem to be written for the benefit of those who are already mystics. Hence Purification, understood as a cleansing from sin, need only be mentioned in passing; the other form of Purification, of a more philosophical order, is dwelt upon at length. This last is effected by mental abstraction from all

35. Op. cit., Sermo III, P. L. T. CLXXXIII, col. 794; Sermo IV, ibid., col. 796.

36. Op. cit., Lib. IV, P. L. T. CLXXV, col. 998.

37. See Mignon, A., Les origines de la Scolastique et Hugues de Saint-Victor, Paris, 1895, T. II, pp. 325 sqq.

things sensible. But, in Bonaventure's hands, the same term is made to stand for the more moral process of cleansing the soul from sin, and thus it is given a meaning better understood of the multitude. None the less, his indebtedness to Pseudo-Dionysius for his terminology remains. He had often met with it in his study of Eriugena's Version of the works,[38] and, taking the substance of the Evangelical and Patristic teaching, he encloses the whole, if the expression may be used, within the three ways: Purgation, Illumination, Union or Perfection.

These three stages do not form, however, a rigid framework excluding one another, in the sense that Purgation necessarily ends where Illumination begins, or that only in the ultimate stage can union with God be experienced. Bonaventure's primary idea is that of a real spiritual evolution. It is, he declares, with these three ways, even as with the various orders of angels. These angelic orders are named in the Scriptures, not so much by reason of characteristics which the others do not possess in any degree, but by their predominating activity. All, for example, have Charity, but in Charity the Seraphim excel, (in Seraphim maior plenitudo charitatis) hence to them alone is the name given. It is the same with the other orders or classes of angels.[39] The Purgative way is so named, because, in the process which it denotes, the predominating spiritual activity is the endeavour to free the soul from sin and sinful habits; the Illuminative way owes its name to the fact that it refers to the stage wherein the principal act is the enlightening of the understanding to know Christ as the most perfect example of the Christian life; to the final stage is given the name 'the way of Union or Perfection,' simply because the predominating activity is that of the will: of the will in possession of its Object. Far from being guilty of a rigid objective schematization, Bonaven-

---

38. There is the oft-repeated comparison of the Power of God with a circle, which, after running its course throughout all created beings, returns to its primal source, having purified, illumined, and perfected them. See, De Divinis Nominibus, cap. IV, P. L. T. CXXII, cols. 1130-1 (Eriugena's Version); and compare P. G., T. III, cols. 697-9.

Also there is the exposition of the Sacraments of Baptism, Eucharist and Unction, as themselves symbolizing this threefold operation of purifying, illumining and perfecting. See De Eccles. Hierarchia, cap. II-IV, P. L. T. CXXII, cols. 1071-1096; compare P. G. T. III, cols. 391-500. Finally ,we have the direct attribution of this threefold operation to the Heavenly Hierarchy. See Coelest. Hierarchia, cap. VII, P. L. T. CXXII, cols. 1050-53; compare, P. G. T. III, cols. 206-211.

39. This idea is taken from Hugo; see De Sacramentis Lib. 1, p. 5, c. XXXII, P. L. T. CLXXVI, col. 262. It is fully explained in II, S. D. IX, a. 1, q. IV ad 2um. T. II, p. 249. 'Quamvis omnes ordines (angelorum) a dono charitatis denominari possent, quia tamen donum illud in supremo ordine praecellit, solus ille ordo ab eo debet denominari . . . .'

ture would be quite willing to admit, both that at no period of the spiritual life can the work indicated by the term 'Via Purgativa' be dispensed with, and that even in the preliminary struggle to obtain mastery over the lower self, the soul may be the subject of those transient divine movements, spoken of by St. Augustine in his *Confessions*.[40] All this is made clear in his *Soliloquium*.[41] Nor is there any question of assigning definite periods of time to each of these three ways. The later and more subjective Richard Rolle of Hampole does this,[42] and had Bonaventure written personally, he too, might have done likewise. As it is, he writes objectively, regarding the development of the spiritual life from the point of view of one who wishes to manifest the normal dealings of God with mankind in general.

It may be objected, that the terms discussed are at first sight mutually exclusive, and that writers like St. Thomas Aquinas who speak of the souls who are taking the spiritual life seriously, as 'incipientes,' 'proficientes' and 'perficientes'[43] are not so open to the charge of rigid schematization. In this there is a certain amount of truth, but it would seem that Bonaventure's terminology expresses with greater force, what is on all hands admitted to take place. Beneath the terms 'purgatio,' and 'illuminatio,' lies a wealth of Platonic and Christian thought. Together, they emphasise the ancient axiom, that before man can obtain any knowledge of the Divinity, he must cleanse the mirror of his mind. Moreover, its worth may be judged from the fact that since the time of Bonaventure, some of the best accredited spiritual writers have adopted his identical terminology, as eminently expressive of the stages through which the soul passes in its journey towards mystical union.[44]

His doctrine on the 'Via Purgativa' takes its natural place in this chapter for several reasons. Though this is the most import-

40. He seems to refer to such a case when he writes, having in mind the first period of Conversion: 'Et cum te primum cognovi, tu assumpsisti me, ut viderem esse quod viderem, et nondum me esse qui viderem.' Op. cit., Lib. VIII, cap. X, P. L. T. XXXII, col. 742.

41. Op. cit., T. VIII, pp. 28 sqq.

42. See the Incendium Amoris, (ed. by Deanesly, Manchester Univ. Press), cap. XV, p. 187.

43. See his Sum. Theol. Secunda Secundae, Quaest. XXIV, art. IX. Opera Omnia S. Thomae, Romae, MDCCCXCV, T. VIII, p. 191.

44. The Author of the Imitation of Christ certainly does so. Consult Raynor Storr, Concordance . . . De Imitatione Christi, Oxford Univ. Press, 1910, for 'purgatio,' 'illuminatio,' 'unio.' So too, it is definitely used in the Theologia Germanica. 'Now be assured that no one can be enlightened unless he be first cleansed or purified and stripped. So also, no one can be united with God unless he be first enlightened. Thus there are three stages: first, the purification; secondly the enlightening, thirdly the union.' Chapter XIV, trans. from the German of Dr. Pfeiffer's Edit. by S. Winkworth, London, 1874, p. 44.

ant point as far as ultimate attainment of mystical union is concerned, it does not offer sufficient matter for a separate chapter. It is appended here, both as giving us a clearer insight into the nature of the threefold division just dealt with, and as emphasising the idea, that this supernaturalism is not developed to the extent of ruling out all individual endeavour. His 'Via Purgativa' stands as a protest against the oft-repeated accusation that mystical writers of his class make the supernatural do what the natural must perform. The supernatural will help in this, but, no matter how necessary it may be, it never assumes the entire burden of the natural. In addition to this, it serves as a warning against that well known temptation to which many so-called mystics have often fallen victims: the temptation to clutch at the fruition of mystical experience before the difficult task of preparation by way of self-discipline. Bonaventure can endorse the declaration of St. Bernard, one which he quite conceivably made after his experience as director of his monks, that it is a reversing of the proper order to ask for the reward before having earned it: to grasp at the mid-day meal before performing the labour.[45]

This truth finds repeated expression in the *Soliloquium*.[46] Here we find him restraining rather than encouraging the soul's longing for spiritual raptures, the restraining element being his insistence upon the arduous preparation required.[47] Whereas moral laxity, and a dreamy form of piety built entirely upon imagination, are too often the characteristics of those lives in which this difficult self-discipline finds no place, those whom by common consent we have come to regard as the great Christian mystics, have been unanimous in asserting, and in demonstrating by their own actions, that the essential first step in the way leading to mystic union, is that implied by the term 'Purgatio.' There may be no unanimity with regard to those extraordinary self-inflicted bodily sufferings familiar to all who have read the lives of types such as St. Peter of Alcantara, St. John of the Cross, and Blessed Henry Suso.[48] There is, however, insistence upon interior purification and self-restraint, to the obtaining of which, the body-buffettings

45. 'Sed et praeposterus ordo est, ante meritum exigere praemium, et ante laborem sumere cibum, cum dicat Apostolus: Qui non laborat non manducet., (II Thess. III, 10), Auct. cit., Sermones in Cant. Sermo XLVI.

46. Op. cit., cap. II, n. 18, T. VIII, p. 51.

47. Ibid.

48. St. Teresa is a witness to the bodily penances of St. Peter of Alcantara, with whom she was personally acquainted. See The Life of St. Teresa of Jesus, written by herself. (Trans. from the Spanish by D. Lewis), London, 1904, p. 232. See, too, the remarkable list of mortifications drawn up for personal use by St. John of the Cross, in 'Saint Jean de la Croix, Vie et Oeuvres,' (Paris, 1893), T. II, pp. 94-9. Suso gives his own list of his

were, for many, such potent means. This stressing of the preliminary purification is the result of a consciousness of the evil of sin, be it the sin under which the whole human race labours, or that directly and personally committed before conversion.[49]

It has already been remarked, but it is necessary to emphasise the fact, that Bonaventure does not consider the 'Via Purgativa' as having any termination in the present life. There is no period in which the soul can afford to abandon self-purification: no period in which self-restraint may be thrown aside in the belief that the lower self has been transformed. In the most exalted states of the spiritual life, there can be no correspondingly lofty disregard of human failings and weaknesses. The downward drag threatens not only the actual mystic, but the very beginner, even though it be conceded that for the first, because of virtuous habits, it is not so powerful. The 'Via Purgativa' is merely the name given to the period when the soul's attention is wholly concentrated upon obtaining that cleanness of mind and heart, without which, not only the vision of God, but the appreciation of spiritual things, is unthinkable.

Psychologists interested in the subject of Mysticism often refer to this as the 'annihilation' of the lower self, and it may be conceded that such an expression finds sufficient warrant in the writings of the mystics, and in Bonaventure's Theology, if it be interpreted in the sense that no progress can be made until there is a genuine abandonment of all that does not lead to God, or cannot be brought into relation with Him. An expression, however, more in keeping with what he has to say, would be 'a reordering of disordered love;' better still, 'a remaking of the entire self,' since 'Purgatio' implies a readjustment of the whole man in conformity with a new and deeper realization of the meaning of life. Life is one long pilgrimage to God: a pilgrimage easy enough in the state of innocence, but now rendered difficult of accomplishment because of sinfulness. It is the first duty of the mystic to restore, as far as is possible, the original state of man.

In the *De Triplici Via,* therefore, the Purgative Life appears as a war upon sin, which, its author maintains, finds its root in 'negligentia, concupiscentia, et nequitia.'[50] This, however, does

---

various forms of self-torture in his autobiography. See The Life of the Blessed Henry Suso by himself, (tr. by T. F. Knox), London, 1865, pp. 49, 54, 77.

49. Bonaventure expresses it: 'Peccata . . . . sive contracta, sive acta.' De Trip. Via, T. VIII, p. 4.

50. Ibid. He adds: 'Fere omnia peccata et mala nostra, sive contracta, sive acta, reduci possunt ad haec tria.'

not exhaust the whole purpose of the preliminary stage. It is not enough that man should obtain full mastery over himself, or an ease in restraining the lower passions. The purgative life must be an attempt to effect a reformation of the interior man. The Patristic teaching is reproduced. Sin both obscures the intellect and weakens the will. The soul must first 'enter into itself' and understand its actual state by contemplating the effects sin has had on these, the two principal faculties.[51] Such introspection he would have result in a genuine effort to restore these faculties to their primitive state; it is designed as revealing to the soul, not only its actual littleness and low estate as a consequence of sin, but its greatness, and high calling.

Its low estate is best described in the *Itinerarium*. The soul of man, in the perfection of its threefold powers, memory, understanding and will, reflected the image of the Blessed Trinity so clearly, that by introspection, it could at once be brought into relationship with God: this without the aid of any special grace, but by simple use of what he calls the 'oculus rationis,' to distinguish it from the 'oculus contemplationis,' so familiar in mystical writings.[52] In its present condition, distracted as it is by mundane cares, the soul cannot use its memory aright; beclouded by sense-images, it cannot use its intellect as it should be used; its will, which should always tend towards God, is drawn away from Him by pleasure in the things of sense. Then, in a beautiful passage, after depicting the soul as lying prostrate among the things of sense, and helpless in regard to the attainment of its true end, Bonaventure shows how it is offered a means of restoration by Christ, the Redeemer: 'Et quoniam, ubi quis ceciderit, necesse habere ibidem recumbere, nisi apponat quis et adiiciat, ut resurgat; non potuit anima nostra perfecte ab his sensibilibus relevari ad contuitum sui et æternæ Veritatis in se ipsa, nisi Veritas, assumta forma humana in Christo, fieret sibi scala reparans priorem scalam, quæ fracta fuerat in Adam . . . . Necesse est igitur, si reintrare volumus ad fruitionem Veritatis tanquam

51. See Soliloq., cap. 1, T. VIII, pp. 29 sqq. 'Quomodo anima per mentale exercitium debeat radium contemplationis reflectere ad interiora sua, ut videat, qualiter sit formata per naturam, deformata per culpam et reformata per gratiam.' Also see De Perfectione Vitae, cap. 1, T. VIII, p. 108 sqq. 'De vera sui ipsius cognitione.'

52. These terms are explained elsewhere. 'Triplicem homo accepit oculum, sicut dicit Hugo de sancto Victore, scilicet carnis, rationis, et contemplationis; oculum carnis quo videret mundum et ea quae sunt in mundo; oculum rationis, quo videret animum et ea quae sunt in animo; oculum contemplationis, quo videret Deum et ea quae sunt in Deo.' Breviloq., cap. XII, T. V, p. 230. Hugo's doctrine is found in De Sacramentis, Lib. 1, p. 10, c. II, P. L. T. CLXXVI, cols. 327-331.

ad paradisum, quod ingrediamur per fidem, spem, et caritatem mediatoris Dei et hominum Jesu Christi, qui est tanquam lignum vitæ in medio paradisi.'[53] The further commission of sin can only increase this helplessness. Not only must this be avoided, therefore, but there must also be a living, full use of the grace coming from God: a continuous self-training in concentrating the mind and heart upon the things pertaining to Him. Various exercises are suggested throughout the *Opuscula Mystica*, as useful to this end. They are chiefly prayer and meditation: prayer being based upon the need of Divine aid in so arduous a task: meditation, centring around the consciousness of the low estate of sinful nature. In the light of such meditation, the soul is to arouse the conscience and stimulate it into activity.[54]

We cannot help noticing that wherever Bonaventure speaks of the 'Via Purgativa' the work contemplated is primarily internal. It is a directing of mind and heart into new channels. This is surely the very essence of asceticism when rightly understood. Yet he has realized that in the concrete life, an internal reördering of this nature can rarely be divorced from what is known as outward or bodily asceticism. We find him dwelling at length, and with manifest approval, upon those typical forms of outward penance, fasting, strict observance of Franciscan poverty and other bodily mortification, so highly valued, in mediaeval times especially. Such outward penances by no means exhaust his notion of asceticism; they remain throughout but as the auxiliaries to the obtaining of internal purity. It is a Manichaean tendency, he maintains, to give them a greater value than this.[55] His doctrine of bodily asceticism is condensed in his principle: 'Tanto magis relevatur spiritus et homo interior, quanto magis mortificatur homo exterior:'[56] a principle which in turn he explicitly derives from St. Paul's statement: 'Though the outward man is corrupted, yet the inner man is renewed day by day.'[57] External mortification of whatever kind it may be, is only a means to an internal renewal of spirit: never an end in itself, and never represented as such. It is intended to bring the body into full subjection to the spirit, and is but the external expression of the great mystical axiom, that he who would gain all must surrender all. There must be, even in those physically incapable of harsh

53. Op. cit., cap. IV, n. 2, T. V, p. 306.
54. See De Trip. Via, passim. Prayer and Meditation are given their due place elsewhere.
55. See Apol. Pauperum, cap. V, n. 11, T. VIII, p. 260.
56. II S. D. XIX. a. 1, q. 1, n. 7, T. II, p. 459.
57. 11 Cor., 4, 16.

external penance, the total sacrifice, not only of the pleasures brought by the satisfaction of the baser instincts, but of the natural instincts too, where these clash with the demands of the higher life of the spirit. Into the asceticism of some, therefore, bodily penance must enter as an integral element. Elsewhere, when dealing with the 'Via Illuminativa,' we shall see how this discipline is not confined to the stage of spirituality with which we are dealing at present, but must be carried on throughout the whole life, since, in an imitation of Christ, the basis of the illuminative life, Our Lord, in His physical sufferings offers Himself as Guide.[58]

In addition to this clear recognition of the fact that bodily austerities are but auxiliaries, we find him extremely moderate in his teaching with regard to them: at least when he is not writing polemically. Thus, the discretion and prudence of St. Francis is frequently commended, as for example when he writes: 'Licet autem pro viribus ad vitam austeram Fratres induceret, non tamen ei placebat districtionis severitas quæ pietatis non induit viscera, nec est discretionis sale condita.' To illustrate this discretion he narrates how on a certain night when one of the brethren, by reason of excessive abstinence, was so tormented with hunger that he could take no repose, Francis, perceiving the danger, called the brother, set bread before him, and, to remove any cause for confusion, began first to eat himself, and then gently bade him partake.[59] He hands down, too, Francis' own advice to follow discretion as the 'charioteer' of all the virtues: 'Docuit (Franciscus) insuper eos discretionem sequi ut aurigam virtutum, non eam, quam caro suadet, sed quam edocuit Christus, cuius sanctissimam vitam expressum constat esse perfectionis exemplar.'[60] His bodily asceticism can never be judged as leading to a stunting of the healthy human life, but rather to the freeing of the self from the shackles placed upon spiritual development, by the constant pandering to the cravings of the body.

This discretion is most noticeable when he is not writing apologetically, as was said: hence in his *Soliloquium* and *De Perfectione Vitæ.* In the *Apologia Pauperum* and the *De Perfectione Evangelica,* he does indeed appear rigid and stern, reminding the reader not so much of the gentle St. Francis of his *Legenda,* as of the Fathers of the Desert, whose example he often quotes. But he is writing both works with a brief, and not as director of souls. The

58. See Itin., Prologus, n. 3, T. V, p. 295.
59. Legenda Sti. Francisci, cap. V, n. 7, T. VIII, p. 518.
60. Ibid.

two works should be called commentaries on the spirituality of the Fathers of the Desert, and of St. Jerome, whose proneness to rigid austerity is marked, rather than the expression of his own doctrine. Augustine and Bernard are only quoted here, when they write enthusiastically on the benefits of self-denial. These works were written after the whole life of the Mendicant Orders had been attacked by Guilllaume de St. Amour; it became his duty, first as a teacher in the University of Paris, and secondly as the Minister General of his Order, to defend its many forms of outward austerity: fasting, poverty, the wearing of sandals and of rough habits. The pivot on which both treatises turn is given, when he writes in the *Apologia Pauperum:* 'Quamquam certum sit omnibus in christiano exercitatis agone, abstinentiæ sanctæ rigorem pernecessarium esse his qui perfectionem adipisci et defensare conantur; quia tamen novæ adinventionis dogma perversum subintroductum est ad probandum contrarium, roboranda est huiusmodi veritas, tam per exempla, quam per documenta Sanctorum.'[61] Not from works written with such a purpose could we reasonably expect to derive his representative doctrines. Their severity should in no way alter our previous estimation of his asceticism. Primarily internal, it is, in its external aspect, moderate and sane.

The end of all asceticism, he declares, is to obtain peace of mind and heart. Only in a state of true peace can the Revelation of Christ in its application to human life be grasped. Hence the 'Via Purgativa' is made to end in peace, 'via purgativa quæ in pacem ducit,'[62] and the constant hope he keeps before the soul in its war upon sin, is the 'tranquillitas et serenitas . . . . . . ex qua oritur spiritualis iucunditas, qua adepta, promptus est animus ut sursum tendat.'[63]

We cannot quote Bonaventure as having added anything to the ascetical doctrine of his day; neither, however, has he narrowed it down. The substance of his doctrine could be traced back to pre-Christian sources, apart, however, from what has been said regarding the grace necessary. Pre-Christian philosophers were almost unanimous in this, that the wise man must reconquer himself, and imitate the Divine Purity, before he can advance in the wisdom that ennobles him. One of the fundamental ideas of Patristic teaching is that the knowledge of God, not only that which is mystical, but any knowledge helpful to the

61. Op. cit., cap. V, n. 1, T. VIII, p. 257.
62. De Trip. Via, T. VIII, p. 3.
63. Ibid., p. 14.

spiritual life, is as a light which cannot penetrate through the darkness created by sin. Quotations in great number could be given to show this. Phrases similar to Origen's 'Cor enim contaminatum Deum contemplari non potest,'[64] are met with again and again in Bonaventurian literature. His ascetical doctrine might easily be reduced to a principle taken from the same source: 'Id quod Deum videt, est cor purum.'[65] He is so much more in sympathy with human failings than Pseudo-Dionysius, to give this mysterious person a special place in connexion with this point. As already remarked, the 'Via Purgativa' of the one, is, in appearance at least, mainly a philosophical process;[66] that of the other is definitely ethical.

In Augustine's *Confessions,* Bonaventure found a living example of a purgative process which was not only a gradual emerging from intellectual error, but also from moral perversity. Throughout his works, St. Augustine is no less practical than theoretical, with regard to the idea that the knowledge of God is as a light which cannot penetrate into the depths of the soul till sin is removed. The theory gives rise to an asceticism similar to Bonaventure's.[67] Gregory's *Moralia in Job,* Bernard's *Sermones,* and the many little works of the Victorines continue the tradition. Finally, in the life of his Father, St. Francis of Assisi, he has seen whither the 'Via Purgativa' will lead.

There is no need to prove that in the case of all the writers mentioned above, bodily mortification of various kinds has been admitted to be the element which gives life to an asceticism which is essentially inward. At least it is upon numerous quotations taken from their works, as well as upon the examples of the saints and the more severe doctrines of St. Jerome, that he constructs the above mentioned apologetic treatises in defense of the Mendicant Friars.

In conclusion: Bonaventure's asceticism, both internal and external, is guided by right reason, aided by the Revelation contained in Sacred Scripture, and by the traditions derived from

64. Auct., cit., Contra Celsum, Lib. VI, n. 69, P. G. T. XI, col. 1404.
65. Ibid., Lib. VII, n. 33, col. 1467.
66. There is of course no intention here of maintaining that Pseudo-Dionysius was unaware of the need of the moral purifying process. There can be no doubt that his 'Via Purgativa,' consisting as it does in an attempt to expel from the mind all sense images, and to create that necessary void wherein grace could have free play, implied a prior effort to rid the soul of sin and its consequences.
67. See Op. S. Augustini: Enarratio in Ps. XLI, P. L. T. XXXVI, cols. 465-6; De Doctrina Christiana, Lib. 1, cap. X, T. XXXV, col. 23; De Trinitate, Lib. VIII, n. 5, T. XLIII, col. 950; In Epist. Joannis, Tract. VII, n. 10, T. XXXV, cols. 2033-4.

Patristic sources. It comprehends the true nature of man, his destiny and his obligations, viewing him as the creature elected to a supernatural state. It seeks to illumine man's mind and to strengthen his will by supernatural grace. Aware that he has to control his lower passions and to withstand many trials and temptations, it not only permits, but upon some it enjoins the practice of bodily penance. In a word, it is a method adopted in a sincere endeavour to observe, and to teach, the full law of God.

CHAPTER III.

The 'Via Illuminativa.'—This the title given to the imitation of Christ. —The title explained.—Bonaventure's doctrine in the major Theological and Scriptural works.—Same teaching in the **Opuscula**.—Christ the central Figure of his spiritual teaching. — Primary element in Bonaventure's 'Imitatio Christi' the renunciation symbolized by the Cross.—Christ in His Human Nature, the Exemplar of the full Christian life. — Love of Our Lord in His Humanity to be spiritualized by thought of His Divinity. — Basis of Bonaventure's 'Imitatio Christi' known to Origen, Augustine, Cassian, and Gregory. — Bonaventure immediately influenced by Anselm, Bernard, and by spiritual tradition set up by St. Francis of Assisi.—His doctrine on the 'Via Illuminativa' criticised.—A Christocentric spirituality. Absence of any Quietistic conceptions of the Humanity of Christ. — Element of renunciation in the 'Imitatio Christi' does not give rise to a one-sided Christianity.—Purpose of renunciation.—Attempted explanation of great efficacy attributed by the mystics to suffering.

From the first it was intended to develope this essay as far as possible, on lines running parallel with Bonaventure's conception of the development of the spiritual life itself, that is, with the 'scala perfectionis' found to be substantially the same in most mystical writings. The next point to be dealt with, therefore, should be the 'Via Illuminativa.' Here the difficulty, due to the fact, that, unlike the Victorines and the German mystics of the fourteenth century, he has left no synthetic treatise on Mystical Theology, is especially felt. There are but few references throughout his works, to the illuminative way, understood as a further stage of spiritual progress,[1] and even when they do occur, no attempt is made to give a full account of what he understands by the term, or to describe the spiritual experiences which objectively constitute the stage in question. This criticism extends even to the *De Triplici Via,* notwithstanding the fact that it deals professedly with the threefold way, and in spite of the further fact, that certain critics have praised it as a compendium of all that is best in Christian Mysticism.[2] On the present matter it is

1. This qualifying clause seems necessary, since frequently his system of knowledge, which is Augustinian in origin, is referred to as the 'Via Illuminativa;' for an exposition of which, see De Humanae Congnitionis Ratione . . . Sti. Bon., ed. studio et cura P. P. Coll. S. Bon. Quarrachi, 1883; also, É. Gilson, Études de Philosophie Médievale, Strasbourg, 1921, pp. 77-95; idem, La Philosophie de Saint Bonaventure, Paris, 1924, chap. XII, L'illumination intellectuelle, pp. 326 sqq.

2. The Quarrachi Editors write: 'Pretium huius opusculi vix satis aestimari potest, cum totam theologicam mysticam in nucleo comprehendat et iure alterum quoddam Breviloquium, sed Theologiae non scholasticae, sed mysticae, vocari possit.' T. VIII, p. 10: an opinion endorsed by P. Robinson,

particularly disappointing, giving as it does, under the title 'Via Illuminativa,' merely a series of pious thoughts and spiritual injunctions obviously intended to serve as aids to meditation.

Bonaventure dwells briefly on the evils from which the soul has been more or less freed during the purgative life: the depths into which it would have fallen, but for the restraining influence of Christ: the benefits, natural and supernatural, supplied by an all-bountiful Providence. Christ in His Incarnation, has been given to man as a brother and friend; in His Passion and Death, He has become for him the sole means of salvation; in the Sacrament of the Eucharist, He gives Himself as a sustaining Food. Christ, moreover, has promised rewards to all who believe in Him and love Him: 'amotionem omnium malorum, associationem omnium Sanctorum, impletionem omnium desideriorum in seipso.'[3]

When, later on, in the same work, he returns to the subject of the illuminative way, we obtain a somewhat deeper insight into his mind. He treats, again in a summary fashion, however, of the 'gradus perveniendi ad splendorem veritatis,' indicating the term of the illuminative life. Beginning, as he also begins his beautiful treatise the *Lignum Vitæ,*[4] by counselling a firm act of faith in Christ as the Son of God, the Supreme Principle of all things, and the Saviour of mankind, he continues by making the many circumstances of Our Lord's Passion and Death the subjects of further affective reflections. Yet it is here that he clearly marks the exact foundation of the second stage of the spiritual life, expressly declaring as he does that its end is attained 'per imitationem Christi.'[5] The problem, therefore, before us, is to ascertain what he implies by an imitation of Christ: no easy one, when it is remembered that in his works are to be found treatises of a purely apologetic nature, concerned at times mainly with discovering in the Christ-life manifestation of particular ideals, to the exclusion of all else.

It is well to remember in connection with the foregoing pious reflections, that they are addressed to those who are making progress in virtue. Compunction of heart, freedom from all sins committed in the past, and from all attachment to the things which lead from God, are presupposed. The struggle is now still

O. F. M., art. St. Bonaventure, in Catholic Encyclopaedia, Vol. II, p. 652. 'What the 'Breviloquium' is to Scholasticism, the 'De Triplici Via' is to mysticism—a perfect compendium of all that is best in it.'

3. Op. cit., cap. 1, n. 14; T. VIII, pp. 6-7. Similar, almost identical thoughts find expression in Sermo X in Pent., T. IX, p. 346; Coll. in Hexaëm: col. XXII, n. 11, T. V, p. 439.

4. Op. cit., T. VIII, pp. 71 sqq.

5. De Triplici Via, cap. III, n. 3, T. VIII, pp. 12 sqq.

more inward than in the 'Via Purgativa' itself. Though Bonaventure makes no mention of such experiences described by St. John of the Cross, as the 'Dark Night of the Soul,' from all that must be said, it will be agreed, that he was quite aware of the trials to be undergone before there could be, normally speaking, any hope of mystic union with God. For, the Illuminative life is an imitation of Christ, and this includes for him, as an integral element, a life of the renunciation which has its symbol in the Cross.

If this imitation of Christ, primarily a devotional stage, be the fundamental idea of the 'Via Illuminativa,' how is the title to be accounted for? Bonaventure gives no direct explanation, but it may be suggested, that it is due to a fondness, which he shares with Hugo of St. Victor, for regarding light as the chief symbol of Christ's influence upon man, and the Sun as itself the symbol of the Word Incarnate, the Source of all Grace.[6] Since Christ's influence, before it is effective, requires free acceptance on the part of a rational creature, the term 'imitatio,' implying as it does for Bonaventure, first of all an acceptance of the graces which flow from Christ, and secondly an effort to advance in virtue according to the example given in His earthly life, admirably expresses the religious experiences he has in mind as coming within the illuminative life.

His imitation of Our Lord furthermore deserves to be coupled with illumination, since it pre-supposes the knowledge by faith, that in the Gospel narrative, the various details of the Christ-life are recorded with direct reference to man's practical edification. This knowledge, we are constantly reminded, is a light from on high. Now, the main supposition is, that in the actual progressive attempt to re-live in our own way Christ's earthly life, by imitating as far as possible, the many virtues of which He is the Archetype, the soul is more and more enlightened, and prepared for the mystic union. With the restoration to holiness of life, through an imitation of Christ, the Pattern of all true holiness, there is a nearer approach to the state of original innocence: consequently, to the original facility in contemplation.

---

6. 'In allegoria . . . per solem intelligitur Christus: Oritur sol et occidit; oritur in nativitate, occidit in morte; gyrat per meridiem, in ascensione; flectitur ad aquilonem in iudicio.' Coll. in Hex. col. XIII, n. 26, T. V, p. 391.

Compare with Hugo's In Eccles. Hom.: Hom. II, P. L. T. CLXXV, cols. 135-6. This acceptation of the Sun as the symbol of Christ, is of course common to writers of an earlier date, but Hugo and Bonaventure show a marked predilection for it. See Keble, J. On the Mysticism attributed to the early Fathers of the Church, Tract. LXXXIX, Oxford, 1868, pp. 159 sqq.

His *Opuscula,* giving as they do, but pious reflections for the purpose of meditation, it seems better to look for his ideas in the major theological works. These contain a Christological doctrine, possessing a warmth not usually associated with Scholastic treatises. Such warmth is undoubtedly due to the importance assumed by the teaching that Christ is given to us for our imitation This is one of the two main themes of his Commentary on the third book of the Sentences, and it is well stressed in that compendium of mediaeval theology, the *Breviloquium.*

There is no need to point out, that with Bonaventure, the Divinity of Our Lord is an indisputable fact. Both works deal with all those questions concerning Him which absorbed the attention of his contemporary theological teachers: with the Hypostatic Union: Christ's special graces and prerogatives. He treats in due order of the grace proper to Christ as Head of the human race, of His knowledge, human life, virginal birth, baptism, doctrines, miracles, Passion and Death: in a word, with all those questions to which St. Anselm's epoch-making *Cur Deus Homo* gave rise. His Christology, as contained in the Commentary, and in the *Breviloquium,* aims at bringing home Christ's Personality to the imagination, intellect and will; all that Christ did and said is valued in the light of what He is believed to be. And He is believed to be the Divine Guide to Christian perfection.

In the introduction to his Commentary, he immediately shows the importance of following this Guide. This introduction is based upon the words of St. Paul: 'But God, (who is rich in mercy) for His exceeding charity wherewith He loved us, even when we were dead in sins, hath quickened us together in Christ, (by whose grace you are saved.)' [7] St. Paul in these words, he maintains, has given us a perfect sum of the economy of grace: 'in qua explicatur nostræ redemptionis sacramentum factum per Christum,'[8] since the whole passage immediately recalls to the mind God, the Author of the Redemption, the fall of the human race in Adam, the Person of the Redeemer, and the means of salvation offered to man, through the grace of Christ.

He now stresses that idea which was to be the basis of the spirituality of future centuries: the imitation of Christ. He writes: 'Postremo secundum Christum nos (Deus) vivificavit, dum ad eius exemplum nos per viam vitæ direxit, iuxta illud Psalmi:

7. Eph. 2, 4-5.
8. S. Exord., T. III, p. 1.

Notas mihi fecisti vias vitæ. Notas nobis fecit vias vitæ, dum nobis fidem et spem et caritatem et dona gratiarum distribuit, et mandata adiunxit. . . . in quibus consistit via vitæ, per quam Christus nos docuit ambulare. Deus igitur nos vivificavit secundum Christum, quia ad vitam dirigit imitatores ipsius.'[9] Throughout the Commentary, there is a faithfulness to the same idea, of the life-giving power of an imitation of Christ; and later, rejecting the division of Christology made by Peter Lombard,[10] he declares it is better to treat, firstly of the life which Christ has assumed for man's salvation, and secondly of the life He has made possible for us, through His grace.[11] The grace He communicates to us, enables us to find in Him, the Exemplar of all virtue: the 'Book' wherein we are to read, not only the things to be believed and hoped for, but also the way we are to tread.[12]

Repeatedly he tells us, that if we desire to respond faithfully to the Christian vocation, we must concentrate our minds upon the historical life of Christ, for in this shall we find certain indication of the road to be trodden. Thus: 'Si volumus ad ultimum prædestinationis terminum pervenire, necesse habemus in auctorem fidei et consummatorem aspicere, qui exemplum dedit, ut quemadmodum ipse fecit, et nos faciamus.'[13] It is evident from the context of this passage, that he has in mind the earthly life of Christ, manifested in the Gospels. Also it is patent, that his 'Imitatio' has a deeper meaning than that ordinarily attached to it, inasmuch as it is rendered possible only through the grace coming from Our Lord,[14] and connotes not a mere conformity in externals with the Christ-Pattern, but an acquiring of Christ's spirit through such external conformity. Beneath this same doctrine, is the conception of the 'Verbum Increatum et Incarnatum' as the Exemplar of the eternal and temporal worlds,[15] and it is as Exemplar of the

9. Ibid., p. 2. The Scriptural reference is to Ps. 15, 10.
10. Ibid., p. 7.
11. Ibid.
12. Ibid. This is also expressed elsewhere: 'Exemplar . . . directivum . . . respectu nostri, tam in credendis, quam in expectandis, quam etiam in operandis.' III S. D. XI, q. II, T. III, p. 246.
13. III S. D. XI, a. 1, q. II, T. III, p. 246. As illustrative of his power of working Scriptural quotations into his text, note how he here connects Heb. 12, 2, with John, 13, 15.
14. See Ibid., D. XXXV, a. I, q. II, p. 776. Knowledge of Christ as Exemplar of all virtue is here attributed to the gift of the Holy Ghost—'Scientia.'
15. This is brought out clearly in the Apologia Pauperum also. 'Intelligendum est igitur, quod cum Christus sit Verbum increatum et incarnatum, duplex est in eo ratio exemplaritatis, aeternae videlicet et temporalis; aeternae, inquam, secundum quod est splendor paternae gloriae et figura substantiae Dei Patris, atque candor lucis aeternae . . . . In quantum autem

temporal world, that is, in His Human Nature, that we are bound to imitate Christ. When, in the Commentary, he deals with the graces obtained for man by Christ, they are represented as so many means placed within our power to produce a likeness to Him.

It is of course, quite possible to conceive of an irrational and purely external imitation of Our Lord, which can be of no great spiritual worth. Needless to say, Bonaventure's doctrine never descends to so low a level. External conformity there must be, but it is given life by the hypothesis that the reward of a progressive attempt to imitate Christ, even in externals, is the correspondingly deeper realization of the inner meaning of it. This is a pre-supposition, which, if it is true, — and to prove whether it is true or not we can only appeal to personal experience —will explain the joyousness with which mystics like St. Francis of Assisi have so literally imitated one or more of the characteristics of Christ, be it His poverty, His self-abnegation, or His patient service of others. Unless we are willing to admit the truth of the Bonaventurian hypothesis, it becomes increasingly difficult to understand their conduct, the more it exhibits the almost passionate attempt to be other Christs, even outwardly. As it is, the nearer they are to the attainment of their end, so much the more do they tend to regard humility, patience, poverty, obedience to others, and suffering of all kinds, as having an almost objective value. These are valued because of their association with Christ: the very fact that Christ deigned to take them to Himself, proves their worth. After all, as Bonaventure admits in his *Apologia Pauperum,* it is not in man's nature to carry the Cross under all these forms, to love it, and to welcome it. It is not in man's nature, he repeatedly declares, to practice that humility, not merely the humility which is the natural characteristic of every sane man, but the humility regarded by St. Augustine [16] and St. Bernard,[17] as the very bed-rock of the Christian virtues. Nor is it in man's nature, to adopt that extreme form of poverty which he regards as the specific element in the Franciscan ideal.[18] Christ in His Incarnation, is the mystic 'Door' leading to union

---

Verbum incarnatum in assumtae humanitatis conversatione, exemplar est et speculum omnium gratiarum, virtutum et meritorum, ad cuius exemplaris imitationem erigendum est tabernaculum militantis Ecclesiae.' Cap. II, n. 12, T. VIII, pp. 242-3.

16. See Auct. cit., Sermo LXIX, cap. 1, n. 2, P. L., T. XXXVIII, col. 441,

17. Auct. cit. In Cant. Cantic. Sermo XXXVI, P. L., T. CLXXXIII, cols. 967-971.

18. See Epist. Officiales, ep. II, T. VIII, p. 471; also Det. Quaest., q. 1. ibid., p. 338.

with the Godhead. Enjoyment of the mystic knowledge and love of the Divinity is vouchsafed only to such as are made like to the Word Incarnate.

This same doctrine of the 'Imitatio Christi' is insisted upon, perhaps still more explicitly, in Bonaventure's Commentary on the Gospel of St. Luke. It is not usual to find mystical doctrines built upon the Synoptics; but here, Luke is represented as showing even more clearly than the other Evangelists, that Christ is not only the Redeemer, in word, of the Christian life, and the Saviour of men through the Cross, but also the Saviour in the sense that He Himself has given to them, in His own actions, a visible example of the perfection within their own grasp. For, in the ninth chapter of St. Luke's Gospel, it is recorded that after St. Peter's confession of faith, Our Lord foretold His Passion and Death, emphasizing the duty of self-abnegation, in those who wished to be saved. 'And He said to all: If any man will come after Me, let him deny himself, and take up his cross daily, and follow Me.'[19] In the same chapter, the Transfiguration is narrated. The Franciscan Doctor couples the two passages together, declaring that in the one, Our Lord is pointing out the nature of the path we are to tread, whilst in the other, He manifests the glories of the rewards which may, in a degree, be anticipated even in this life. These rewards await a genuine attempt to imitate Christ.[20]

The way therefore, leading to God, implies principally two things: a knowledge of Christ by faith, and a perfect imitation of Him through the sharing in His Cross.[21] By faith, the soul realizes all that Christ is to itself: that He is the supreme source of spiritual well-being. The more intense the faith, so much the more is His life revealed as being possible of imitation, by use of the means possessed by every soul acknowledging His dominion. The significance therefore of the definition he gives of saving faith, is now more fully understood: 'Fides est habitus quo intellectus noster captivatur in obsequium Christi.' For the intellect must needs be brought into subjection to the obedience of Christ, if it is to find in His lowliness and poverty and sufferings, sure means to be adopted in the attainment of fullest spiritual fellowship with

---

19. 9, 23.

20. See: Com. in Luc.: cap. IX, n. 29, T. VII, pp. 225. 'In parte ista exprimit viam proficiendi. Ad profectum autem isti duo consideranda concurrunt, scilicet asperitas viae, in qua consistit meritum, et suavitas patriae, in qua consistit praemium.'

21. 'Via autem ad patriam potissime in duobus consistit, scilicet, in perfecta cognitione Christi per fidem, et perfecta imitatione per crucem.' Ibid.

Our Lord. In the light of such a faith in Him, every action of His earthly life recorded in the Gospels has a distinct value, as directive of man's spiritual affairs.

Bearing in mind these fundamental ideas, culled from his major Theological and Scriptural treatises, we may return to the *Opuscula*. Since they are for the most part addressed to Religious, to those bound by the three vows of Poverty, Chastity and Obedience, it is well-nigh impossible to gather from them the material representing his full conception of the imitation of Christ to which all are called. Certainly he makes no attempt to impose upon all men precisely the same form of imitation. Thus, not all, in a desire to follow Our Lord, need adopt His counsels of perfection, upon which the religious vows of Poverty, Chastity and Obedience are founded. Even with those who have adopted the counsels, not all need regard the form of poverty peculiar to the Franciscan Order as the only true imitation of Christ's poverty. The Church Militant, being the body of Christ, must, as a whole, be assimilated to Him.[22] Within it, must be found members who reproduce in their lives His Penance and sufferings: others who continue His life of service to mankind in general: still more, who continue His life of prayer and intercession. Every characteristic of the Christ-life must be reflected in the whole body of the faithful.

In general, it may be said of the *Opuscula*, that there is an immediately noticeable endeavour to make the Gospel narrative live vividly in the minds of his readers: not, however, by way of departing from the strict details contained therein, in favour of the imaginary and fanciful incidents beloved of mediaeval spiritual writers.[23] All Christ's human experiences are treated of with loving thought, and with an eagerness to draw from them spiritual direction. His Birth, Infancy, Manhood, Life and Passion, are presented in the light of a faith which beholds Him calling men to a mode of life, by Himself first living that same life. Bonaventure's *Opuscula* present to us a Christ, truly God, and truly Man, voluntarily accepting all human weaknesses save those which are the direct consequences of sin, and

---

22. 'Ad cuius exemplaris imitationem erigendum est tabernaculum militantis Ecclesiae.' T. VIII, p. 243, cf. De Sex alis Seraphim, ibid., p. 137.

23. Examples abound in the Meditationes Vitae Christi wrongly attributed to him. Contained in Editions of Bonaventure's works printed before that of the Quarrachi Fathers. Portions of these Meditations, which were popular over the whole of Europe, were rendered into English by Nicholas Love, prior of the Carthusian house of Mount Grace de Ingelby, Yorks, before 1410. See The Mirrour of the Blessed Lyf of Jesu Christ, ed by L. F. Powell, Oxford, MCMVII.

proving that nothing He Himself has done is too difficult for man.

Because of this, Bonaventure can spur the Poor Clares on to a generous love of Franciscan poverty. 'O Deus meus! quomodo possumus esse ita duri contra Christum, qui exivit de terra sua, ... et factus est pro nobis pauper, abjectus et despectus? Et nos nolumus pro eo relinquere unum miserum et fœtidum mundum?' [24]

In a sense, we can re-live, inwardly, the special events recorded in the Gospel story. Of Christ's conception, birth, and infancy, he writes: 'Incidit menti meæ secretius, quod anima Deo devota, benedictum Dei Patris Verbum et Filium unigenitum mediante gratia Spiritus sancti spiritualiter posset virtute Altissimi concipere, parere, nominare, cum beatis Magis quærere et adorare et demum Deo Patri secundum Legem Moysi in templo feliciter præsentare, et sic tanquam vera Christianæ religionis discipula quinque festa, quæ de puero Jesu agit Ecclesia, mente devota cum omni reverentia valeat celebrare.'[25] He continues his work by making these events the basis of his doctrine.

In the *Vitis Mystica,* after showing how all the events of the Christ-life are recorded for man's spiritual benefit, he represents Christ as addressing the devout soul thus:- 'Conformaveram te imagini Deitatis meæ, cum te crearem; conformatus sum imagini humanitatis tuæ, ut te reformarem. Tu ergo, qui non retinuisti formam Deitatis meæ tibi impressam in tua formatione, retine saltem formam humanitatis tuæ mihi impressam in tua recreatione; si non retines, qualem te creaveram, retine saltem qualem te recreaveram; si non capis, quantas virtutes tibi dederim te creando, capis saltem, quantas in humanitate tua miserias propter te acceperim te recreando, et ad potiores quam ad quas te formaveram delicias reformando. Nam propterea homo visibilis factus sum, ut a te visus amarer; qui in Deitate mea invisus et invisibilis quodam modo non amabar. Da ergo præmium incarnatione meæ et passioni te, pro quo incarnatus simul sum et passus. Dedi me tibi, da te mihi.' [26] These quotations, the length of which, it is hoped, will be pardoned, will sufficiently prove that the central Figure of Bonaventure's spiritual doctrine, is our Divine Lord.

A judgment often passed on Mediaeval Mysticism in general, is that it can view no incident in Christ's life, except His actual

---

24. De Perfect. Vitae, cap. III, n. 8, T. VIII, p. 114.
25. De Quinque Festiv.: Pueri Jesu, Prologus, T. VIII, p. 88.
26. Op. cit., cap. XXIV, n. 3, T. VIII, p. 189.

sufferings, as a subject of meditation, or as an incentive to Christian practice: that it gives rise to a one-sided Christianity, and fails to realize that the ordinary life of man, which must needs be lived in such a way that a literal imitation of those sufferings is impossible, can also find its ennoblement in the very fact of the Incarnation. How far is this true of Bonaventure?

It is unquestionable, that the aspect of the human life of Our Lord which he emphasises, is that which is centralized in His absolute renunciation. Most often it is to Christ's self-denial, culminating in His Passion and Death that he makes appeal. The whole of Our Lord's earthly life presents itself to him as leading up to the Cross, so that he can write: 'Passionem vero, non illum unum diem appellamus, quo mortuus fuit, sed totam vitam illius; tota enim vita Christi exemplum fuit et martyrium;'[27] and elsewhere: 'A prima enim die nativitatis suæ usque ad ultimum diem mortis semper fuit in passionibus et doloribus.'[28] Moreover, he dwells upon the idea that in a sinful world, an experience of Christianity transcending the Cross, is never granted. His main object throughout the *Opuscula* is, therefore, to arouse a deep practical love of Christ Crucified. This gives rise to an asceticism, moulded and formed by the Cross, and it is the asceticism of Christ's Cross, more than the asceticism of His service of others, which becomes in his Mysticism the sure road to Contemplation.[29] The love which makes the saint, is the practical love of Christ Crucified, which seeks to find expression in suffering and self-abnegation.[30]

So persuaded is he of the power of this form of devotion, that a whole chapter of the *De Triplici Via* is employed in showing how meditation on the Cross leads up to the 'splendor veritatis,' the privilege of the contemplative state.[31] It is, moreover, when treating of the Passion of Our Lord, that he exhibits the emotionalism of a St. Bernard, or a St. Francis. The following passage is typical: 'Accede ergo tu, O famula, pedibus affectionum tuarum ad Jesum vulneratum, ad Jesum spinis coronatum, ad Jesum patibulo crucis affixum, et cum beato Thoma Apostolo non solum intuere in manibus eius fixuram clavorum, ... non solum mitte manum tuam in latus eius, sed totaliter per ostium lateris ingredere usque

27. Vitis Mystica, cap. V, n. 2, T. VIII, p. 169.
28. De Perf. Vitae, cap. VI, n. 8, T. VIII, p. 122.
29. See Sermo II, Feria Sexta in Parasceve, T. IX, pp. 262-7.
30. See De regimine animae, T. VIII, p. 130, and compare De Perf. Vitae ad Sorores, 'De passionis Christi memoria,' cap. VI, T. VIII, pp. 120-124, quoted infra.
31. 'De septem gradibus, quibus pervenitur ad splendorem veritatis.' Op. cit., T. VIII, pp. 12-14.

ad cor ipsius Jesu, ibique ardentissimo Crucifixi amore in Christum transformata, clavis divini timoris confixa, lancea præcordialis dilectionis transfixa, gladio intimæ compassionis transverberata, nihil aliud quæras, nihil aliud desideres, in nullo alio velis consolari, quam ut cum Christo tu possis in cruce mori. Et tunc cum Paulo Apostolo exclames et dicas: Christo crucifixus sum cruci. Vivo iam non ego, vivit vero in me Christus.'[32]

Bonaventure's devotion to Christ, then, is unquestionably centralized in His Passion and sufferings. And it means for him all that it meant for the mediaeval mind in general — the voluntary undertaking of internal and external mortification, not indeed for its own sake, but because of its association with Christ. Participation in His sufferings, effects a union between Him and the soul: 'Verus Dei cultor Christique discipulus,' he writes, 'qui Salvatori omnium pro se crucifixo perfecte configurari desiderat, ad hoc potissimum attento mentis conatu debet intendere, ut Christi Jesu crucem circumferat iugiter tam mente quam carne, quatenus præfatum Apostoli verbum (Christo crucifixus sum cruci) veraciter valeat in semetipso sentire. Porro huiusmodi affectum et sensum is duntaxat apud se vivaciter experiri meretur, qui, dominicæ passionis non immemor nec ingratus, laborem et dolorem amoremque crucifixi Jesu tanta memoriæ vivacitate, tanto intellectus acumine, tanta voluntatis caritate considerat, quod veraciter illud sponsæ proferre potest eloquium: Fasciculus myrrhæ dilectus meus mihi, inter ubera mea commorabitur.' [33]

The foregoing may be displeasing to those who would prefer to see the Christ 'going about doing good and spending Himself in the service of others,' put to the forefront as an object of imitation. If this aspect of Christ's life were entirely neglected, an adverse criticism, would, we venture to think, be perfectly justified. Elsewhere we deal with the spiritual worth of the renunciation based upon the Cross, in relation to the Christian activity which is, or should be, based in turn upon the labours of Our Lord. For the present, it suffices to instance Bonaventure's conception of the ideal Franciscan life, to show that his Christianity is not wholly one-sided. The perfect Friar can only fulfil his vocation by equally emphasising in his

32. De Perf. Vitae, cap. VI, n. 2, T. VIII, p. 120. The words of St. Paul are from Gal. 2, 19-20.

33. Lignum Vitae, Prologus, T. VIII, p. 68. The Scriptural reference is to Canticles, 1, 12.

personal imitation of Our Lord both characteristics of the supreme Archetype.[34]

A further question to be asked is this: is it in His Divinity or in His Humanity that Our Lord is the central Figure of Bonaventure's spirituality? We ask this question in view of the oft-repeated assertion, that with mystical writers there is a great temptation to forget altogether the Humanity of Christ, or to pass beyond it as quickly as possible, to the 'vacant ground of the undifferentiated Godhead.' The very quotations already given, to show how the great lesson of renunciation is to be learnt in Christ, should suffice to answer this question. Of course, the desired end of this love of Christ suffering in His human nature, is always the attainment of union with His hidden Divinity. So persuaded is Bonaventure that faithfulness to meditation upon the Humanity will ultimately lead to mystic union, that he uses the idea to illustrate other facts: 'Sicut in Christum pie intendentibus aspectus carnis, qui patebat, via erat ad agnitionem Divinitatis, quæ latebat; sic ad intelligendam divinæ sapientiæ veritatem ænigmaticis ac mysticis figuris intelligentiæ rationalis manuducitur oculus.'[35] Nor is there any indication in his writings of a doctrine that the time may come in the spiritual life when meditation upon the Humanity can be a stumbling-block to further development. One has only to study the *Itinerarium* to arrive at this conclusion. Here the mystical union itself is continually mentioned in direct conjunction with devotion to the Crucified: 'Via autem non est nisi per ardentissimum amorem Crucifixi' is met with again and again.[36] The following is so precise that, in spite of its length, it may be quoted in full. He has been discoursing 'de excessu mentali et mystico, in quo requies datur intellectui, affectu totaliter in Deum per excessum transeunte,'[37] that is, of the mystical experience, and he writes: 'Cum tandem in sexto gradu ad hoc pervenerit, ut speculetur in principio primo et summo et mediatore Dei et hominum, Jesu Christo, ea quorum similia in creaturis nullatenus reperiri possunt, et quæ omnem perspicacitatem humani intellectus excedunt: restat, ut hæc speculando transcendat et transeat non solum mundum istum sensibilem, verum etiam semetipsam: in quo transitu Christus est via et ostium, Christus est

34. Apologia Pauperum, T. VIII, pp. 234-330; also Determinationes Quaest. ibid., pp. 337-374; and Quare Fratres Minores praedicent, ibid., pp. 375-385.

35. Tractatus de Plantat. Parad., n. 1, T. V, pp. 574-5.

36. Op. cit., Prologus, n. 3, p. 295; compare: cap. II, n. 13, p. 303; cap. IV, n. 2-5, pp. 306-7; cap. VI, n. 4-7, pp. 311-12; cap. VII, n. 4, n. 6, pp. 312-13. All in T. V.

37. The title of his last chapter in the Itinerarium, T. V.

scala et vehiculum tanquam propitiatorium super arcam Dei collocatum et sacramentum a sæculis absconditum. Ad quod propitiatorium qui aspicit plena conversione vultus, aspiciendo eum in cruce suspensum, per fidem, spem et caritatem, devotionem, admirationem, exsultationem, appretiationem, laudem et iubilationem; pascha, hoc est transitum, cum eo facit, ut per virgam crucis transeat mare rubrum, ab Aegypto intrans desertum, ubi gustet manna absconditum, et cum Christo requiescat in tumulo quasi exterius mortuus, sentiens tamen, quantum possibile est secundum statum viæ, quod in cruce dictum est latroni cohærenti Christo: Hodie mecum eris in paradiso.'[38]

It would be difficult to find in any other mystical treatise a passage dealing with an equally lofty experience of communion with the Godhead, and yet showing forth more explicitly still the fundamental tenet of Christianity, namely, that Christ in His twofold Nature is the sole foundation upon which any true form of spirituality may be built. In view of it, we may declare with confidence that though ultimate mystical attainment must be union with the Divinity, Bonaventure makes no attempt to get beyond the manifestation of the Divinity in the concrete fact of the Incarnation. Christ in His human nature, is as much his Guide to the fulness of the Christian life, as He was to His Apostles while still on earth. To that same Evangelical Figure he looks for guidance, whether it be with regard to ordinary details of everyday Christian life, or to the fulfilment of the highest aspirations of the Christian soul.

But whilst all this is undoubtedly true, there is an insistence, that if the love of Our Lord in His human nature is to lead to any deeper experience of religion, it must be spiritualized by the ever present thought of His Divinity. Upon this, his friend Saint Thomas is equally explicit.[39] If it be not spiritualized in this way, it will degenerate into a profitless emotionalism; of this he is fully persuaded. History testifies to the truth of his conviction, for where what St. Bernard called the 'amor carnalis' has not been regarded as a step to a higher love of Christ, the literary

38. Ibid., n. 1—n. 2.

39. Auct. cit. 'Corporalis praesentia Christi in duobus poterat esse nociva. Primo, quantum ad fidem: quia videntes Eum in forma in qua erat minor Patre, non ita de facili crederent Eum aequalem Patri, ut dicit glossa super Joannem. Secundo, quantum ad dilectionem, quia Eum non solum spiritualiter, sed etiam carnaliter diligeremus, conversantes cum Ipso corporaliter, et hoc est de imperfectione dilectionis.' Comm. Sent. Lib. III, D. XXII, q. 3, a, 1, ad. Vum. Divi Thomae Scriptum in Tertium et Quartum sententiarum. Venetiis, MDXCIII, f. 77b. The only edition available.

results have been justly condemned as the outpourings of misguided imagination.[40] Bonaventure takes the opportunity to emphasise the need of thus spiritualizing the devotion to Christ's Humanity, when he explains why Our Lord, after His Resurrection appeared to Mary Magdalen, yet did not permit her to touch Him: 'Maria ante passionem Christum Deum esse credebat, tamen vehementissime eum in carne amabat; et ideo in passione tantum dolorem concepit, ut jam absorpta non nisi de humanitate et morte cogitaret, et ideo non recoleret opera Maiestatis, sed pœnas humanitatis.'[41] Between the principle underlying the above explanation of Our Lord's conduct, and the Quietistic doctrine that all thought of His Humanity is a barrier to mystical progress, there is no conceivable relation. The two ideas are poles asunder.

The foregoing represents an attempt to bring to light the chief elements worthy of note in connection with the Franciscan's 'Via Illuminativa.' On the authority of the references found scattered throughout his works, this stage of the spiritual life has been regarded as a genuine endeavour to imitate Jesus Christ in His Humanity, as the supreme example of all human perfection. According to that example is every life to be shaped in some form or other. The measure of grace and variety of vocation will determine the precise characteristics to be especially imitated. But for all who are striving after mystical union with the Divinity, there must be imitation of the Christ-life. In the affective piety to which this doctrine gives rise, the chief element is an ardent love of the suffering Redeemer: a love which seeks to find expression in voluntary suffering in union with Him: a love never wholly absorbed in His Humanity, but formed, purified, and balanced by the faith which finds in Him, at once, true Divinity and true Humanity.

All this, however, is purely impersonal; it is purely dogmatic. But it is necessarily so. For we should look in vain for the expression of any subjective states which would enable us to attempt a constructive criticism from this point of view. We repeat: Bonaventure is the spiritual geographer, and this not in the sense that he explains the inward experiences we are to expect in the path to God, but in the sense that he gives us the means, and

40. A typical example of what we mean will be found in the works of Maria D'Agreda (b. 1602, d. 1665), a Franciscan nun. Authoress of La mistica ciudad de Dios, historia divina de la Virgen Madre de Dios, Madrid, 1670. Her so-called 'revelations' concerning Christ, are obviously the result of dwelling upon Christ's sacred humanity, to the entire exclusion, at least in practice, of any thought of His Divinity.

41. Comment. in Joan., cap. XX, n. 34, T. VI, p. 511.

points out the way, which, he is convinced, will lead to an enlightenment of the understanding, and an inflaming of the will, in preparation for the fullest Christian life known to the great mystics. The practical utility of his doctrine on the 'Via Illuminativa' can only be judged by a personal application of it. From the various points of view naturally suggesting themselves, we elsewhere criticise the teaching. Meanwhile Bonaventure's principal sources may be briefly indicated.

These, it is suggested, are the Gospels, the writings of St. Anselm and St. Bernard, and the characteristically Franciscan traditions begun by the 'Poverello.' Yet, in suggesting that it is to these that he is indebted for his conception and presentation of the mystical value of this practical devotion to Christ, we do not wish to rule out the earlier Fathers and spiritual writers. Both in the dogmatic and in the scriptural treatises already mentioned, and in the *Opuscula,* he constantly appeals to the earlier writers for confirmation. The *Soliloquium* is but a mosaic of Patristic texts.

Among the earlier Fathers whom he quotes most frequently, it has been noticed that he favours Origen, Augustine, Cassian and Gregory, all of whom seem to be well acquainted with the form of spirituality, centred in the Christ-life, which was to characterize the mediaeval writings in general. Thus, it is undoubtedly true that for Origen, the earthly career of our Lord is the classic exhibition of human possibilities, as it is for Bonaventure. We find Origen stressing the spiritual value of entering by way of imitation into the life which Christ taught by word and deed, in order to attain to communion with the Divinity. Bonaventure only quotes, in their Latin form of course, Origen's Scriptural Commentaries. Though the following is taken from his apologetic treatise *Contra Celsum,* we do not for a moment venture to assert that the Franciscan was acquainted with this work. The passage in question has been chosen, as best illustrating the spirit underlying Origen's Commentaries. 'Voluit enim Jesus ipse et ejus discipuli, ut qui accedebant, non ita ejus divinitati et miraculis haberent fidem, ac si non consociasset sibi naturam humanam, et carnem, quæ in hominibus concupiscit adversus spiritum, non suscepisset. Noverant enim conferre ad fidelium salutem, si, ut res diviniores, sic etiam crederent virtutem se ad humanam naturam humanasque miserias demisisse, et animam humanumque corpus assumpsisse. Quippe qui hinc discunt ab illo incœpisse divinæ naturæ cum humana conjunctionem; ut humana sua cum re diviniori societate fieret divina non in solo Jesu, sed et in omnibus, qui cum fide vitam amplectuntur quam Jesus edocuit, et quæ ad amicitiam Dei ejusque communionem perducit quicunque suos mores ex Jesu præceptis composuerint.'[42] Here at least the purpose of all imitation of Christ is seen. However, Bonaventure has not pushed to so extreme a limit the distinction which Origen makes between those who know Christ according to the flesh, that is, in His sufferings and death, and the higher class, the 'Gnostici' who, on the basis of this knowledge, can rise to the spiritual Essence of the Word. In Origen's distinction, the imperfection of devotion to the Humanity of Christ, as contrasted with the mystical union itself, which must be a union between the soul and the Divinity, is vividly shown forth. Bonaventure, convinced as he is of the power of devotion to Christ's humanity, when duly spiritualized by the thought of the Divinity to which it is conjoined, manifests no keen desire to emphasise the distinction.

St. Augustine, too, recognizes the basis of Bonaventure's 'Imitatio Christi': that the temporal works of the Lord were both performed, and written in the Gospels, for man's practical edification. The following, whilst showing no doubt his own preference for the spirituality of St. John, nevertheless marks the twofold method of viewing Our Lord's life on earth: 'Tres tamen isti Evangelistæ in his rebus maxime diversati sunt; quas Christus per humanam carnem temporaliter gessit: porro autem Joannes ipsam maxime divinitatem Domini, qua Patri est æqualis, intendit, eamque præcipue suo Evangelio, quantum inter homines sufficere credidit, commendare curavit. Itaque longe a tribus istis superius fertur, ita ut hos videas quodammodo in terra cum Christo homine conversari; illum autem transcendisse nebulam, qua tegitur omnis terra, et pervenisse ad liquidum cœlum, unde acie mentis acutissima atque firmissima videret, in principio Verbum Deum apud Deum, per quem facta sunt omnia; et ipsum agnosceret carnem factum ut habitaret in nobis.'[43] Elsewhere, he can build up a spiritual doctrine upon the basis supplied by the Synoptics, finding in Our Lord's earthly life the pattern to which we must conform, if we hope for a higher Christian experience.[44] All this supposes a love of Christ in His Human Nature, but again

---

42. Contra Celsum., Lib. III, P. G., T. XI, col. 955.
43. De Consensu Evangel., Lib. I, cap. IV, n. 7, P. L., T. XXXIV, col. 1045.
44. See De Utilitate Cred., cap. XV, P. L., T. XLII, cols. 88-89. 'Sapientia Dei incarnata, via ad religionem commodissima.'

we find an insistence that such love must be in some way spiritualized. St. Augustine emphasizes this when commenting upon the words of Our Lord, as narrated by St. John: 'But I tell you the truth: it is expedient to you that I go. If I do not go, the Paraclete will not come to you.'[45] Christ was unwilling, declares the great Western Doctor, that His disciples should merely love Him with a carnal love; such carnal love could not make them fit to receive the Holy Ghost.[46]

For Cassian in his Institutes and Conferences, written for monks, Christ in His human life is the Exemplar all virtues,[47] and Gregory can base much of his teaching upon the example given 'humano modo' by Him.[48] Yet it seems safe to assert that the spirituality of all these lacks the warmth found in Bonaventure's doctrine. They are not, it is quite true, ignorant of the piety, devotion, and prayer, centred in Our Lord's Humanity, which he places so much to the forefront, but with them, the intellectual, as opposed to the affective element, prevails. In St. Anselm we find the first worthy representation of Mediaeval piety.

His importance in the history of the development of spirituality has not yet been fully realized, but few attempts having been made to coördinate his doctrine, or to treat it from a critical point of view.[49] In his Meditations he has shown how his systematic teaching on Christ's Atonement, far from being barren, may become the fruitful source of confidence and love: that the union between intellectual speculation and affective piety, for which he had prayed, is possible.[50] The speculative thought contained in his major works inspires him with a deep practical love of Christ in His Human Nature: 'Certe nescio, quia nec plene comprehendere valeo, unde hoc est quod longe dulcior es in corde

45. John, 16, 7.

46. 'Expedit vobis ut haec forma servi auferatur a vobis: caro quidem factum Verbum habito in vobis; sed nolo me carnaliter adhuc diligatis, et isto lacte contenti semper infantes esse capiatis . . . si carni carnaliter haeseritis, capaces Spiritus non eritis.' Tract. XCIV, in Joan. Evangel., cap. XVI, n. 4, P. L., T. XXXV, col. 1869.

47. See especially Collatio X, cap. VI, P. L., T. XLIX, cols. 826-7.

48. The following is characteristic:—'Hinc est quod humani generis Redemptor per diem miracula in urbibus exhibet, et ad orationis studium in monte pernoctat, ut, perfectis videlicet praedicatoribus innuat quatenus nec activam amore speculationis funditus deserant, nec contemplationis gaudia penitus operationis nimietate contemnant; sed quieti contemplantes sorbeant, quod occupati erga proximos loquentes refundant.' Moral. in Job, Lib. VI, cap. XXXVII, P. L., T. LXXV, col. 760.

49. It is, however, assigned an important place in La Spiritualité Chrétienne, T. II, (Le Moyen Age), par P. Pourrat, 1921. See pp. 19-28; cf. The Devotions of Saint Anselm, ed. by C. C. J. Webb, London, 1903. The Introduction deals with Anselm's spirituality.

50. 'Fac, precor, Domine, me gustare per amorem, quod gusto per cognitionem; sentiam per affectum quod sentio per intellectum.' Medit. XI, P. L., T. CLVIII, col. 769.

diligentis te, in eo quod caro es, quam in eo quod Verbum; dulcior in eo quod humilis, quam in eo quod sublimis. Siquidem longe dulcius est memoriæ diligentis te videre te ex matre Virgine in tempore natum quam in splendoribus ante luciferum a Patre genitum, temetipsum exinanivisse, servique formam accepisse quam in forma Dei æqualem te Deo esse.'[51] St. Augustine could not have been the author of this, which demonstrates so admirably the trend of mediaeval piety. Anselm writes as emotionally on the Passion and Death of Christ, albeit his emotion is always kept within reasonable bounds by clear thinking, as in any of the later mediaeval writers.[52] Coming as it does from the author of the *Cur Deus Homo,* and the *Proslogion,* his affective piety, centred on the figure of Christ, makes a greater appeal than that of St. Bernard, who did not particularly favour speculative thought. It is in this aspect that he is a forerunner of Bonaventure, who, in his own great theological works, and in the *Opuscula,* makes the same attempt to combine intellectual activity with Christian fervour.[53] The end of Anselm's fervent devotion is the union of the soul with God, through an imitation of the virtues exhibited in the life of Christ.

Of St. Bernard it has been written: 'His great achievement was to recall devout and loving contemplation to the image of the crucified Christ, and to found that worship of our Saviour as the 'Bridegroom of the Soul' which in the next centuries inspired so much fervid devotion and lyrical sacred poetry.[54] Bernard in this sphere seems to have been anticipated in no little degree by Anselm. He condenses the whole mediaeval theme into few words when he writes: 'Vita Christi, vivendi mihi regula extitit: mors, a morte redemptio. Illa vitam instruxit, mortem ista destruxit.'[55] Consequently, his teaching on mortification, humility, meditation, and prayer, is everywhere explained in direct reference to the actions of Christ, narrated in the Gospels. He can dwell lovingly upon the mysteries of Our Lord's life, His infancy,[56] His thirty-three years of retirement,[57] His Passion and death,[58] having

51. Medit. XII, ibid., col. 770.
52. See Med. de Passione Christi, ibid., col. 761.
53. Indeed, we think that the too frequent use of the term 'affective' in connection with St. Bonaventure is misleading. Many think that it means he is emotional and does not possess the same intellectual basis as St. Thomas, which, of course, is absurd.
54. W. R. Inge, Christian Mysticism, p. 140, note 2.
55. Lib. ad milites templi, cap. XI, P. L., T. CLXXXII, col. 932; compare Sermo VI, T. CLXXXIII, col. 803.
56. See Sermones in Vigil. Nativit. Domini, P. L., T. CLXXXIII, cols. 87-116.
57. See Sermones in Epiphan., ibid., cols. 141-152.
58. See Sermo in Feria IVa Hebdom. Sanct., ibid., cols. 263-270.

always in mind the idea that the Humanity of Christ draws men to love Him, till their love is purged of all carnality, and exalted to a perfect love of God. For Bernard has the clear cut distinction between the 'amor carnalis Christi,' and the 'amor spiritualis,' the one having as its object Christ in His human activity, which love, he surmises, motived the Apostles to leave all things, and to follow Him: the other, rising above Christ in His Humanity, to that more spiritual love demanded by Christ Himself, when He said: 'It is the spirit that quickeneth; the flesh profiteth nothing.' But Bernard insists that the 'amor carnalis' has its worth; it is indeed in itself a great gift. Only through the attainment of the higher 'amor spiritualis,' however, will the soul enter into mystical contemplation.[59] Bonaventure has carried on this same doctrine, which, in Bernard's sermons on the *Canticle of Canticles,* finds its highest mystical expression. The same Christ-love permeates subsequent devotional literature, and constitutes the chief characteristic of the spirituality of St. Francis.

In the career of Francis which he had studied so carefully before writing his own *Legenda,* Bonaventure discovered a concrete example of the mystical heights to which this same devotion, encouraged by Anselm and Bernard, could lead. The basic principle of that career was undeniably the realization of the spiritual worth of true imitation of Christ. Sufficient has been written to show how literal and sincere was his imitation of Our Lord's Life. So literal was it, that Francis, who, to himself, seemed ever the 'poor little man,' became to his immediate followers, and to the first generation of Friars, nothing less than a new manifestation of the spirit of Christ. His literal imitation of Christ is the first note in his life that strikes the anonymous author of the *Fioretti:* 'In prima è da considerare che il glorioso san Francesco in tutti gli atti della vita sua fu conforme a Cristo benedetto.'[60] This

---

59. All this is explained in Sermo XX in Cant., n. 6—n. 8, P. L., T. CLXXXIII, cols. 870-I. 'Et nota amorem cordis quodam modo esse carnalem, quod magis erga carnem Christi, et quae in carne Christus gessit vel jussit, cor humanum afficiat. . . . Astat oranti Hominis Dei sacra imago, aut nascentis, aut lactentis, aut docentis, aut morientis, aut resurgentis, aut ascendentis; et quidquid tale occurrerit, vel stringat necesse est animum in amorem virtutum vel carnis exturbet vitia, fuget illecebras, desideria sedet. Ego hanc arbitror praecipuam invisibili Deo fuisse causam, quod voluit in carne videri, et cum hominibus homo conversari, ut carnalium videlicet, qui nisi carnaliter amari non poterant, cunctas primo ad suae carnis salutarem amorem affectiones retraheret, atque ita gradatim ad amorem perduceret spiritualem . . . . Licet vero donum, et magnum donum Spiritus sit istiusmodi erga carnem Christi devotio; carnalem tamen dixerim hunc amorem, illius utique amoris respectu, quo non tam Verbum caro jam sapit, quam Verbum Sapientia, Verbum Justitia, Verbum veritas, Verbum sanctitas, pietas, virtus; et si quid aliud quod sit, hujusmodi dici potest.'

60. Op. cit., ed. Leopoldo Amoni, Roma, 1889, cap. 1, p. 1. The Latin is not to hand at the moment of writing,

conformity was based upon the knowledge, acquired by faith, that Christ, when He took upon Himself the burdens of our fallen humanity, became the moulding form of our earthly life, in the striving to regain true relationship with God. For Francis, the very fact that Our Lord in His appearance upon the earth had taken to Himself all those hardships to which the human race is heir, had endowed these with a spiritual significance and power; through Christ's adoption of them, they became in a sense the revealed means whereby men may produce within themselves the image which all must bear, who, through Him, seek communion with the Divinity.[61] The only illumination he claimed was the enlightenment which comes from a practical knowledge of Christ: practical, in that it was acquired through an imitation of His life.

An incident occurred towards the end of his career, affording him an opportunity of indicating the devotion which had absorbed him for years, and which had made him the mystic he is acknowledged on all hands to be. To console him in his sufferings, one of the brethren suggested that he should have recourse to the Scriptures, knowing the strength and comfort he usually derived from them. Francis answered with wonted simplicity, that it was indeed good to read the Scriptures, and to seek God therein, but that he himself had mastered so much of them, that he had ample store for meditation. Then he added, as if it were final and supreme for him, that he needed no more, for he *knew* Christ, the Poor Man Crucified.[62] For, to know Christ in this sense, it did not suffice, as he expressly states, to read the Scriptures, to find therein a mode of life taught by Him, and to preach that life to others by word of mouth. They alone have the true spirit of the Scriptures, and know Our Lord, who interpret 'materially' every text they find,

---

61. Thus Celano writes of him: 'Summa eius intentio, praecipuum desiderium, supremumque propositum eius erat sanctum evangelium in omnibus et per omnia observare, ac perfecte omni vigilantia, omni studio, toto desiderio mentis, toto cordis fervore, domini nostri Jesu Christi doctrinam sequi et vestigia imitari. Recordabatur assidua meditatione verborum eius, et sagacissima consideratione ipsius opera recolebat. Praecipue incarnationis humilitas et charitas passionis ita eius memoriam occupabant ut vix vellet aliud cogitare.' Legenda Prima, cap. XXX, (ed. Alencon), p. 85. In this same chapter Celano shows that Francis' devotion to the Crib was but the outcome of his ruling form of spirituality.

62. 'Infirmanti sibi et undique pervaso doloribus dixit aliquando socius eius: Pater, semper ad scripturas confugium habuisti, semper illae tibi dolorum praebuere remedia. Fac, oro, et nunc tibi de prophetis aliquid legi; fortassis exsultabit spiritus tuus in Domino. Cui sanctus: Bonum est scripturae testimonia legere, bonum est dominum Deum nostrum in ipsis exquirere; mihi vero tantum iam ipse de scripturis adegi, quod meditanti et revolventi satissimum est. Non pluribus indigeo, fili. Scio Christum pauperem crucifixum.' Legenda Secunda, cap. LXXI, ibid., p. 249.

and by word and example 'give them back to God, from Whom all is good.'[63]

And we need have no hesitation in saying what was the element predominating in his imitation of Christ's life; it was assuredly the Cross, for him, as for Bonaventure, the symbol at once of the renunciation demanded of all who wish to follow Christ fully, and of the promise of everlasting life, contained in His Revelation. 'Let us all,' he writes, 'consider the Good Shepherd, Who, to save His sheep, bore the sufferings of the Cross. The sheep of the Lord followed Him in tribulation and persecution and shame, in hunger and thirst, in infirmity and temptations and in all other ways; and for these things they have received everlasting life from the Lord.'[64] Hence the passionate devotion to the sufferings of Christ witnessed to, in his *Office of the Passion of the Lord.*[65] This, composed as it is, of a combination of Scriptural texts, gives evidence, not only of his ardent devotion to the Crucified, but also of the method and source of his prayer. The Seraphic Doctor reflects the same devotion, and an approval of a like method, in his own *Officium de Passione Domini.*[66]

Finally, in support of our contention that Bonaventure both realized the extent and warmly approved of the nature, of Francis's imitation of the Christ-life: that he was moreover influenced by that same example, in the exposition of his own doctrine, we can make appeal to his writings, wherein all that Francis did and said with regard to man's duty of following Christ is accepted as final. The most enthusiastic 'Spiritual', anxious to find in the 'Poverello' a new manifestation of the Divine Spirit, could scarcely be more appreciative than Bonaventure when he writes: 'Hunc Dei nuntium (i. e. the Angel referred to in *Apoc. VII, II.)* amabilem Christo, imitabilem nobis et admirabilem mundo servum Dei fuisse Franciscum, indubitabili fide colligimus, si culmen in eo eximiæ sanctitatis advertimus, qua, inter homines vivens, imitator fuit puritatis angelicæ, qua et positus est perfectis Christi sectatoribus in exemplum. Ad quod quidem fideliter sentiendum et pie, non solum inducit officium, quod habuit, vocandi ad fletum et planctum, calvitium et cingulum sacci signandique thau super

63. See The Writings of St. Francis of Assisi, trans. by P. Robinson, 1906, pp. 11-12.
64. Ibid.
65. Ibid., pp. 154, sqq. See also his psalm, called The Praise of the Most High God, ibid., pp. 146-9. This, as Fr. Cuthbert has noted, should more fittingly be styled, The praise of the Crucified. Auct. cit., Life of St. Francis of Assisi, 1912, p. 345.
66. Contained in T. VIII, pp. 152 sqq.

frontes virorum gementium et dolentium signo pœnitentialis crucis et habitus cruci conformis; verum etiam irrefragibili veritatis testificatione confirmat signaculum similitudinis Dei viventis, Christi videlicet crucifixi, quod in corpore ipsius fuit impressum non per naturæ virtutem vel ingemium artis, sed potius per admirandam potentiam Spiritus Dei vivi.'[67]

We may conclude, then, that after the Gospel, Bonaventure is influenced in his exposition of the 'Via Illuminativa' by the writings of Anselm and Bernard especially, and what is of greater importance, he has seen in the life of the Founder of his Order, that devotion to Our Lord—and here the word 'devotion is used in a wide sense, embracing all that has been said in this present chapter—can be used as a sure means of establishing those relations between God and the human soul, usually designated mystical. References to Pseudo-Dionysius are markedly absent, though it is admitted that he too taught that if we aspire to communion with the Divine, we must first fix our eyes upon Christ in the flesh.[68] But Pseudo-Dionysius's form of Mysticism, is distinctly a Theocentric, as opposed to the Christocentric spirituality shared in by Anselm, Bernard, and Bonaventure, and lived with such whole-hearted sincerity by St. Francis of Assisi. If special mention of the Victorines is likewise omitted, it is not because they in no way exhibit this devotion to Our Lord in His Humanity. It is simply because their symbolism too often robs the doctrine of the warmth it possesses in the literature upon which we have dwelt.

It seems necessary to remark, that if those who are at once admirers of St. Francis and students of the works of Bonaventure are impressed by the fact, that in his exposition of the practical spiritual injunctions based upon the doctrine of the 'Imitatio Christi,' he retains much of the old monastic spirit, it must be remembered, as we asserted before, that it was Bonaventure the Legislator who was writing most often. He was writing at a time when it was painfully apparent that the personality of Francis is not easily reproduced: that not all calling themselves Franciscans had the same Christ-like spirit of their Founder.[69] This fact, leaving his own personal spirit untouched, led him to repeat with vigour many of the monastic principles of St. Bernard

67. Legenda Sti. Francisci, cap. 1, n. 2, T. VIII, pp. 504-5.

68. See Epistola VIII, Eriugena's Version, P. L., T. CXXII, cols. 1181 sqq., compare P. G., T. III, cols. 1083 sqq.

69. See supra.

and others.[70] Where these are stressed, the picturesqueness associated with Francis' living imitation of Our Lord, will necessarily be lacking. Granted though it is, that this element is absent in his doctrine, it cannot be denied, that this doctrine will give rise to an essentially Christocentric form of Mysticism, manifesting no tendency to pass over the Humanity of Our Lord, over the God revealed to men in the Flesh, in an eagerness to attain to the 'undifferentiated ground of the God-head.'

That a temptation in this direction does assail some souls, is made clear by the emphasis with which writers like Saint Teresa, and Saint John of the Cross, command meditation upon the Sacred Humanity.[71] Within the Catholic Church, attention has been called to the tendency, or rather, to the temptation, chiefly through the teachings of the Quietists, who were charged with positively excluding such meditation, in the preparation to be made for mystical contemplation.[72] Bossuet, who was very familiar with the writings of Bonaventure, which he quotes again and again, in his well known *Instruction sur les États d'oraison,* fully represents the Franciscan's teaching in the following fine passage: 'Eloigner de notre pensée un si parfait exemplaire de notre union (Jesus-Christ), c'est, au lieu de s'avancer à la perfection en croissant dans la charité, renoncer au plus haut principe de l'unité chrétienne, et perdre à la fois la plus belle idée de l'amour de Dieu envers nous, qui consiste dans cette parole du Sauveur: Il faut, mon Père, que le monde sache

---

70. This reversion to pre-Franciscan monastic principles has been shown by G. Coulton, quoting Bonaventure, Bernard of Besse, and David of Augsburg, to have been a characteristic of the generation of spiritual writers within the Order, succeeding St. Francis. See Mediaeval Studies, 1st Series, London, 1915, pp. 27-36.

71. St. Teresa mentions the temptation she once experienced, but which she happily overcame, to remove from her mind the thought of all bodily objects, the Humanity of Christ included. Recognition of her error leads her to emphasise the necessity of dwelling lovingly upon that aspect of Our Lord's Life, in which He appears most human, viz.: in His Passion. See The Life of St. Teresa of Jesus written by herself, trans. by D. Lewis, London, 1904, pp. 177-189.

St. John of the Cross declares that deliberate forgetfulness and rejection of all knowledge and forms (the mystical 'Via Negativa'), must never be extended to Christ's Humanity. See his Ascent of Mount Carmel, trans, by D. Lewis, London, 1906, Bk. III, cap. 1, p. 248. I have been unable to obtain further information regarding the interesting question raised by Montgomery Carmichael (art. The Works of St. John of the Cross, in Dublin Review, vol. 174, pp. 84-97), as to the authenticity of St. John's words. But they certainly reflect the spirit of this great mystical writer.

72. Vaughan is not quite fair when he declares that the Church canonized St. Teresa, and condemned the Quietist Molinos, for teaching the same thing. St. Teresa only says that in the mystic union itself, the Divine Essence and the soul are concerned; we must do nothing positive to exclude Christ's Humanity. Molinos said this exclusion is a positive duty on our part. The two statements are quite different. See Hours with the Mystics, II, p. 172.

que vous les avez aimés comme vous m'avez aimé.'[73] Bonaventure's position is also represented with perfect fidelity, when Bossuet calls all positive exclusion of Christ's Humanity 'une degradation du Fils de Dieu incarné, et un renversement du fondement de la foi.'[74] Ultimately, both Bonaventure and Bossuet rely upon St. Paul's declaration: 'For other foundation no man can lay, but that which is laid; which is Christ Jesus.'[75]

Whilst the distinction between God, considered in His Essence, and God manifested in His Incarnation, being, as it is at the very root of Christianity itself, is ever before Bonaventure's mind, it is to the 'Verbum Incarnatum' that he looks for guidance in the mystic path. If Christ took to Himself a Humanity, identical in all, save in sin, and in those things which are the direct consequences of sin, with the humanity common to all men; if through and in that Humanity He intended our Redemption from sin; then we may confidently look to Him for guidance with regard to everything that concerns our own earthly existence. In His Humanity we may justly expect to find reflected the possibilities of our own nature, atoned for by His grace. To pass it over in any sense would be to miss the very foundation of the Revelation He came to deliver. Those who deny as well as those who accept the Divinity of Christ admit the advantages following upon the constant remembrance of the lessons taught by His earthly life. All admit that He appears as the perfect bloom of faultless humanity: that nothing can be more uplifting than the endeavour to imitate Him, in His love of God, love of man: in His forbearance, courage, and self-sacrifice. All these are shown forth in conditions to which we ourselves are subjected. In realizing the full significance of the truth, that God's supreme revelation of Himself took the form of an ordinary life, lived on a level in which we may live, and under conditions to which we are subjected: in setting forth Christ's Humanity as the perfect Pattern of all human life, Bonaventure has overcome, if ever he experienced it, the temptation to which we have just referred. When we find him, in the last chapter of his *Itinerarium,* which deals with the actual union of the soul with God, making constant use of such expressions as 'Christus est via et ostium,' 'Christus est scala et

73. Op. cit., Seconde Traité, Paris, 1897, p. 25. He refers to John, 17, 23. It would be interesting to discover to what extent Bossuet is indebted to Bonaventure; we do not know of any work dealing with this point, though there seems to be room for a treatise on the subject. Bossuet's familiarity with the writings of St. Bonaventure is frequently shown in his other and better known works.

74. Ibid., p. 27.

75. I Cor. III, 11.

vehiculum,' 'transeamus cum Christo crucifixo ex hoc mundo ad Patrem,'[76] we must certainly exclude him from the number of those referred to by Herrmann when he declares that when the mystic has found God, he has left Christ behind.[77]

However, it may be objected, that Bonaventure only, or at least primarily, finds the lesson of Renunciation taught in the Christ-life: that in consequence, he gives us an un-Christ-like form of asceticism. It may appear, that in making the lesson of the Cross the primary element in his imitation of Our Lord, he forgets the lesson of service of others, taught by the very fact of Christ's dwelling among men. The perpetual carrying of the Cross, upon which he dwells, like the later A Kempis, seems incompatible with the service of others, and with the inherent dignity of human nature, in revolt against the idea, that the body, an integral part of that same nature, must be continually suppressed and 'buffetted,' that the other part, the soul, may the more truly reflect the image of Christ. Christianity, it is said, should surely tend to the perfection of the whole man.

All these are objections constantly raised with regard to the whole mediaeval scheme of spirituality. They could be, and indeed they often are, expressed with greater force. We are only thrown back upon what we have already said in our attempted explanation of his asceticism.[78] The statements already made need not be qualified. External suffering, endured in the literal imitation of the suffering Christ, in itself, can be of no avail. Endured, however, with the spirit of Christ, or assumed explicitly in an endeavour to realize that spirit, it is regarded by Bonaventure as giving life to Christianity. And if we would prove that the result of all this is not a wholly one-sided form of religion, we need appeal only to the lives of those mystics, who have carried this lesson of the Cross to the farthest extent. These have surely been of the greatest service to their fellow men. Francis' influence in the rebuilding of Christendom in his own century is generally acknowledged, yet no one treated his body more harshly than he. Nor have these mystics in all their self-inflicted penances forgotten the inherent dignity of the human body; they have

76. Op. cit., T. V, pp. 312-13.

77. Auct. cit., The Communion of the Christian with God, trans. by R. W. Stewart, London, 1906, p. 30. This author's position seems to be that Roman Catholic piety is essentially such, that at the highest point to which it leads, not only cultus and doctrine, but also our conception of the Person of Our Lord Himself, must vanish along with all else that is external. That this is false is apparent to all who are familiar with the writings of our Saints.

78. See supra, chap. II.

recourse to the same Revelation telling them that the body is the temple of the Holy Ghost, to justify the fact that they chastise it daily and bring it into subjection. The truth inspiring them is simply this, that only after they have thoroughly mastered the lesson of the Cross, only after a long crucifixion of the self, can they be worthy to enter into the service of their fellow men.

Need their renunciation inspired by the Cross take the 'crude material' form they have given it? Cannot renunciation itself follow upon the attempt to serve others, in that it inevitably brings with it so much forbearance, self-control, self-discipline and patience in disappointments? All this is suffering in the real sense of the word, and it can be borne in the Christ-like spirit which effects union with the Divinity. Mystics like the Seraphic Doctor, would readily admit all this, and declare it to be essential. Yet they go still further. Teresa's 'aut pati aut mori' voices the unanimous interpretation of our personal duty of following Christ, given by generations of mystics before her time. To us it seems, that it is in this interpretation, rather than in their claim to have been mystically united to God, that they present the critic with his greatest difficulty. The intensity of their devotion to the Passion and Death of Christ to which they attach so great a value, could, if desired, be explained on purely natural grounds. Nor would anyone quarrel with this devotion in itself, since, when it is free from a harmful morbidity, it can be a welcome proof of human sympathy. There is no problem here, for the sight of One Whose Life was so good and holy, suffering torments to atone for others, tends of its very nature to arouse sympathy, love, and, in the believer, grateful adoration.

The problem presents itself when it comes to the question of entering literally into those same sufferings, not in any Buddhistic spirit which looks forward to an extinction of all existence, but in a spirit of faith and trust and joyousness.[79] Yet the solution is at hand if we look to the faith inspiring the mystics. The relations they conceive to exist between themselves and Christ are those, elevated indeed to a higher plane, which exist between ordinary human lovers. Love naturally tends to similarity in all things; it spontaneously seeks to enter, not only into the thought, but into the very conditions of the Beloved. The more arduous those conditions are, the more joyously are they embraced. Applying this principle to the mystics,

79. St. Francis used to call sadness in such voluntary sufferings, the 'Babylonish' malady.

with their faith on the one hand, and with their conception of the Christ-life, as one of prolonged suffering on the other, we find an explanation of their deeds and doctrine. Even a Platonic conception of love as the outcome of wealth and poverty, need not be destructive of the argument. Christ is viewed as the all-wealthy, and all that they, in their poverty, have to give back to Him, is the pledge of love, finding expression in a joyous suffering in union with Him.

Less satisfactory, apparently, from the psychological point of view, is the explanation to be found in the doctrine, dwelt upon by St. Paul, and reproduced so often by Bonaventure, that the Church is the Body of Christ. The mystics, as members of the Church, are also members of Christ. As it behoved Christ to suffer, so too, must they. This, however unsatisfactory it may seem, leads to that which we regard as the final explanation. We must credit the mystics with a more vivid conception of the work which Christ came into the world to perform: with a keener sense of the enormity of personal sin, and of the sin of the world, than that usually experienced by ordinary Christians. They are united to Christ by love as co-heirs and as co-partners with Him in His redemptive work upon earth, and since it was precisely in His life of suffering, culminating in the Cross of Calvary, that Christ effected the work of the Atonement[80] which must be continued within His Church to the end of time, they joyously continue what they consider to be His work, by themselves living a life of suffering. In coöperating in this fashion with Our Lord as members of His Mystical Body, their minds are enlightened to realize the worth of the Humanity which brought the Son of God, in the depths of His Love, to endure so great a sacrifice. After thoroughly mastering the lesson of the Cross, they can return to the service of men, though even in their suffering, because of the motive impelling them to endure it and to love it, they have rendered that service in their own peculiar, and, to many, incomprehensible fashion.

To go beyond this, and to comment upon the nature of the illumination they claim as a result of their endeavours to follow Christ so closely, is not within our power. Certainly it is never

80. We are aware of the speculative Theology which arose in answer to the question: What was the principal reason of the Incarnation? For Bonaventure, and for the majority of Theologians, it was the Redemption through the sacrifice on the Cross. See III S. D. I, a. II, q. II, T. III, pp. 23 sqq. As is well known, Duns Scotus taught that in all probability, the Word would have been made Flesh, even though Adam had never sinned. See his III S. D. VII, q. III, Schol. II, ed. Vivès, T. XIV, pp. 354 sqq.

revealed in Bonaventure's Theology. We have but the oft-repeated declaration, which can be proved only by personal experience, that they alone who are willing to be crucified together with Christ know Divine truths fully, and can understand the right relations existing between God and the soul. It is this which determines the limits of Mystical Philosophy. The truth seems to be contained in the words of a recent writer: 'It is possible to be a mystical philosopher in an armchair, to be a mystic only on a Cross.'[81] It is the mystic himself, not the philosopher, who can speak of the 'Illuminatio' which follows upon the imitation of Christ.

81. Watkin, E., Philosophy of Mysticism, London, 1920, p. 14.

CHAPTER IV.

Meditation and Prayer.—Discursus on Liturgical Practice.—Meaning of Meditation.—Meditation in the three ways.—Meditation upon creatures.—These stepping-stones to God.—Bonaventure's doctrine on 'Mediate Contemplation' best expressed in the **Itinerarium.** — Characteristics of the **Itinerarium** to be noted.—The main conclusion to the fundamental principle, that creatures are stepping-stones to God. — 'Mediate Contemplation' explained.—Prayer.—Bonaventure's Philosophy of Prayer.—The degrees of Prayer.—'Mediate Contemplation' the only element demanding special comment.—Bonaventure's appreciation of its spiritual worth, the result of general tendency of former writers.—The special influence of Augustine.—Pseudo-Dionysian influence relatively unimportant.—Augustine's influence continued through the Victorines, Hugo and Richard. — St. Francis of Assisi, and his sensibility to nature.—Importance of 'Mediate Contemplation.'—Its spirit contrasted with tendencies of later Mysticism.—Symbolism.—Symbolism does not lead to a natural, as opposed to a supernatural Mysticism.—Bonaventure's doctrine of 'Mediate Contemplation' free from all Pantheism. — His idea of Divine Immanence and Transcendence explained.—Worth of 'Mediate Contemplation' in the spiritual life.

So far, an effort has been made to point out Bonaventure's ideas as to what must take place within the soul in its ascent to mystical union. True mystical experience is the fullest development of the life of grace, but there is no question of God drawing to Himself, by means of an irresistible agency, a wholly inert and passive subject. On the contrary, the soul must work, up to a certain degree, together with grace. Bonaventure, like the majority of Franciscan theologians, emphasises the necessity of correspondence with grace; hence the asceticism, the imitation of the Christ-life, the meditation and prayer, all of which, though depending for their salutary value upon Sanctifying grace, nevertheless demand that which may rightly be called conative activity. Such is the spirit underlying his axiom, 'Qui enim vult esse perfectus amator Dei, prius debet se exercere in amore proximi, sicut qui vult esse bonus contemplativus prius debet esse bonus activus, sicut docet Gregorius.'[1] The same idea is to be found throughout the Sermons, expressed in various forms,[2] and everywhere, in his minor works, we find reference to the need of

1. III S. D. XXVII, art. II, q. IV, T. III, p. 610. Gregory's teaching will be found in Moral. Lib. VI, CXXXVII, P. L., T. LXXV, cols. 760-761, and in Homil. in Ezech. Lib. I, Hom. III, n. 9, P. L., T. LXXVI, col. 809.

2. See Sermo in Dom. II Quadrag., T. IX, p. 216; cf. also Sermo de S. Agnete, Sermo II, ibid., p. 510.

spiritual activity, to the numerous spiritual exercises which demand genuine effort.[3] Principally, however, he dwells upon Meditation and Prayer, which are to be used in all the stages of the spiritual life, and are viewed as leading the soul on to union with God. Meditation and prayer are singled out for special mention, when he is treating of the preparation to be made for Contemplation. He writes: 'Qui igitur vult in Deum ascendere, necesse est, ut vitata culpa deformante naturam, naturales potentias supradictas exerceat ad gratiam reformantem, et hoc per orationem, ... ad scientiam illuminantem, et hoc in meditatione.'[4] To these two forms of spiritual activity, he devotes greatest attention, in the *De Triplici Via*, and in the little work written for the guidance of new Religious, the *Regula Novitiorum*.

However, like many of the religious reformers of his generation, he attaches great importance to that more external form of devotion, liturgical practice, and during his Generalate, he did his best to arouse an active interest in it, among the Friars.[5] This fact is worthy of mention, since pure Franciscanism has been regarded as a revolt against all monastic customs, and, as is well known, the Liturgy has not only been at its best in the monastic orders, but within such orders it has been regarded as having great spiritual value. No doubt, Bonaventure's insistence upon the full observance of the Liturgy, upon the singing of Divine Office in Choir, and the various practices familiar within monastic establishments, had much to do with the dissatisfaction expressed by the 'Spirituals' in connection with his general policy. Nor is it difficult to understand their attitude. Apart altogether from the fact that they claimed the liberty to live more inward lives, the full observance of the Liturgy demanded large communities. Large communities not only diminished opportunities for the eremitical life to which so many of them clung, but they also brought with them breaches of that poverty, upon which Francis of Assisi had built his order. Bonaventure can readily find excuses for all these things: not so the 'Spirituals.' His love of liturgical practice is also worthy of note, since it is sometimes considered, that true Mysticism is quite incompatible with the

3. See De Perfectione Vitae, T. VIII, pp. 109 sqq.; De Reductione artium ad Theol., T. V, p. 324 sqq.: Soliloq., T. VIII, p. 50.

4. Itin., cap. 1, n. 8, T. V, p. 298.

5. For his teaching on the necessity and utility of liturgical practice, see Regula Novit., T. VIII, pp. 475-6: De Sex Alis Seraphim, ibid., p. 149 As to his general influence in this matter, see Gesta e dottrina del serafico dottore S. Bonaventura, Gaspare de Monte Santo, Macerata, 1793, pp. 101-4: and Statuta liturgica seu rubricae Breviarii, auctore divo Bonaventura, art in Archiv. Francis. Histor., T. V, pp. 62-73.

external religion for which it stands. Bonaventure sees no such incompatibility; external worship is to accompany the more internal forms of devotion, meditation and prayer being but an aid to the one,[6] and the outward expression of the other.

By meditation, he does not merely imply that which is sometimes understood by the term, the reflection upon various religious truths. This is but one element in his more comprehensive use of the term; it is but the starting point of true meditation. Sometimes it is used to cover the whole spiritual life, wherein an attempt is made to realize the final destiny of man, and wherein all truths, of whatever kind they may be, are viewed in their relation to that destiny. In meditation, every faculty possessed by the soul is to be used. Thus, in the *De Triplici Via,* after proposing certain religious truths as matter for pious reflection, he indicates what must take place in efficacious meditation: 'In huiusmodi autem meditatione, tota anima debet esse intenta, et hoc secundum omnes vires suas, scilicet secundum rationem, synderesim, conscientiam et voluntatem. Nam in huiusmodi meditatione ratio percunctando offert propositionem, synderesis sententiando profert definitionem, conscientia testificando infert conclusionem, voluntas præeligendo defert solutionem. Verbi gratia, si quis velit meditari circa viam purgativam, debet ratio quærere, quid debeat fieri de homine, qui templum Dei violaverit; synderesis respondet, quod aut debet disperdi, aut lamentis pœnitentiæ purgari; conscientia assumit: Tu es ille: ergo vel oportet te damnari, vel pœnitentiæ stimulis affligi; deinde voluntas præelegit, scilicet, quia recusat damnationem æternam, assumit voluntarie pœnitentiæ lamenta. Juxta hunc modum in aliis viis est intelligendum.'[7]

Here we have a steadying of the whole personality, a gathering in, and an application of every force, a clear proof that genuine meditation, to be spiritually useful, implies much more than haphazard reflection upon religious truths. It implies real work. At no period does such meditation become wholly unnecessary. When Contemplation is denied it, the soul must ever engage itself in meditation. Apart from these indications of the method to be followed in profitable meditation, we do not find in his works the hard and fast rules known to a later generation of spiritual writers. Bonaventure allows free play to the

6. It is easy to see how the liturgical recitation or singing of the Psalms, etc., could furnish matter for meditation. See Butler, C. Benedictine Monachism, pp. 58 sqq., and elsewhere.

7. Op. cit., cap. I, n. 19, T. VIII, p. 7.

pious imagination, being very familiar with the method known as 'composition of place' used to such great advantage in St. Ignatius' famous *Exercitia Spiritualia.* The imagination may construct for itself some definite and appropriate scene, in connection with the truths to be reflected upon, to the end that the same truths may be grasped with a greater vividness, and sense of reality. We have an example of this in his *Lignum Vitæ.*[8] Here, the truths centring around Our Lord's earthly career, are illustrated in connection with imagined scenes based upon the Gospel narrative. Departing from exact Scriptural data, the author of the *Meditationes Vitæ Christi,* already referred to, continued the method. There can be little doubt that it has much to recommend it. For the majority of people, pious reflections remain vague and shadowy, with feeble energising force to affect the will; yet, when the imagination is appealed to, the same reflections possess a greater power.

Bonaventure gives meditation its due place in each of the three ways. In the first stage, the 'Via Purgativa,' as we would expect, the soul is to concentrate upon its faults and failings, upon the enormity of sins committed, and the penalties incurred, apply- as a remedy sincere contrition, and a steadfast re-formation of the interior man.[9] In the illuminative way, the intellect is to recall the benefits brought to the world by the advent of Christ, His claim to the world's homage and gratitude, and man's personal duty of imitating His earthly life, as far as possible.[10] Lastly, in the unitive way, every consideration is brought forward, to inflame the will with love of God, and to withdraw its affection from the things that do not lead to Him. It is here that his Franciscanism reveals itself. The devotion underlying and inspiring the following passage gained for him the titles 'Doctor Devotus' and 'Doctor Seraphicus.' He writes: 'Postremo sequitur, qualiter nos exercere debemus ad igniculum sapientiæ. Hoc autem faciendum est hoc ordine: quia iste igniculus est primo congregandus, secundo inflammandus, tertio sublevandus. Congregatur autem per reductionem affectionis ab omni amore creaturæ . . . . Secundo, inflammandus est, et hoc ex conversione affectionis super amorem sponsi . . . . Tertio, sublevandus est, et hoc supra omne sensibile, imaginabile, et intelligibile.'[11]

8. T. VIII, pp. 68 sqq.
9. See De Trip. Via, cap. I, n. 3-9, T. VIII, pp. 4-6.
10. Ibid., pp. 6-7.
11. Ibid., p. 7.

We see in this, how Pseudo-Dionysius' 'Via Negativa' can be the outcome of love.

Such are the general directions given in the *De Triplici Via;* yet Bonaventure does not content himself with merely giving directions. A comparison between this little work, and the more extensive *Soliloquium,* has led to the conclusion, that the latter is but the *De Triplici Via,* written with the express purpose of showing how the given directions may be put into practice. The care with which the *Soliloquium* has been drawn up, demonstrates the importance given to meditation in his spiritual system.

In the last passage quoted from the *De Triplici Via,* it would seem, that Bonaventure is over-anxious to pass with Pseudo-Dionysius beyond all creatures, and to shut out from the mind all thought of contingent being. That this has to be done in a certain stage of spiritual development he insists elsewhere,[12] but he does not advise his reader to enter upon such a course at once. Creatures may do valuable work in leading the soul to God, and one of Bonaventure's characteristic forms of meditation, one which must be mentioned especially, is that which seeks traces of God in the creatures of His Hands, and makes of creatures so many stepping-stones to the final contemplation of the Divinity. This form of meditation, of a more intellectual order than that contained in the works already quoted, finds its finest, and most magnificent expression, in the *Itinerarium,* frequently, though incorrectly referred to, as a wholly mystical treatise. The *Itinerarium* has indeed a mystical bearing, yet because of its contents, it must be ranged among Bonaventure's philosophical and theological works. Its object is to lead the soul by ways of reflection, up to the highest point at which it may, with the grace of God, abandon itself to pure Contemplation. In doing this, it passes over the well-trodden roads of natural philosophy and theology. No doubt the general tone of the *Itinerarium* has led to its being regarded as of a primarily mystical value. It is mystical in the end viewed by the author; it is mystical in the dispositions he declares to be requisite in the reader, which dispositions could scarcely be expected in the case of the purely scientific student. These points are well emphasised in the Prologue, and in the first chapter of the book to which we refer. In view of the attitude taken up by Bonaventure, we have concluded, that while the *Itinerarium* is neither wholly mystical, nor wholly scientific, it contains within it a form of meditation, useful to those who are gifted

12. See infra.

with greater intellectual powers, which can be helpful in preparing the soul for mystical union.

In the Prologue he declares that his intention is not to impart a purely theoretic science, nor to confute error, but rather to present to the reader certain considerations, which will increase devotion, and the love of divine things: 'Volentibus ad Deum magnificandum, admirandum et etiam degustandum, speculationes subiectas propono.' [13] And, as dispositions in the reader, for the right understanding of his treatise, he does not deem sufficient the use of reason alone, however trained it may be. The student of the *Itinerarium,* is to be a 'homo desideriorum,' 'præventus gratia, humilis et pius, compunctus et devotus.'[14] His whole thought is condensed in few words, when he writes: 'Parum aut nihil est speculum exterius propositum, nisi speculum mentis nostræ tersum fuerit et politum.'[15] He indicates how the 'mirror of the mind' is to be cleansed, when he adds: 'Exerce igitur te, homo Dei, prius ad stimulum conscientiæ remordentem, antequam oculos eleves ad radios sapientiæ in eius speculis relucentes, ne forte ex ipsa radiorum speculatione in graviorem incidas foveam tenebrarum.'[16] These no doubt, are the sentiments, expressed as they are continually throughout the *Itinerarium,* which gave the work such power in the eyes of Gerson, years later, at a time when Bonaventure's writings were being neglected.[17] Yet Gerson's enthusiastic appreciation, owes much to his own ability to follow the Franciscan in his speculative flights. For the theme of the work is lofty indeed. In passing over the relationship, which he considers to be existent between all created beings, in the natural and supernatural orders on the one hand, and the Primary, Efficient, Exemplary and Final Cause of all these things, on the other, he is not content with the bare presentation of that relationship. He binds all things together in a wonderful unity.

It is beyond the scope of this essay to give a complete commentary on the *Itinerarium.*[18] This would carry us into a wide philosophical and theological field. It will suffice, if his main conclusions from his principle, so finely expressed in the first

13. Op. cit., Prologus, n. 4, T. V, p. 296.
14. Ibid.
15. Ibid.
16. Ibid.
17. See his De examinatione doctrinarum in Opera Omnia, J. Gersonii, Parisiis, MDCVI, T. I, cols. 553 sqq.
18. Such commentaries abound. See for the complete list, Opera, T. V, Prolegomena, cap. IV, p. 26. All these commentaries are not available. A more recent one, based upon those mentioned by the Quarrachi Editors has been used for our present purpose—that of P. A. Delaporte, Étude sur l'Itineraire de l'âme à Dieu, de Saint Bonaventure, Paris, 1863.

chapter, be followed: 'Secundum statum conditionis nostræ ipsa rerum universitas sit scala ad ascendendum in Deum.'[19] This principle underlies much of his teaching in his other works. In the *Collationes in Hexaëmeron* for example, the whole world is made to speak of the Wisdom of God: 'Totus mundus est sicut unum speculum plenum luminibus præstantibus divinam sapientiam, et sicut carbo effundens lucem;'[20] and in the *Breviloquium,* the 'liber creaturæ' is represented as having been quite sufficient for man in the state of innocence, to attain to the knowledge of his Maker.[21] Now, however, he would remind all who wish to follow him in his 'pertinent speculations,' of the love of the Crucified, without which, no-one can approach unto God: of the necessity of prayer and compunction of heart, since reading without unction, speculation without devotion, research without admiration, knowledge without charity, avail nothing. To readers of a mind like his own, he will, in the *Itinerarium,* present seven chapters, dealing with the degrees of ascent to God, each degree being a search after evidence of the Divine in some special sphere.

As we have said, the fundamental principle of the *Itinerarium,* underlies many of his other major works, but it was not till he could enjoy the peace and quiet of Mount Alvernia, that he had an opportunity of illustrating the principle fully, and with required devotion. He tells us how he came to write the work, in his Prologue: 'Cum igitur exemplo beatissimi patris Francisci hanc pacem anhelo spiritu quærerem, ego peccator, qui loco ipsius patris beatissimi post eius transitum septimus in generali fratrum ministerio per omnia indignus succedo; contigit, ut nutu divino circa Beati ipsius transitum, anno trigesimo tertio ad montem Alvernæ tanquam ad locum quietum amore quærendi pacem spiritus declinarem, ibique existens, dum mente tractarem aliquas mentales ascensiones in Deum, inter alia occurrit illud miraculum, quod in prædicto loco contigit ipsi beato Francisco, de visione scilicet Seraph alati ad instar Crucifixi.'[22] In all eagerness to discover symbolism wherever possible, he goes on to show how this vision, vouchsafed to St. Francis of Assisi, typifies the way leading to mystical Contemplation. The six wings of the Seraph symbolize the six illuminations—all forms of knowledge being viewed in his philosophy as illuminations—which are given to

19. Op. cit., cap. I, n. 2, T. V, p. 297.
20. Op. cit., col. II, n. 27, T. V, p. 340.
21. Op. cit. cap. XII, T. V, p. 230: and compare II S. D. XXIII, art. II, q. III, T. II, p. 545.
22. Op. cit., n. 2, T. V, p. 295.

man, when he reflects upon certain truths, in the natural, and supernatural orders. His task is to show how creatures are the stepping-stones to God.

Not all beings in this Universe possess the same power of leading the soul to God; they do not for example, all possess in an equal degree, a resemblance to Him. Some things there are, presenting themselves to the mind as His Vestiges (Vestigia); others may be regarded as His very Image; some are corporeal, some are spiritual; some temporal, some eternal; some are outside ourselves, others are within us, and to attain to the Frst Principle of all these things, which is altogether Spiritual, Eternal and Transcendent, we are to proceed in due order. We must pass over the vestiges of God, which are corporeal, temporal, and outside ourselves; then we are to enter into our own souls, and reflect, that inasmuch as they are immortal, and spiritual, they form the Image of God; and finally, we are to transcend all, to the Eternal and purely Spiritual Cause of all these things.[23]

Man was created of his very nature to make such meditation, and for this purpose, he was endowed at the beginning, with six faculties, wonderfully adapted to rise to contemplation by way of these six stages. Bonaventure here refers to sense, imagination, reason, intellect, intelligence, and the 'apex mentis' or 'synderesis scintilla,' which we meet with elsewhere.[24] These powers, naturally given to us, are deformed and weakened by sin, and reformed by Grace. They are to be purified by righteousness, exercised by knowledge, and made perfect by Wisdom.[25] Though they have not been rendered totally incapable by the Fall, they now need the assistance of Divine Grace, to aid them in their quest. Grace is to be obtained by means of devout prayer.

From 'Prolegomena' such as these, the first chapter proceeds over well-worn ground, giving little that is new. When Bonaventure passes from the consideration of the greatness and the beauty of created things to the greatness and beauty that is

23. Itin., cap. I, n. 5, T. V, p. 297.
24. He writes: 'Juxta igitur sex gradus ascensionis in Deum sex sunt gradus potentiarum animae, per quos ascendimus ab imis ad summa, ab exterioribus ad intima, a temporalibus conscendimus ad aeterna; scilicet sensus, imaginatio, ratio, intellectus, intelligentia et apex mentis seu synderesis scintilla.' Ibid. This psychological doctrine is taken from the little work De Spiritu et Anima, attributed at one time to St. Augustine, and now proved to be of mediaeval origin. See Jungmann. Institut. Patrol., T. II, pars 1, nota 3, p. 337. The work itself is contained in Minge, P. L., T. XL, cols. 779 sqq. Bonaventure does not positively attribute it to St. Augustine, admitting that it may come from another source. See II S. D. XXIV, a. II, q. 1, T. II, p. 560.
25. Itin., cap. I, n. 6, T. V, p. 297. 'Hos gradus in nobis habemus plantatos per naturam, deformatos per culpam reformatos per gratiam; purgandos per iustitiam, exercendos per scientiam, perficiendos per sapientiam.'

Divine, we are but re-tracing the thought of St. Augustine, or more approximately, of Hugo of St. Victor. The origin, magnitude, multitude, beauty, plenitude, operation, and wondrous order of things contained in the Universe, elicit his praise. Those who cannot join in his admiration are blind, deaf, dumb, and foolish.[26] Not only is this meditation useful; it is a positive duty. He concludes his first chapter with an exhortation to his reader: 'Aperi igitur oculos, aures spirituales admove, labia tua solve et cor tuum appone, ut in omnibus creaturis Deum tuum videas, audias, laudes, diligas et colas, magnifices et honores, ne forte totus contra te orbis terrarum consurgat. Nam ob hoc pugnabit orbis terrarum contra insensatos, et econtra sensatis erit materia gloriæ, qui secundum Prophetam possunt dicere: Delectasti me Domine, in factura tua, et in operibus manuum tuarum exsultabo. Quam magnificata sunt opera tua, Domine! omnia in sapientia fecisti, impleta est terra possessione tua.' [27]

In his second chapter, he deals with a more particularized theme: with the meditation upon the traces to be found of God in the world of sense. God is in the objects which we see and touch, by His Essence, Power and Presence.[28] It would be impossible to reduce his reasoning to few words, for he here dwells at length upon the processes of sense and intellectual knowledge. The thought, however, is the same. He passes through all these intricate and difficult reasonings, to prove: 'quod omnes creaturæ istius sensibilis mundi animum contemplantis et sapientis ducunt in Deum æternum, pro eo quod illius primi principii potentissimi, sapientissimi et optimi, illius æternæ originis, lucis et plentitudinis, illius . . . . artis efficientis, exemplantis et ordinantis sunt umbræ, resonantiæ et picturæ, sunt vestigia, simulacra et spectacula nobis ad contuendum Deum proposita et signa divinitus data.'[29]

Entering within the soul by way of reflection, he finds there the image of the Blessed Trinity. The trinity of faculties in the unity of the soul is but a shadow of the Blessed Trinity.[30] Even viewed in its natural state, therefore, the soul, with its memory, understanding, and will, speaks to him of the Triune God. When the same soul is considered precisely as 'restored' by grace, and endowed with the gifts of the Holy Ghost, he seeks the aid of

---

26. Qui igitur tantis rerum creaturarum splendoribus non illustratur caecus est; qui tantis clamoribus non evigilat surdus est; qui ex omnibus his effectibus Deum non laudat mutus est; qui ex tantis indiciis primum principium non advertit stultus est.' Ibid., cap. I, n. 15, T. V, p. 299.
27. Ibid.
28. 'Est in eis per essentiam, potentiam et praesentiam,' cap. II, ibid.
29. Ibid., n. 11, p. 302.
30. See the whole of Cap. III, T. V, pp. 303 sqq.

Faith, Hope and Charity, to bring him still nearer to the Divine. Now he attempts to fathom the Scriptural teaching, that the soul in the state of grace, is the 'Dei filia,' 'Dei sponsa et amica,' 'Christi capitis membrum, soror et cohæres,' 'Spiritus Sancti templum.'[31] He declares that the least understanding of what is implied by these terms will be sufficient, when conjoined with the continuous use of grace, to elevate the soul to a higher stage in the spiritual life.

Still examining the evidence of Scripture, he proceeds to dwell upon the first name assigned to God in Holy Writ, which he finds to be *Being*.[32] He can now consider Him in the Unity, wherein there is neither privation nor bound,[34] passing on to the consideration of the Divine Goodness, the highest communicability of which may be contemplated, though never comprehended, in the mystery of the Blessed Trinity: 'In quibus necesse est propter summam bonitatem esse summam communicabilitatem, et ex summa communicabilitate summam consubstantialitatem, et ex summa consubstantialitate summam configurabilitatem, et ex his summam coequalitatem, ac per hoc summam coeternitatem, atque ex omnibus prædictis summam cointimitatem, qua unus est in altero necessario per summam circumincessionem et unus operatur cum alio per omnimodam indivisionem substantiæ et virtutis et operationis ipsius beatissimæ Trinitatis.'[35]

We have quoted this latter passage to give some idea of the form which his reasoning frequently takes. No matter what devotion he may infuse into such arguments, they remain, because of their intricacy, above the understanding of the less educated reader. From similar speculations, he comes to the mystery of the Incarnation: 'Hæc est vita æterna, ut cognoscant te solum verum Deum, et quem misisti Jesum Christum. Nam admirari debemus non solum conditiones Dei essentiales et personales in se, verum etiam per comparationem ad supermirabilem unionem Dei et hominis in unitate personæ Christi.'[36] In Christ he discovers the most perfect illumination given to man concerning things Divine. Christ is the very 'Bridge' joining the Eternal to the temporal. He is the most perfect 'Image' wherein we may contemplate the Divinity: 'In

31. Cap. IV, n. 8, T. V, p. 308.
32. 'Primus modus primo et principaliter defigit aspectum in ipsum esse, dicens, quod qui est est primum nomen Dei.' Cap. V, n. 2, ibid.
34. 'Quia primum, aeternum, simplicissimum, actualissimum, ideo perfectissimum; tali omnino nihil deficit, neque aliqua potest fieri additio,' n. 6, p. 309.
35. Cap. VI, n. 2, p. 311.
36. Ibid., n. 4. The Scripture reference is to John, 17, 3.

hac autem consideratione est perfectio illuminationis mentis, dum quasi in sexta die videt hominem factum ad imaginem Dei. Si enim imago est similitudo expressiva, dum mens nostra contemplatur in Christo Filio Dei, qui est imago Dei invisibilis per naturam, humanitatem nostram tam mirabiliter exaltatam, tam ineffabiliter unitam, videndo simul in unum primum et ultimum, summum et imum, circumferentiam et centrum, alpha et omega, causatam et causam, Creatorem et creaturam, librum scilicet scriptum intus et extra; iam pervenit ad quandam rem perfectam, ut cum Deo ad perfectionem suarum illuminationum in sexto gradu quasi in sexta die perveniat; nec aliquid iam amplius restet nisi dies requiei, in qua per mentis excessum requiescat humanæ mentis perspicacitas ab omni opere, quod patrarat.'[37]

Thus does Bonaventure represent his six degrees of ascent to God. We are to contemplate Him in the wonderful mirror of His Creation: to behold His reflection in the soul, considered both naturally, and supernaturally: to rise as high as possible in theological speculation, concerning His Unity and Goodness: to view Him in the mystery of the Incarnation, and, if this direct reflection upon Him be accompanied by true devotion and love, it will lead to the point, at which reason may take her rest, and give place, if God sees fit, to a more mystical operation. Reason has done her work; now love alone can bring the soul further. Love will declare to reason that the God Who was the Object of Francis' mystical transports transcends all that her researches have revealed, even though those researches have been guided by Revelation. Love will therefore throw the reason back upon the 'Pseudo-Dionysian' negative path. Bonaventure concludes his *Itinerarium* by insisting on the ineffability of the mystical experience to which God invites all Christians, in the person of the Blessed Francis,[38] and by reproducing the well known exhortation of Pseudo-Dionysius to Timothy: the exhortation to leave the senses, and the operations of the intellect, and all things sensible and intelligible, and things that are, and things that are not, that the soul may rise by ways above knowledge, to union with Him Who is above all knowledge and being. It is in freedom, and in the abandonment of all things, that the soul is borne, through pure, entire and absolute abstraction from all things, into the supernatural radiance of the Divine Darkness.[39]

37. Cap. VI, ad conclus., p. 312.
38. Cap. VII, n. 3, T. V, p. 312.
39. Cap. VII, n. 5, T. V, p. 313.

It remains to be added, that if at times Bonaventure refers to these efforts to discover traces of God in the whole of creation, as the 'degrees of Contemplation,' he is not using the word 'Contemplation' in the strict sense to be defined later. They are but steps leading to Contemplation strictly so called; they are preparatory thereto. Richard of St. Victor, in his *Benjamin Major,* used the same expression, 'gradus contemplationis' of his own more subjective considerations. The remark made by St. Thomas Aquinas, in reference to Richard's terminology, 'per illa sex designantur gradus quibus per creaturas in Dei contemplationem ascenditur,'[40] applies with equal significance to the degrees set forth in the *Itinerarium.* Nevertheless, the subject-matter of the *Itinerarium* may justly be styled the 'Mediate Contemplation' of God, and such 'Mediate Contemplation' assumes so important a place in Bonaventure's Theology, that it cannot be passed over in silence. Before attempting to show by whom he has been influenced in this love of 'Mediate Contemplation,' we must deal briefly with his teaching on prayer.

It is of course realized that the word 'prayer' may be, and is, used to signify any, and every act, which has direct relationship with God. Thus, it includes meditation itself. Tradition has rightly elevated to the sphere of prayer every form of human activity, which has as its end the glorifying of the God-head. The word is sufficiently comprehensive to include all that has been said up to the present. Contemplation may therefore be called the supreme development of the life of prayer. All this is fully appreciated; but since Bonaventure makes distinct and separate mention of prayer, 'meditatio et oratio' occurring frequently, it seems right that it should receive separate, if but brief treatment.

He is well acquainted with prayer in all its forms; from that which is understood of the multitude, vocal prayer, with its petitions by means of extemporary or traditional locutions addressed to God, to the more advanced, and the more difficult and rare wordless communings of the soul with its Maker. In those *Opuscula* which seem to contain the essence of his doctrine on prayer, the *De Triplici Via,* the *Soliloquium,* and the *De Perfectione Vitæ ad Sorores,* as well as in his Sermons, he exhausts all the resources of his imagination to illustrate the rewards awaiting those who will undertake in all earnestness the difficult work of prayer. The true end of prayer, like the end of the mystical life of the soul

40. Auct. cit. Secunda Secundae, Q. CLXXX, art. IV, ad. III (Leonine Edition), T. X, p. 428.

which it cultivates, is represented as the meeting between the soul and God: between the lover and the Beloved. What might be called his 'Philosophy of Prayer' is contained in the *Breviloquium*, and is couched in the more restrained language of the scholastic.

He is writing with especial reference to the spirit and the letter of the Lord's Prayer: 'De petitionibus autem orationis dominicæ hoc tenendum est, quod licet Deus sit liberalissimus et promptior ad dandum quam nos ad accipiendum; vult tamen orari a nobis, ut occasionem habeat largiendi dona gratiæ Spiritus sancti. Vult autem orari non solum oratione mentali, quæ est 'ascensus intellectus in Deum,' verum etiam vocali, quæ est 'petitio decentium a Deo' . . . . Ratio autem ad intelligentiam prædictorum hæc est; quia primum principium, sicut est summe verum et bonum in seipso, sic misericors et iustum in opere suo. Et quoniam misericordissimum est, ideo libentissime condescendit humanæ miseriæ per infusionem gratiæ suæ. Quia vero simul cum hoc iustum est, ideo donum perfectum non dat nisi desideranti, non dat gratiam nisi regratianti, non impendit misericordiam nisi miseriam cognoscenti, ut salva sit libertas arbitrii, et non vilescat nobilitas doni, et integer perseveret cultus honoris divini. Quoniam ergo orantis est divinum affectare subsidium, proprium allegare defectum et gratias agere propter beneficium gratis datum; hinc est, quod oratio disponit ad susceptionem divinorum charismatum, et Deus orari vult ad hoc, ut munera largiatur.'[41] Principles such as these, he applies to every form of prayer.

There seems to be no need to reproduce the various degrees of prayer, which he so carefully tabulates in many places. Like many mystical writers, for example Richard of St. Victor,[42] he is not consistent in this matter, giving sometimes five, sometimes three degrees. It is most probable that his fine shades of difference are emphasised at various times, not in order to set up objective norms whereby his reader may ascertain the progress made, but in a purely arbitrary spirit. Broadly speaking, there are three degrees of prayer, found in the Purgative, Illuminative, and Unitive Ways respectively.[43] These degrees are consequently progressive. As there is a gradual approximation of the soul towards union with God, and a production within it, of those conditions under which this union can take place, so there is a

41. Op. cit., Pars. V, cap. X, T. V, pp. 263-4.

42. See his De quattuor gradibus violentae charitatis, passim, P. L., T. CXCVI, cols. 1207 sqq.

43. See De Triplici Via, T. passim, VIII, pp, 1 sqq.

higher degree of prayer. Whilst the soul is engaged in the removal of obstacles to union with God, its degree of prayer will be primarily characterized by compunction of heart. In the Illuminative way, during which the soul becomes, through the imitation of Christ, more appreciative of the meaning to be given to the Divine mysteries, and of the need of Divine guidance, through, and in Christ, petition and gratitude give to prayer its chief characteristics. Finally, in the Unitive way, when the soul realizes its closeness to God, and experiences mystical joys with greater or lesser intensity, it will send forth its love to God in joy and gratitude: in secret, silent communings, as to One Who is thought of as continually present, even though at times He may not be experienced as present. Until this stage is reached, until the soul can commune with God alone, with no thought or care for anything outside Him, prayer, according to Bonaventure, is not wholly perfect.

All the above is but a tentative coördination of his teaching on prayer contained in the *De Triplici Via*. It is found to be substantially the same in the fifth chapter of his *De Perfectione Vitæ ad Sorores,* wherein he deals expressly with the prayer proper to the mystical life. There is no need to dwell upon this point. Bonaventure has nothing that is original or striking to offer us, with regard to prayer. Familiar exhortations abound. Let the soul be continually in prayer; let it not attempt to abandon vocal prayer before the habit of recollection, necessary in the higher stages of the spiritual life, be acquired; let it pray constantly that the gift of mystical contemplation may be granted; let every philosophical and theological speculation or argument, every scientific investigation, every form of duty, be consecrated by genuine prayer—by the referring of all to the glory of God. Obedience to these, and similar exhortations, he is persuaded, will bring the soul nearer to the fullness of the Christian life.[44] Perhaps no one could be more insistent than Bonaventure, upon the necessity of prayer. The way of perfection, as he repeatedly states, demands much work. In the present state of fallen nature, obstacles abound, and the strength needed to overcome them can be obtained only by perseverance in prayer.

Once again we find Bonaventure following with fidelity the general teaching of the Fathers. We need not prove by means of quotations the statement that they have all emphasised the efficacy of meditation and prayer in the development of the spiritual

44. See De Perfect. Vitae, cap. V, T. VIII, pp. 117-120.

life. By the time we come to the Victorines, we find that the tabulations and divisions, now so common in text-books of Ascetical or Mystical Theology, are quite well known. There is, however, one element in all the foregoing, which may be particularized, since it is among the characteristics of Bonaventurian Theology. We refer to that which has been called 'Mediate Contemplation:' his view of the external world as a vast mirror, wherein the face of God is reflected. Even in this, he does not appear original. St. Thomas Aquinas attributed equal importance to this 'Mediate Contemplation' in the spiritual life.[45] Yet it is to Bonaventure's credit, that he put to the forefront, making it the subject-matter of one of his major works, an idea which was to be shunned not so many years later. There is no originality in his conception, indeed, for from age to age the religious soul has sought to find traces of its God in Nature, and in its inmost self. The ways of finding Him have changed with the prevailing currents of philosophical thought, but generally speaking, whatever the philosophy, the 'vestigia' have been sought, and found. Scripture, old and new, has urged the religious soul on to this as it urged Bonaventure. Baron von Hügel has shewn that the Synoptics are especially insistent upon the observation and love of the external world which is at the root of the whole subject.[46]

Whilst it remains true that the 'Mediate Contemplation' embodied in the *Itinerarium,* only represents the general tendency in the literature with which the Franciscan was familiar, it bears marked traces of Augustinian and Victorine influence especially. Moreover, we are convinced that in itself, the work is but the philosophical expression of that love of Nature, and that reverence for the Divinely revealed mysteries associated with St. Francis of Assisi.

The same quest of which the *Itinerarium* speaks, the same final silencing of those very faculties which made the quest

45. See Secunda Secundae, Q. CLXXX, art. IV. 'Utrum vita contemplativa solum consistat in contemplatione Dei, an etiam in consideratione cuiuscumque veritatis.' Leonine Edition, T. X, pp. 427-8.

46. The Mystical Element of Religion. He writes: vol. 1, p. 30) 'Thus the 'Petrine' group gives us, as evidence for the observation and love of the external world: 'Behold the birds of the heaven, how they sow not, neither do they gather into barns;' 'Consider the lilies of the field how they grow; they toil not, neither do they spin; yet I say unto you, that even Solomon in all his glory was not arrayed like one of these;' 'The seed springeth up and grows, the man knoweth not how; the earth beareth fruit of itself, first the blade, then the ear, then the full corn in the ear;' 'When the fig-tree's branch is become tender and putteth forth its leaves, ye know that the summer is nigh;' and, 'When it is evening, ye say: 'It will be fair weather: for the heaven is red.' And in the morning: 'It will be foul weather to-day: for the heaven is red and lowering.' The texts are: Matt. vi, 26, 28; Mark, IV, 27-28; XIII, 28; Matt., XVI, 2, 3. The author declares on p. 28 that he has sought the Petrine type in the Synoptic Gospels.

possible of achievement, are commonplaces in the writings of St. Augustine. The quest runs throughout his philosophical works. He has expounded in his *De Libro arbitrio,*[47] how the things of Nature can be the pledges of further spiritual realities, and from this work, as well as from his *De Trinitate,*[48] much information might be gathered. Both works are quoted continually in the *Itinerarium.* Here, however, for the purpose of showing Augustine's thought, we have used his *Confessions,* in which the quest is placed in a more mystical setting. We find in the *Confessions* repeated descriptions of the soul's search for God through the ascending grades of creation, the turning of the mind upon itself, to mount through its more spiritual faculties, till it finds God within itself, by the most mysterious agency of grace, and yet still above itself. He writes in one place: 'Eramque certissimus quod invisibilia tua, a constitutione mundi, per ea quæ facta sunt, intellecta conspiciuntur; sempiterna quoque virtus et divinitas tua (Rom. I. 20). Quærens enim unde approbarem pulchritudinem corporum, sive cœlestium, sive terrestrium; et quid mihi præsto esset integre de mutabilibus judicanti, et dicenti: Hoc ita esse debet, illud non ita: hoc ergo quærens unde judicarem, cum ita judicarem, inveneram incommutabilem et veram veritatis æternitatem, supra mentem meam commutabilem. Atque ita gradatim a corporibus ad sentientem per corpus animam; atque inde ad ejus interiorem vim, cui sensus corporis exteriora annuntiaret; et quosque possunt bestiæ: atque inde rursus ad ratiocinantem potentiam ad quam refertur judicandum quod sumitur a sensibus corporis. Quæ se quoque in me comperiens mutabilem, erexit se ad intelligentiam suam; et abduxit cogitationem a consuetudine, subtrahens se contradicentibus turbis phantasmatum, ut inveniret quo lumine aspergeretur, cum sine ulla dubitatione clamaret incommutabile præferendum esse mutabili; unde nosset ipsum incommutabile, quod nisi aliquo modo nosset, nullo modo illud mutabili certo proponeret.'[49] Then it would seem that this quest, with the final abstraction, brings him to what may be called the mystic experience, for now he declares that in the flash of a trembling glance, his mind arrived at that which is. He is unable to sustain his gaze, but is relegated to his ordinary experience, bear-

---

47. See Op. cit., Lib. II, cap. XVI, P. L., T. XXXII, col. 1263, where he gives instances in the works of Nature and Art, in the beauty of motion and of form, and in the very science of numbers, tracing all to their mysterious origin—God.

48. See especially Op. cit., Lib. VI, cap. X, P. L., T. XLII, cols. 931-2. 'Trinitas in rebus factis repraesentatur.'

49. Op. cit., Lib. VII, cap. XVII, P. L., T. XXXII, col. 745.

ing with him but a loving memory, and a longing for that of which, he had, as it were, but perceived the odour, and was not yet able to feed upon.[50]

The same idea is more elaborately, and perhaps more beautifully worked out, in his description of the scene at Ostia, just before his mother's death, when mother and son opened to each other their most secret thoughts. The passage is too well known and too often quoted to need more than a passing reference here. He tells again how they passed through all material things, through Heaven itself, where sun and moon and stars shed their radiance upon earth: how they began their more inward ascent by thinking of, and marvelling at God's works: how, coming to their own minds, they passed beyond them again, to the Wisdom, whereby all things came to be.[51] Then comes the successive silencing of the faculties. They seek refuge in blind elevations to God, and in the 'quiet' thus produced, the very beings of their souls come into relation with the Ultimate Reality, which is God. Then, when their souls had gone out in longing for the Wisdom to which they had been led, they ask: 'Si cui sileat tumultus carnis, sileant phantasiæ terræ et aquarum et æris: sileant et poli, et ipsa sibi anima sileat, et transeat se non se cogitando, sileant somnia et imaginariæ revelationes, omnis lingua et omne signum, et quidquid transeundo fit, si cui sileat omnino; quoniam si quis audiat, dicunt hæc omnia: Non ipsa nos fecimus, sed fecit nos qui manet in æternum (Ps. XCIX. 3-5): his dictis si jam taceant quoniam erexerunt aurem in eum qui fecit ea, et loquatur ipse solus, non per ea sed per seipsum, ut audiamus verbum ejus, non per linguam carnis, neque per vocem angeli, nec per sonitum nubis, nec per ænigma similitudinis; sed ipsum quem in his amamus, ipsum sine his audiamus, sicut nunc extendimus nos, et rapida cogitatione attigimus æternam Sapientiam super omnia manentem; si continuetur hoc, et subtrahantur aliæ visiones longe imparis generis, et hæc una rapiat et absorbeat et recondat in interiora gaudia spectatorem suum, ut talis sit sempiterna vita, quale fuit hoc momentum intelligentiæ, cui suspiravimus; nonne hoc est: Intra in gaudium Domini tui?' (Matth. XXV, 21).[52]

It is perfectly true that we can find nothing in Bonaventure's works to compare in beauty with this, and with similar passages

---

50. 'Et pervenit ad id quod est, in ictu trepidantis aspectus . . . . . sed aciem figere non evalui: et repercussa infirmitate redditus solitis, non mecum ferebam nisi amantem memoriam, et quasi olfacta desiderantem quae comedere nondum possem.' Ibid.

51. Ibid., Lib. IX, cap. X, col. 774.

52. Ibid.

in Augustine's *Confessions:* nothing which reflects so lofty a conception of the Majesty of God. Yet Augustine's thought seems to have inspired the greater part of the *Itinerarium.*

Nor has it been forgotten that, to express the need of final abstraction from all the 'data' of intellectual search, Bonaventure seeks refuge in Pseudo-Dionysian language: a fact which may seem to remove his thought from Augustinian influence. Now careful examination of the *Itinerarium,* and of the *Collationes in Hexaëmeron,* will reveal how relatively unimportant in this matter is the influence of the *Dionysiaca.* We venture to think that in the last chapter of the *Itinerarium,* where he reproduces Eriugena's version of the famous prayer, and the exhortation to Timothy, he has done so, simply because he has found the best authority at hand, and the most forcible authority, for his previous statement that in precise relation to the mystical union, 'modicum potest industria, parum est dandum inquisitioni, et multum unctioni.'[53] The whole content of the *Itinerarium,* with its eager intellectual search after traces of God, is the best explanation of what he himself understands by the 'modicum' and the 'parum.' Little though the result may be, when compared with the Light revealed in mystical union, the search has been prolonged with his beloved Augustine. At the end of his quest, realizing with St. Augustine that God transcends all that his intellect has revealed, he merely makes use of Pseudo-Dionysian language. Pseudo-Dionysius and Augustine are, after all, at one with regard to the need of abstraction from the 'given' of sense and intellect. The point of difference between them is this, that Pseudo-Dionysius shuts out from his mind as soon as possible the revelation given in created things; the wise man is he who can speedily attain to a facility in this negative process. St. Augustine, even though knowing that the same negative process must eventually take place, pursues the Light revealed by sense and intellect as long as he can. The last chapter, therefore, of the *Itinerarium,* in which Pseudo-Dionysius is introduced with his negations, need not cause us to alter the opinion already expressed, that in his 'Mediate Contemplation,' Bonaventure is primarily inspired, on the intellectual side, by St. Augustine.

This opinion is strengthened, when we find him having recourse to the Victorines, Hugo and Richard, to illustrate, by way

53. Itin., cap. VII, n. 5, T. V, p. 312.

of authority, the idea that the Universe is as a great 'Book,' wherein the Wisdom of the Maker may be read. Both Hugo and Richard owe much in turn to St. Augustine, the former having gained the name of a 'second Augustine.'[54] For Hugo, as for Bonaventure, the works of Creation have the sacramental quality of similitude, and, in a general, wider way, they possess, like the real sacraments, the quality of institution, since their similitude to spiritual things was intended by the Creator. He has much to say concerning the 'decor' and the 'pulchritudo' of the created world; we should meditate upon it, because of the suggestions given in such meditation. The visible will suggest to us, and help us fix our minds upon the invisible. Consequently, Hugo's path leads upwards, like Bonaventure's, beginning with 'cogitatio' through 'meditatio' to 'contemplatio,' this last lying beyond all meditation, and attained only after the abstraction of which we have spoken. All this is everywhere evidenced in his works.

Perhaps the most concise exposition of his mystical process, wherein the chief ideas of Bonaventure's *Itinerarium* appear, is to be found in the last book of his *Eruditionis didascalicæ libri septem,* that comprehensive treatise, which embraces so many subjects. The Goodness and Wisdom which made the World, he says, is manifested in the contemplation of creatures. The Word was invisible, but He has made Himeslf visible by His work: 'Quamvis multis et variis modis creaturarum pulchritudo perfecta sit, quattuor tamen præcipue sunt, in quibus earumdem decor consistit. Hoc est in situ, in motu, in specie, in qualitate. Quæ quidem si quis investigare sufficeret, mirabilem in eis sapientiæ Dei lucem inveniret. Et hoc utinam ego tam possem subtiliter perspicere, tam competenter enarrare, quam possum ardenter diligere. Delectat enim me quia valde dulce, et jucundum est de his rebus frequenter agere, ubi simul et ratione eruditur sensus, et suavitate delectatur animus, et æmulatione excitatur affectus, ita ut cum Psalmista stupeamus, et admirantes clamemus: Quam magnificata sunt opera tua, Domine! omnia in sapientia fecisti. (Ps. CIII).'[55] Compare this with the opening chapters of Bonaventure's *Itinerarium,* and the similarity of thought and expression is striking. Yet this is only the beginning.

Like the later Franciscan, Hugo passes upwards through the natural works of God to the supernatural works: to the Incarna-

54. Leibner's Hugo of St. Victor, p. 21; cited by Vaughan, 'Hours with the mystics,' bk. 1, p. 154.
55. Op. cit., Lib. VII, cap. IV, P. L., T. CLXXVI, cols. 813-14.

tion itself, viewed as a fact. In the Incarnation, we are given the second 'Book' wherein we may read the Divine designs. He writes: 'Universus enim mundus iste sensibilis quasi quidam liber est scriptus digito Dei, hoc est virtute divina creatus, et singulæ creaturæ quasi figuræ quædam sunt non humano placito inventæ, sed divino arbitrio institutæ ad manifestandam invisibilium Dei sapientiam.' [56] This is the first 'Book.' God, however, wished to do more than this. We turn to his *De Sacramentis,* where he best expresses his teaching: 'Voluit autem postea adhuc aliter scribi foris sapientia ut manifestius videretur et perfectius cognosceretur, ut oculus hominis illuminaretur ad scripturam secundam, quoniam caligaverat ad primam. Fecit ergo secundum opus post primum et illud evidentius erat, quoniam non solum demonstravit sed illuminavit. Assumpsit carnem non amittens divinitatem, et positus liber scriptus intus et foris; in humanitate foris, intus in divinitate, ut foris legeretur per imitationem, intus per contemplationem; foris ad sanitatem, intus ad felicitatem . . . .' [57]

The mystical value of this meditation upon the works of God is fully recognized, for when his thought has climbed to the work of the Incarnation, he counsels, like Bonaventure, the usual 'burying of the self'—the abstraction from all things, to enjoy the ineffable delights of mystical union.[58] We may remark, before leaving Hugo, that it was probably due to his influence that Bonaventure makes meditation stand, not so much for mere reflective activity, as for a work in which every faculty takes part, the reflections adduced being merely the starting point. For Hugo certainly emphasised this idea; with him, meditation was useless, if it did not set the whole man at work upon a re-building of the self.[59] We acknowledge, therefore, Bonaventure's debt to Hugo, but when it comes to the question of accounting for the tendency to enclose the foregoing doctrine within certain well defined degrees, we must turn to the next great figure in the Victorine School, Richard.

Richard works upon the material supplied by Hugo, and carries his master's passion for symbolism to an almost puerile extent. He, like Bonaventure, leads the soul up to mystical Contemplation by six stages, the reflective activity on the part of the

56. Ibid.
57. Op. cit., Lib. I, pars. VI, cap. V, P. L., T. CLXXVI, cols. 266-7.
58. See for this the last five chapters of the seventh book of Erudit. Didasc.: ibid., cols. 833-836.
59. See his Hom. in Eccles. Hom. I, P. L., T. CLXXV, cols. 117 sqq., where he developes the idea that 'in meditatione quasi quaedam lucta est ignorantiae cum scientia,' ignorance and knowledge, standing for sinfulness, etc., and a more perfect Christianity, respectively.

soul in these stages being symbolized by the wings with which it is endowed to ascend to the mystic heights:[60] a touch of symbolism borrowed by Bonaventure in his Prologue to the *Itinerarium*. The Augustinian doctrine handed down by Hugo forms the warp and woof of Richard's *Benjamin Major*. Here he treats firstly of Contemplation, and then of its degrees. The degrees, as St. Thomas noted, are only forms of meditation, conducive to the mystical state. The first degree consists in the consideration and admiration of corporeal objects; the second, in the further study of the products of nature and art. In the third degree, the soul is raised to the moral order by meditation upon Divine and human laws; in the fourth, to the knowledge of incorporeal and invisible objects, the soul itself, and angelic spirits. So far, human wisdom has sought manifestation of the Divine Wisdom, but human industry, in the height of its success, must give place to a more mystical operation. For, in the fifth degree, the soul must rise above itself, by transcending itself and all the limitations of its thought, till, in the sixth and last stage, it is rapt in mystical ecstasy. In relation to this, he declares, in language again borrowed by Bonaventure, penitence avails more than science; sighs are more potent than reason. Reason has done its work; it has done the work which Augustine and Hugo made it perform. Now it needs Divine assistance to enable it to pierce the clouds enveloping the Divinity.[61]

Substantially, it is clear, the above is the same as the doctrine expounded in Bonaventure's *Itinerarium*. The identity of thought is such that many have seen in it but a reproduction of Richard's work.[62] Others, while admitting similarity, give Bonaventure credit for an additional originality in his treatment of the subject.[63] It is not within the scope of this essay to attempt a detailed examination of the two treatises. In both, the degrees are six in number; in both, the starting point is the same; in both, the end to be attained is mystical Contemplation. The similarity lessens when we begin to compare degree

---

60. 'His sex sane contemplationum alis a terrenis suspendimur et ad coelestia levamur.' Benjamin Major, Lib. 1, cap. X, P. L., T. CXCVI, col. 75.

61. See for all this, Op. cit., Lib. IV, cap. VI, P. L., T. CXCVI, col. 139. Quoted infra, chap. VI.

62. See Andes, F., art. Die Stufen der Contemplatio in Bonaventuras Itinerarium mentis in Deum und im Benjamin maior des Richard von St. Viktor, in Franziskanische Studien, Festnummer, 1921, pp. 189 sqq.

63. Thus Étienne Gilson writes, art. La Conclusion de la Divine Comédie et la Mystique Franciscaine, in Revue d'histoire Franciscaine, T. I, p. 56: 'Le Benjamin Major de Richard de Saint-Victor et l'Itinerarium mentis in Deum de saint Bonaventure . . . . il est evident que l'opuscule mystique de saint Bonaventure est lui-même une interprétation, d'ailleurs profonde et originale, de celui de Richard de Saint-Victor.'

with degree. Richard has as his basis, when mapping out his degrees, the subjective outlook upon created things.[64] Bonaventure is compelled to make his degrees, because of a mysterious appeal in Nature itself: an appeal which nature makes to every reflective mind. His attitude towards created things is less metaphysical than that of either of the Victorines. With them he admits that created things are symbols; but their symbolism does not exhaust their worth. Here and there in the *Itinerarium,* we find traces of St. Francis' own addition to the symbolism of the Victorines: traces of the love which, in view of the Incarnation, may legitimately go forth to all Nature.

We are far from attributing to the 'Poverello,' a knowledge of the above ideas in their correct scientific setting, but it remains true, that in Nature he spontaneously hews out the steps that will lead him to God. Francis spent much of his time in loving meditation upon the beauties of Nature,[65] and upon the wondrous work of the Incarnation which had endowed all things, even the most minute and insignificant, with a new splendour and magnificence. It would be a mistake to refer to any pious sentimentality, his blithe love of animals, birds, and flowers, and his regard even for the things devoid of sense. This love was but part of a deeper, personal philosophy, which viewed these things as the creatures of the hand of God:[66] as symbols in their loveliness of the Beauty which is Divine: yet not symbols to be spurned when their work was done, but to be loved still, because of their origin and their value derived from the very fact of the Incarnation. Francis' mystical movement is from creatures to God, and from God, with renewed fervour, to the world in which he is set. This removes him to a different plane from that of the Victorines. The *Legenda* of Bonaventure, may not depict the St. Francis who has

64. Richard writes: 'Sex autem sunt contemplationum genera a se et inter se omnino divisa. Primum itaque est in imaginatione et secundum solam imaginationem. Secundum est in imaginatione secundum rationem. Tertium est in ratione secundum imaginationem. Quartum est in ratione et secundum rationem. Quintum est supra, sed non praeter rationem. Sextum supra rationem, et videtur esse praeter rationem.' Benj. Maior, Lib. I, cap. VI, P. L. T. CXCVI, col. 70.

65. 'Contuebatur in pulchris pulcherrimum et per impressa rebus vestigia prosequebatur ubique dilectum, de omnibus sibi scalam faciens, per quam conscenderet ad apprehendendum eum qui est desiderabilis totus. Inauditae namque devotionis affectu fontalem illam bonitatem in creaturis singulis tamquam in rivulis degustabat, et quasi coelestem concentum perciperet in consonantia virtutum et actuum eis datorum a Deo, ipsas ad laudem, Domini more Prophetae David dulciter hortabatur.' Leg. Sti. Francisci, St. Bon., Cap. IX, n. I, T. VIII, p. 530.

66. 'Consideratione quoque primae originis omnium abundantiori pietate repletus, creaturas quantumlibet parvas fratris vel sororis appellabat nominibus, pro eo quod sciebat, eas unum secum habere principium.' Ibid., cap. VIII, n. 6, p. 527.

gained the respect of succeeding generations; the spirituality of the Saint with whose life he is occupied may, in his description, lack the freedom associated with Franciscanism in its purity; but at least this may be said of his work, that he has succeeded in representing the true Nature-philosophy of the 'Poverello,' where others, who made greater pretensions, Ubertino da Casale for example, miserably failed.[67] Bonaventure can single out this love of St. Francis for creatures, and show how his meditation upon them led him to God; he can exult in it, with the best accredited among the early chroniclers,[68] and later critics of the Franciscan spirit.[69] It is due to his own appreciation of this characteristic of St. Francis, that his doctrine of 'Mediate Contemplation,' though inspired by Augustine and the Victorines in its scientific bearings, has become, in the *Itinerarium,* a little more appealing, a little more in touch, perhaps, with true human life.

Bonaventure's doctrine, we may conclude, seems to derive on its philosophical side, from Augustine and the Victorines, and in its more devotional aspect, from St. Francis of Assisi. The influence of Pseudo-Dionysius has not been stressed for reasons already given; the ultimate transcending of all knowledge given by sense and intellect concerning the Supreme Cause of all things has been shown to be an element common to the writers mentioned. Needless to say, though this transcending process finds no expression in St. Francis' *Opuscula,* it remains true, that the God with Whom he finally enjoyed mystical union, was viewed as essentially raised far above the things which had led him upwards. Francis himself would admit, even in his most enthusiastic creature-love, that they would serve him in his path to God, only as long as their inadequacy to satisfy the highest human aspirations, was fully recognized.

The point upon which we have dwelt at some length is considered to be the only one worth particularizing in any critical treatment. All else Bonaventure says with regard to meditation, and with regard to prayer, is too commonplace to demand special notice. The point also assumes an importance, in the light of subsequent mystical teaching. There have been mystics, who, as we

---

67. See for full evidence as to this statement, L'Idéalisme Franciscain Spirituel au XIVe siècle. Étude sur Ubertin de Casale, par F. Callaey, O. F. M. C., Louvain, 1911, pp. 95-99.

68. E. g. Celano, Legenda Prima; see cap. XXIX (ed. Alencon), pp. 81 sqq.; also the author of the Speculum Perfectionis (ed. P. Sabatier), caps. C-CI, pp. 195 sqq.

69. See P. Sabatier, Vie de S. François d'Assise, Paris, 1894, pp. 341 sqq.; F. Cuthbert, St. Francis of Assisi, 3rd ed., London, 1921, pp. 19, 55, 351, passim; also The Romanticism of St. Francis, 2nd ed., London, 1924, pp. 13 sqq.

have said, whilst admitting in theory the truth that creatures may be stepping stones to God, have nevertheless in practice found the contemplation of concrete realities to be a veritable stumbling-block to their progress. This has frequently been due to an extraordinary sense of the enormity of sin. Sin, original sin in particular, has cast a shadow of gloom over the whole Universe; or if the gloom is not thought of, the delights of creatures are only so many snares, whereby the unwary may be trapped. Not all mystics have been able to join with St. Francis in his delight and comfort derived from the thought, that the whole of Nature, hitherto over-clouded by the darkness of sin, had in some mysterious way, participated in the great atoning work of Christ. Ubertino da Casale has already been mentioned as an example. The God of his *Arbor Vitæ* is, if we may use the expression in all reverence, an Egoist, Who has made all things absolutely for Himself and who rests content in the knowledge that because of Original Sin, creatures, far from leading men to Him, take them still further from Him. Even if, in all fairness to Ubertino, we mention his appreciative commentary on St. Paul's 'Every creature of God is good,' we must in all truth add that he tends to destroy the spiritual worth of such a belief, when he remarks with customary bitterness: 'Comedant carnes qui carnalibus deserviunt.' [70]

This is an attitude which characterizes to some extent, the first three books of the *Imitatio Christi,*[71] and which was developed by mystics like Eckhart, Tauler, Suso, and Ruysbroeck. To some the meditation upon created things has brought positive pain, and an intense longing for something more permanent. Thus, St. John of the Cross, whilst admitting that creatures exhibit traces of God, the impress of His Beauty and Magnificence and Power, declares that in contemplating them, the love of the soul increases indeed, but so does the pain at the absence of the Beloved. The soul must therefore pray for the full fruition of His Presence, and St. John represents the soul as praying thus: 'Entertain me no more with any knowledge of communications or impressions of Thy grandeur, for these do but increase my longing and the pain of Thy absence; Thy presence alone can satisfy my will and desire.'[72] Such a repulsion from natural beauty was expressed also by St.

---

70. Op. cit., Lib. III, cap. III, ff. 149-150. The ref. to St. Paul is I. Tim. IV, 4.
71. See Op. cit., bk. I, chap. VII, bk. III, chaps. XXI sqq.
72. Auct. cit., A Spiritual Canticle of the Soul, trans. by D. Lewis, London, 1909. Explanation of Stanza VI, p. 54.

Catherine of Genoa in her *Vita.* She writes: 'The sun, which at first seemed so clear to me, now seems obscure; what used to seem sweet to me, now seems bitter: because all beauties and all sweetnesses that have an admixture of the creature are corrupt and spoilt.' [73]

All this is in sharp contrast with the spirituality of Saint Francis, and his disciple Bonaventure. Yet such uterances as these need not be condemned. Mysticism is preëminently personal; the individual mystic, must, to a great extent, hew out his, or her, own path. Neither is the other attitude to be reproached: that of finding symbolism everywhere, and in everything. To the mystic, two great truths are of absorbing interest; they cover his whole outlook upon life—one is that God exists, the other, that the only happiness possible is that which is attained in union with Him. With that union as his supreme goal, he is free to regard the world and all its contents, as nothing but a stumbling-block, and if he does not consent to such a step, so repulsive to many, what is more natural than that he should make use of creaturely objects in relation to his own end? Symbolism follows logically upon this latter choice. Such was the choice of the Victorines; such too, was the choice of St. Francis, who added to Symbolism the results of his own conception of Christ as the Lord of the World, and influenced Bonaventure to a certain extent. True it is, that symbolism can lead to certain abuses — to fanciful puerilities, and to an artificial outlook upon all life. But once we admit the validity of the two great truths, quoted as absorbing the whole interest of the mystic, there is little to quarrel with in the root principle of symbolism. Some who are intent upon defending the supernatural element in Mysticism, might quarrel with it on the ground that it leads to a 'Natural Mysticism.' It certainly did not do so in the cases of Bonaventure and his predecessors. There is no hint of a belief, that the mystical experience may be attained to, by any mere use of the natural powers. These can but prepare the way. To see the reflections of Divine Beauty and Power in Nature is one thing; to see God is another. The beholding of such reflections may lead to feelings of awe and reverence towards Nature in its symbolical aspect; yet awe and reverence do not constitute the basis of the mystical experience described by the Franciscan.

---

73. Quoted by Baron Von Hügel in The Mystical Element of Religion, vol. 1, pp. 276-7.

Nor is there latent beneath this outlook upon the world which forms the basis of Bonaventure's doctrine of 'Mediate Contemplation' any trace of Pantheism. Many passages might be quoted from the *Itinerarium,* and elsewhere, as savouring of Pantheism. Thus he writes: '(Deus) est simplicissimum et maximum, ideo totum intra omnia et totum extra, ac per hoc est sphæra intelligibilis cuius centrum est ubique et circumferentia nusquam;'[74] and again: 'Deus magis est intimus unicuique rei quam ipsa sibi.'[75] These, and similar passages which might be multiplied, are only forcible expressions of his own conceptions of Divine Immanence. All creatures are in a state of immediate dependence upon God, and it is only in virtue of that dependence that they exist. In a certain sense, therefore, God is immediately present among, and in creatures, for they are the continual result of His Power, and Wisdom; where these are at work, there God in His uncreated Essence must needs be. In this sense, Bonaventure admits, is God immanent in creatures. He is not mixed with them, yet they possess a likeness to Him, inasmuch as they reflect His Beauty and Wisdom. He can write of creatures: '(Deus) est in eis per essentiam, potentiam et præsentiam,'[76] but he always insists that God is by Nature absolutely distinct and separate from all creaturely existence, not merely in the way in which one creature differs in kind from another, but in virtue of the unique Nature of His Being, which is absolute, self-dependent, and thus altogether incommensurable with created things, which are necessarily dependent and derived. Though all creatures are in the similitude of God by virtue of their being, communicated to them by Him, they are absolutely unlike Him in His independence; no imaginable greatness or perfection in any creature can give it any kind of resemblance to this essential and fundamental attribute of the Divine Nature. Hence Bonaventure is forced to the point that God is really known best only after intellectual separation from all creaturely existences; He cannot moreover be expressed in terms of anything but Himself, nor brought under any category which has any other content.

If, therefore, we find the 'Mediate Contemplation' expounded above, leading to the consideration of God's Intelligence, Wisdom, Beauty and Power, together with other attributes, it must always be remembered that the Franciscan

74. Op. cit., cap. V, n. 8, T. V, p. 310.
75. II S. D. XXIX, art. I, q. III, n. 6, T. II, p. 643.
76. Itin., cap. II, n. 1, T. V, p. 299.

Theologian recognises the Divinity as still being none of these things in precisely the same sense in which they are predicated of creatures. Creatures can only be intelligent, wise, and the rest, by participation, even as their very existence is only participation in the Being of God.[77] The speculative knowledge that God exists, possessing in a transcendent manner the attributes found reflected in creatures, is, in the Bonaventurian synthesis, what may be called the theoretical preparation for the mystical experience, which, in turn, is only possible in a manner consistent with Divine Transcendence. Hence his final adoption of the 'Via Negativa:' hence too, his references to the soul in mystical union, as being 'lifted above itself,' 'taken out of itself,' and not as realizing itself as part of a universal Divinity. In the realm of grace it is the same; mystical experience is ever the full realization of the inherent possibilities of the 'given.'

It is fully realized that this is but an inadequate treatment of the most difficult problem presented by Divine Immanence and Transcendence. There are gaps in the brief presentation of Bonaventure's doctrine, which demand much careful thought and reading, before they can be filled; still wider reading and deeper study would be demanded before his doctrine could be criticised from the philosophical point of view. It is only hoped that so far, sufficient has been said, to remove him from the number of those mystical writers who are represented either as fully Pantheistic in thought, or at least, as in expression trembling on the edge of Pantheism.[78]

We are more concerned with the value to be attributed to the doctrine of 'Mediate Contemplation' in the devotional sphere. It must needs have a special worth, inasmuch as it aids the soul to keep in constant, albeit indirect, communion with God. The practice of the 'presence of God,' beloved of many mystics, becomes easier of accomplishment, when, in addition to the belief that He is present within the soul of every devout Christian by His grace, the truth and potency of the 'manuductio' illustrated in the *Itinerarium,* is fully realized. Also, the attitude taken up by Bonaventure in regard to the external world, gives rise to an

---

77. For all the above, see I S. D. XXXVII, P. I, Art. III, Q. I,—P. II, Art. I, Q. III—T. I, pp. 646-657; and cf. Breviloquium adjectis illustrationibus, etc. P. Antonii Mariae a Vicetia, Friburgi, MDCCCLXXXI, pp. 110 sqq. Here, Bonaventure's works are examined with reference to Pantheism, and the commentator concludes that there is no evidence of Pantheistic tendencies.

78. With many non-Catholic writers on the subject of Mysticism it has become the fashion to read Pantheism into the most innocent expressions of Nature-love. This need not be dealt with too seriously. It is too often a case of wilful misunderstanding.

optimism, present indeed in the writings of some of our own English mystics, yet painfully lacking elsewhere—in the works of later Continental mystics[79] for example. It is only a pessimistic philosophy that would make of the beauties of Nature so many stumbling blocks to communion with the Divine: so many distractions in prayer. Moreover such an attitude of pessimism is surely difficult of reconciliation with the belief that Christ is the Lord of all Creation. It seems more in keeping with the spirit of Our Lord's Gospel, to regard the external world with Francis of Assisi, and his spiritual son, Bonaventure, as capable of being used in the great task before the mystic—the attainment of the contemplation of the God Who made not only the human soul, but all else.

79. By 'Continental Mystics' we here mean those who lived their lives or wrote their works in countries other than England.

CHAPTER V.

Contemplation the reward of the ascetical life.—Meaning of the term and its synonyms.—Bonaventure's inconsistency in use of the term 'Contemplatio.' — The question of 'acquired' Contemplation. — Bonaventure manifests no acquaintance with later distinction between 'acquired' and 'infused' Contemplation. — His teaching that no special vocation is demanded for the attainment of mystical union.—Accessibility of the mystical state.—His encouragement of desire in relation thereto.—This desire balanced by making it extend to a strenuous preparatory asceticism. — The nature of mystical union or contemplation.—Some modern attempts to explain it. — Bonaventure's teaching that the experience of God in normal mystical union is indirect.—The soul conceived to commune with God, through the medium of a special interior effect. — Apparently contrary passages explained.—The two constitutive elements of the mystical act. — The enlightenment of the intellect. — This at once an 'Illuminatio' and a 'Docta Ignorantia.'—The consummation of the mystical act, found in the will-union of the soul with God.—The enlightenment of the intellect a subordinate factor.—Effects of mystical union.—The illumination of the intellect and the inflaming of the will, attributed to the gifts of the Holy Ghost, Understanding and Wisdom respectively.—The gift of Understanding founded upon Faith. — Bodily phenomena find no necessary place in mystical union. — Terms apparently implying external phenomena, explained.

We have now to treat of the highest state in the development of the spiritual life: that of Contemplation. So far, it has been seen, that Bonaventure insists upon a genuine process of purgation as a preliminary to this state. It has likewise been pointed out that he places in the forefront, among the necessary preparatory steps, that peculiarly Franciscan 'Imitatio Christi,' which, in a later age, was to become the basis of what was known as the 'New Devotion.' All this was followed by a discussion on his ideas of prayer and meditation, the form of meditation known as 'Mediate Contemplation' being particularly stressed.

It is undoubtedly Bonaventure's opinion that from these, and from kindred spiritual exercises demanding by their nature not only the aid of grace, but also individual conative activity, there develops within the soul that life of complete union with God, which is called the Contemplative life: a life which may or may not be accompanied by those extraordinary external phenomena met with in many ascetical and mystical treatises, such as ecstasy in its common acceptance, and rapture. With external phenomena we need not concern ourselves. Bonaventure manifests no tendency to dwell upon them as if they represented in any sense the mystical dealings between God and the human soul. External phenomena neither prove, nor make for sanctity; even the Bonaventurian 'ecstasis' implies no necessary bodily effect, as we shall see. The Franciscan Doctor teaches that, as a reward for its fidelity, for its stern self-discipline, and steadfast exercise of virtue, the soul is at last endowed with an ability to enjoy, with greater or less frequency, with greater or less intensity, according to progress made, the act of mystical Contemplation. It is this that gives the name to the state now attained; it is also called the state or 'way' of Union, since the essential act of the Contemplative life is viewed as an act of will-union with God.

Since we have now come to the principal and most difficult part of our treatise, it is proposed to make this act, and all connected with it, the subject matter of the whole of the present chapter.

Again, it must be noted the doctrine is very much scattered in the sources whence it has been drawn. Moreover, when Bonaventure mentions 'Contemplatio,' it cannot always be ascertained with immediate certainty whether he is referring to a truly mystical act, rendered possible only through the operation of a special grace, or to the mere discursive act of the intellect which is co-natural with it. There is great confusion of terminology. 'Contemplatio' is made to stand for the mystical and the natural acts, and in all probability, the confusion is only part of the heritage received from the Victorines, particularly from Richard, whose *Benjamin Major* offers a striking example of a similar carelessness.[1] In view of this confusion, great care has been taken in choosing quotations. Nothing is cited which has not undoubted reference to that act of the soul which is regarded as the fullest enjoyment of the Christian life. Again, whilst the act itself admits of degrees in intensity, there are, and must be, within the spiritual life, other acts, which, though they approach in character the essential will-union with God, nevertheless fall short of being mystical in reality. Thus, there are periods of intense spiritual exaltation, hardly distinguishable from true mystical Contemplation; but spiritual exaltation can be, and very often is, due to purely natural causes. On the other hand, mystical

1. Thus Richard writes in one place: 'Possumus tamen illam quae in hac vita haberi potest, Dei cognitionem, tribus gradibus distinguere et secundum triplicem graduum differentiam per tres coelos dividere. Aliter siquidem Deus videtur per fidem, aliter cognoscitur per rationem, atque aliter cernitur per contemplationem. Prima ergo visio ad primum coelum, secunda ad secundum, tertia pertinet ad tertium . . . Ad primum itaque et secundum contemplationis coelum homines sane ascendere possunt.' Op. cit., P. L., T. CXCVI, col. 53.

Contemplation, in its essence, is due solely to grace. It is viewed in Bonaventure's theology as the super-structure built by God Himself, on the foundation laid by the soul when aided by the ordinary graces common to all Christians. The soul has, as far as may be, cleansed itself from sin; it has made advances in virtue in an imitation of the Christ-life; it has acquired habits of prayer and meditation. Now God directly adds the power to commune with Himself, in a more exalted and in a mystical manner.

Furthermore, it must be remembered that we are dealing with a progressive development implying multitudinous degrees; to search out, and to tabulate with precision every such degree, to mark those which are on the border-line of the mystical, and to determine to what extent each and every one falls short, would carry us into far too wide a field. We venture to think, that all that is really necessary will be done, if, keeping well in mind the truth that we are concerned with a spiritual growth, we discover what Bonaventure has to tell us concerning the act of truly mystical Contemplation.

Some mention must be made, however, of a particular state, which has largely occupied the attention of writers since the seventeenth century. The result of a laudable and painstaking attempt to analyse the whole spiritual process, and to sift the non-mystical from the mystical, is found in the importance attached by most moderns to what is called 'acquired' or 'active' Contemplation. This is frequently regarded, sometimes on the authority of Bonaventure himself, as an integral part of the spiritual life: as a step which must necessarily be taken before further progress can be made. Unfortunately, all are not unanimous with regard to this, and it seems better to define at once the position taken up here. We are not concerned with the question: Is there such a state as that of 'acquired' Contemplation? This would be out of place. The only question that concerns us is: Does Bonaventure make it a necessary step in spiritual development? If he does, it must be carefully noted; if not, we are perfectly justified in using, without any further qualification, the word 'Contemplation' as referring to the highest act of union with God, attained to in this life. In this act, all individual conative activity ceases, in the sense that it is God, Who, according to the Franciscan Doctor, acts upon the soul by some mysterious operation.

When descriptive writers began to busy themselves with the known experiences of others, when they began to work upon the material supplied to directors of souls, they declared that in ordinary cases, before this higher level acknowledged as mystical was reached, the soul experienced a type of communion with God, akin to the act of mystical union, yet falling short of it for a particular reason. The reason why it could not be called truly mystical, was simply that considerable scope was still given for individual conative activity; human effort still played a large and conscious part in such communion with God. Contemplation therefore becomes twofold — 'acquired' and 'infused.' Only the latter variety is acknowledegd on all hands to be properly speaking mystical. Attempts are made to discover the distinction in Patristic and earlier scholastic writings. In the seventeenth century, a certain Philip of the Blessed Trinity[2] in his *Summa Theologiæ Mysticæ,* made the distinction famous, and we find the Dominican, Thomas of Vallgonera[3] and the Franciscan, Tempesti,[4] reading it, with apparent ease, into the writings of St. Thomas Aquinas and St. Bonaventure respectively. Opposition quickly arose, and to-day there is a school grouped round the learned French scholar, M. Saudreau,[5] vigorously asserting that such a distinction cannot possibly be found in the early mystical writings, unless considerable violence be done to the texts in question. The absence of any direct mention of this state expressed in modern terminology, in the earlier treatises, cannot of course, serve the purpose of those who wish to rule the so-called 'acquired' Contemplation out of court. This is fully recognized. We can only work upon the absence of any clear recognition of a state corresponding to that denoted by the terminology invented by the modern writers, and all that is asserted here, is, that in the

---

2. A Discalced Carmelite Theologian; b. 1603, d. 1671. Author of other works besides the one mentioned, e. g. Summa Philosophiae, Summa Theologiae Thomisticae. See Henricus a S. Sacramento, Collectio Scriptorum Ord. Carmel. Excalc., T. II, p. 110, N. B. Pourrat in his La Spiritualité Chrétienne, T. II, p. 476, declares that the distinction referred to was first elaborated in the fifteenth century by Denys the Carthusian.

3. Born in Catalonia, c. 1595, d. 1665. His most important work is a treatise similar in type to that of Philip of the Blessed Trinity, entitled Mysticae Theologiae D. Thomae, utriusque theologiae scholasticae et mysticae principiis, etc. The original work is very rare. The Edition used is that published at Turin, 1890.

4. C. Tempesti — a Conventual Friar Minor. His Mistica teologia, already quoted, seems to have been his greatest work. But it is practically useless, as it is based for the most part upon spurious writings.

5. Author of many works on the subject of Mysticism. His attitude towards the present point is summed up in his work La vie d'union à Dieu, et les moyens d'y arriver d'aprés les Grands Maiitres de la Spiritualité, Paris, 1921, pp. 23-4. 'Beaucoup d'auteurs des derniers siècles ont adopté une division différente des oraisons contemplatives; ils distinguent la contemplation infusé ou passive et la contemplation acquise ou active. Comme on ne trouve pas trace de cette distinction chez les Maiitres de la mystique, il n'y a pas lieu d'en parler ici.'

works of Bonaventure, the state known as 'acquired' Contemplation, finds no place.

'Acquired' Contemplation as it is generally described by its exponents seems to refer to a state of prayer or communion with God, forming a 'via media' between ordinary discursive meditation, and what we call mystical or 'infused' Contemplation. It is akin in simplicity to acknowledged mystical prayer, but since the conative element plays an important part, and the consciously 'given' is absent, it is not strictly speaking mystical. Because, in a word, it has many of the characteristics of mystical Contemplation, yet remains without that secret working of God upon the soul deemed necessary to constitute the mystical act, it has been termed 'acquired,' being, 'ex hypothesi,' the highest point to which the soul, with the aid of ordinary grace, may rise.[6]

Perhaps it would be better to give as briefly as possible the position adopted with regard to the point, by one of the best acredited exponents of Mysticism in modern times—Père Poulain, whose *Graces of Interior Prayer* is a veritable monument of patient research in matters mystical. He defends the existence of 'acquired' Contemplation, and with great skill he traces its development from ordinary meditation by a process of gradual simplification. Meditation, usually a complex of considerations and affective acts, grows naturally into 'acquired' Contemplation, by a gradual reduction of the number of considerations. He writes: 'This degree (of 'acquired' Contemplation) differs from meditation, therefore, merely as from the greater to the less. *(sic)* It is a discourse, only less varied and less apparent and leaving more room for sentiments of love, praise, gratitude, respect, submission, contrition, etc., and also for practical resolutions. The deduction of truths is partly replaced by intuition. From the intellectual point of view, the soul becomes simplified.'[7] Père Poulain continues: 'The simplification can be carried farther still, and may extend, in a certain measure, to the will, which then becomes satisfied with very little variety in the affections. There is nothing to prevent them from being very ardent at times, but they are usually produced without many words. This is what we call the prayer of simplicity, or of simple regard. It can be defined thus: a mental prayer where 1° intuition in a great

---

6. A full account, with criticism, will be found in La Science de la Prière, par Ludovic de Besse, Paris, 1924.

7. Op. cit., Authorized English Translation by Leonard L. York-Smith, London, 1921, pp. 7-8. The original French edition is not available to the present writer.

measure replaces reasoning; 2° the affections and resolutions show very little variety and are expressed in few words.'[8] This definition being primarily negative in character, Père Poulain completes it by saying: 'In the prayer of simplicity there is a thought or a sentiment that returns incessantly and easily (although with little or no development) amongst many other thoughts, whether useful or no. This dominant thought does not go so far as to be continuous. It merely returns frequently and of its own accord. The prayer of simple regard is really only a slow sequence of single glances cast upon one and the same object.'[9] Elsewhere,[10] he identifies the state he has been describing with 'acquired' Contemplation, and still further on in his treatise, he endorses the definition given by Scaramelli, which makes it, 'that contemplation, which, with the aid of grace, we can acquire by our own endeavour, and particularly by a long practice of meditation; although, strictly speaking, it is not due to all these efforts.'[11]

Père Poulain speaks on the authority of first hand material obtained during years of patient labour. The 'acquired' Contemplation of which he treats offers many attractions to one who is trying to trace the development of the spiritual life, and to-day it has assumed such an importance that the majority take it for granted. It may or may not be a special degree in spiritual growth. Does it find a place, as described by Père Poulain and others, in the theology of Bonaventure?

If they are referring only to what frequently appears to be a form of meditation attenuated to a point, and therefore capable of explanation by the laws of psychology, doubtless it could be discovered therein. Tempesti, however, regarding it as a 'via media' between the non-mystical and the mystical communion with God, decided that it could easily be traced. Unfortunately for his case, it is built up almost entirely upon works now judged spurious, for example, the *Stimulus Amoris* of James of Milan, and the *De Septem Itineribus Aeternitatis* of Rudolph of Biberach.[12]

One genuine quotation is brought to bear upon the problem, and at first sight it does indeed appear that Bonaventure considers that a form of communion with God, corresponding to that described by Père Poulain and others as 'acquired' Contemplation, is an integral and necessary

8. Ibid.
9. Ibid.
10. Ibid., p. 11.
11. Ibid., p. 61.
12. See Mistica Teologia, T. I, Trattato III, pp. 340-77.

step in the spiritual scale. The whole context whence Tempesti has drawn his quotations, shows clearly that the Franciscan Doctor is pointing out the path leading to the fullest Christian experience. Bonaventure writes: 'Nota, quod hic est status sapientiæ christianæ; unde cum Dionysius multos libros fecisset, hic consummavit, scilicet in Mystica Theologia. Unde oportet, quod homo sit instructus multis et omnibus præcedentibus. De mystica theologia Dionysius: 'Tu autem,' inquit, 'O Timothee amice, circa mysticas visiones forti actione et contritione, sensus derelinque, etc.; vult enim dicere, quod oportet, quod sit solutus ab omnibus, quæ ibi numerat, et quod omnia dimittat; quasi diceret: super omnem substantiam et cognitionem est ille quem volo intelligere. Et ibi est operatio transcendens omnem intellectum, secretissima; quod nemo scit, nisi qui experitur. In anima enim sunt virtutes multæ apprehensivæ: sensitiva, imaginativa, æstimativa, intellectiva; et omnes oportet relinquere, et in vertice est unitio amoris, et hæc omnes transcendit . . . . Hæc autem contemplatio fit per gratiam, et tamen iuvat industria, scilicet ut separet se ab omni eo, quod Deus non est, et a se ipso, si possibile esset.'[13]

It is perfectly obvious that Bonaventure is thinking of that form of Contemplation, distinguished to-day as 'infused' or 'passive:' of an act which is most secret, being known only to him who has experienced it. Everything he says, points to the ineffable character of the act he is describing. This being so, it is far removed in nature from what is now called 'acquired' Contemplation; no-one claims ineffability for this. Our theory is confirmed, when, enumerating according to the mediaeval conception the various faculties of the soul, he declares that the state he has in mind transcends them, and finally singles out grace as the efficient cause: 'Hæc contemplatio fit per gratiam.' It is, however, upon the immediately adjoined clause that Tempesti relies, 'Tamen iuvat industria,' for he interprets this to mean that human effort can, with ordinary grace, acquire an experience akin to the 'operatio secretissima.' For him, the same clause affords conclusive proof of Bonaventure's acquaintance with the distinction. This, we think, is claiming far too much. By the clause in question, Bonaventure merely excludes all Quietistic tendencies. The grace of Contemplation is indeed an exalted one; it transcends the capacities of unaided soul-faculties; it is in its very essence, due to Divine Benignity. Nevertheless, he would not have it thought

---

13. Collat. in Hexaëm., col. II, n. 29-30, T. V, p. 341. Quoted by Tempesti, op. cit., p. 343.

that all effort can be dispensed with, or that to attain it, the mere suppression of all activity is necessary. It seems more correct to find in the above quotation, but one more proof of the voluntaristic character of Franciscan theology, rather than an acquaintance with the state upon which moderns dwell so much. Here too, it may be remarked, that it is because of Bonaventure's insistence that, no matter how exalted the grace of Contemplation may be, it is the duty of the soul to work, that in the previous chapters we have concerned ourselves so much with the various forms of spiritual activity of which he treats.

Nor do we find anything approaching the nature of 'acquired' Contemplation, where he professedly gives the steps leading to the mystical experience. In the *Collationes in Hexaëmeron,* he makes these steps or degrees correspond, in characteristically mediaeval fashion, with the nine choirs of angels: this, after rejecting the division given by the Abbot of Verecelli.[14] The operation of the first three choirs of angels corresponds with the threefold activity of the natural powers; the operations of the next three correspond with the activity of the soul when aided by grace; finally, Bonaventure makes it clear, that in the only mystical state known to him, all conative activity ceases: 'Tertia hierarchizatio est gratiæ super naturam et industriam, quando scilicet anima supra se elevata est et, se deserta, suscipit divinas illuminationes et supra se speculatur quod sibi datum est; et ex hoc surgit in divina sive sursum agitur.'[15] This, the last stage, is the exclusive work of grace; the conscious, deliberate working of the faculties finds no place; they are acted upon by Divine Power, and it is this that makes them mystical in their operation. There is given no step or degree before this, which is recognized as semi-mystical, or which is so described that we may identify it with 'acquired' Contemplation. Surely, had he known the state, or considered it to be an integral step in religious development, he would have marked it out here. Since the 'via media' finds neither explicit nor implicit mention, it seems only right to say that for Bonaventure, the only state to which the term 'mystical' can in any sense

14. He writes: 'Abbas Vercellensis assignavit tres gradus, scilicet, naturae, industriae, gratiae. Sed non videtur, quod aliquo modo per naturam anima possit hierarchizari. Et ideo nos debemus attribure industrie cum natura, industriae cum gratia, et gratiae super naturam et industriam.' Op. cit., col. XXII, n. 24, T. V, p. 441. This 'Abbas Vercellensis' was Thomas, Abbot of St. Andrew's, Vercelli, from its foundation in 1219, until his death in 1246(?). He was a Canon Regular of the Congregation of St. Victor. Author of Extractiones libri S. Dionysii areopagitae de coelesti seu angelici hierarchia, Extractationes Libri S. Dionysii de divinis nominibus, Extractationes . . . de mystica theologia, Commentarius super Cantica canticorum, etc. See Histoire Littéraire de la France, T. XVII, pp. 356 sqq.

15. Collat. in Hex., col. XXII, n. 27, T. V, p. 441.

be applied, is that which is now distinguished as 'infused.' We may concede that the above arguments are negative in character. We are not in the position to judge whether in his opinion, the modern exponents are correct or not. The least we can claim on the strength of the arguments adduced, is that we are justified in excluding from this treatise any lengthy discussion on the interesting, albeit intricate psychology, involved in the problem of the Prayer of Simple Regard, or 'acquired' Contemplation.[16]

Positively speaking, the thought of the Franciscan Doctor seems to be that the mystical union follows upon the above mentioned ascetical practices, and hence upon every state wherein individual activity plays a part, immediately, without any 'via media,' and whenever God is so pleased to bestow the special grace necessary.

Nor is there any question of special vocation. Mystical union is represented as a state of grace offered to all, though few attain to it.[17] It is 'special' only in the sense, that it requires a given element, which is not present where ordinary grace is concerned. On the other hand, the tendency of those who attach great importance to 'acquired' Contemplation has assuredly been in the direction of making mystical union a great and extraordinary gift, to be ranged, it would seem, among such gifts as prophecy, and the power of working miracles. Ordinarily speaking, it is held, the soul does not proceed, without a special vocation from God, beyond 'acquired' Contemplation. The step beyond this leads the soul into the realms of the extraordinary, and the rarely given. Bonaventure must consequently be represented as being in opposition to those, who, to quote a recent exponent, regard true, or 'infused,' mystical Contemplation as 'une de ces faveurs, semblables aux graces extraordinaires, qui s'appellent gratiæ gratis datæ, faveur très spéciale et rarement accordée.'[18] By all means, Bonaventure would agree, it is a great gift, but it is not an essentially extraordinary one, on a level with the gifts of prophecy and miracle, which are typical examples of 'gratiæ gratis

---

16. Many, however, go still further than this, and not only declare that Bonaventure does not treat either explicitly or implicitly of 'acquired' Contemplation, but that on his authority it may be judged, that such a state does not exist at all. This is the thesis of P. Vicente de Peralta in his art. El pensamiento de San Bonaventura sobre la contemplacion mistica. Estudios Francescanos, 1912, pp. 426-442. He also examines the works, once attributed to Bonaventure, and now traced to James of Milan and Rudolph of Biberach, and shows that even these did not know the state.

17. See Itin., cap. I, n. 8, T. V, p. 298; also II Sermo de S. Agnete, T. IX, p. 510.

18. P. Marie-Joseph, art. Il existe une contemplation acquise, in Études Carmélitaines, 1920, p. 3.

datæ.' He constantly reveals his attitude towards the problem, as, for example, when he writes: 'Nota, quod quadruplex est modus cognoscendi Deum, videlicet per fidem, per contemplationem, per apparitionem, et per apertam visionem. Et primum est gratiæ communis, secundum est *gratiæ excellentis,* tertium gratiæ specialis, et quartum gloriæ consummantis.'[19] There is no room in a synthesis of his doctrine for a special vocation, as antecedently necessary for the enjoyment of mystical experience. He can certainly have no thought of the need of such a vocation, when, in all his *Opuscula,* having true mystical experience as his goal, he dwells upon the dispositive value of purgation, imitation of the Christ-life, prayer and meditation, in their relation to the highest spiritual experience accorded to men on earth. To set so high a value upon such forms of piety, and nevertheless to think that they are useless, unless the special vocation be given, would demand an express statement to that effect. This statement is lacking in the works already examined.

On the hypothesis too, that this special vocation is a pre-requisite to the enjoyment of mystical experience, we are thrown back upon a breach of continuity between the ascetic and mystic lives: a breach which cannot be reconciled with his theory of grace, already expounded. The ascetic, on such a hypothesis, may progress indefinitely in his asceticism, but he may never reach any fuller enjoyment in the spiritual life, beyond the continual cleansing of the self, the rigorous self-discipline, the facility in prayer and discursive meditation—in a word—beyond all those spiritual exercises, possible to every one with the aid of ordinary grace, unless he be made subject to an entirely new Divine economy. The breach between the ordinary and the extraordinary would have to be clearly marked; mystical union, or Contemplation, would have to be treated of in the same manner as miracle and prophecy, and, even though acknowledged as less rare than these two phenomena, the special vocation necessary thereto would have to be clearly stressed. In the absence of these and other necessary qualifying statements, passages like the following, which are constantly found in Bonaventure's works, would be certainly misleading. For they imply that from the very first periods of asceticism, till the enjoyment of the mystical union itself, there is a steady progress, without any breach of continuity. He addresses the devout soul: 'Nec debes ab oratione spiritum relaxare, sed tamdiu

---

19. II S. D. XXVII, a. II, q. III, T. II, p. 545; and compare ibid., ad 6, p. 546.

per devotionis ardorem sursum ascendere, donec ingrediaris in locum tabernaculi admirabilis usque ad domum Dei, et ibi utcumque cordis oculo dilecto tuo viso et utcumque degustato, quam suavis est Dominus, et quam magna multitudo dulcedinis eius, in amplexus eius ruas, impressis labiis intimæ devotionis oscula figas, ut sic tota a te alienata, tota in cœlum rapta, tota in Christum transformata, non valeas cohibere spiritum tuum, sed exclames cum propheta David et dicas: Renuit consolari anima mea; memor fui Dei, et delectatus sum.'[20] He is not referring to ordinary outbursts of love as the goal of the soul's striving, but to real mystical union.

In perfect agreement with this, we find him dwelling upon the accessibility of the highest level of spirituality. Mysticism is often regarded as an intellectual search, the Object of which must needs remain hidden from the uncultured. We can mention cases in which it is so presented; the writings of Pseudo-Dionysius afford an example. Conceivably, there are but few who can follow whither the *Dionysiaca* would lead, for only the intellectually trained could understand his import. Also, Bonaventure himself in his *Itinerarium,* like St. Augustine in several of his treatises, frequently co-mingles his mystical teaching, with arguments understood only by those gifted with a more philosophical turn of mind.[21] Nevertheless, the Franciscan Doctor is most careful to indicate that philosophy, even when conjoined with most ardent devotion, is not the only road. For the ignorant and the unlettered, there always remains the safe and equally sure method of uprising to God, by way of prayer and devotion. To all is open the imitation of the Christ-life, with its concomitant richness of spiritual experience. Inability to follow his more learned theological speculations, by no means spells failure in the realization of the end to which they are directed. It is probably because of the mystical experience of St. Francis of Assisi, and his first companions, Brother Giles for example, who certainly possessed nothing approaching the intellectual capacity of some of the earlier mystical writers, and who nevertheless attained to precisely the same levels, that he fully develops this truth. He does

20. De Perf. Vitae, cap. V, n. 5, T. VIII, p. 119. The Script. references are to Ps. 41, 5; Ps. 33, 9; Ps. 76, 3-4.

21. It must not be inferred from this, that the most intense intellectual speculations, divorced from what is commonly understood by devotion, can ever be of use in relation to the mystical experience. Certainly this is never taught by Pseudo-Dionysius or by Augustine and Bonaventure. All that is implied here, is that there are treatises, coming from the pens of these and from others, which contain philosophical arguments difficult to follow, and which are couched in language, removing them from the understaing of all but the cultured.

this in one of his sermons. He has been preaching on the way of approach to God, and had enumerated the various steps leading to mystical union. But, up to a point, he has done so, in a manner comprehensible only to the trained intelligence. Then, almost apologetically, he falls back upon the evidence of Brother Giles, to show how devotion, without intellectual search, can lead with equal efficacy in the same direction: 'Sed quidam frater laicus, qui per triginta annos habuit gratiam excessus mentalis et qui mundissimus fuit et virgo et tertius frater post beatum Franciscum, sic dixit, quod septem gradus contemplationis devotæ sunt isti, scilicet, ignis, unctio, extasis, contemplatio, gustus, amplexus, requies, et octava sequitur gloria.'[22] Consequently, he can exhort his hearers thus: 'Modo non debetis desperare, vos simplices, quando audistis ista, quia simplex non potest ista habere, sed poteritis postea habere. Nos non facimus nisi dicere. Sed quando anima sancta habet ista sex, tunc disponitur ad videndum gloriam. Hæc est requies, quam quærere debemus .... Si vis esse tabernaculum sapientiæ, studeas istas dispositiones habere; et si homo non velit ad istam perfectionem pervenire, magnum tamen est, quod lex christiana habet tales.' [23]

All that is required, is that the soul should do whatever is in its power; this done, Divine grace will supply that which is still wanting: 'Quando enim anima facit quod potest, tunc gratia facile levat animam, et Deus ibi operatur.'[24] We here find the keynote to his theory. All, independently both of special vocation and of special intellectual endowments, may attain with equal ease to the fulness of the Christian life. In the 'Poverello,' especially in the reception of the Stigmata, he finds an example of the mystical possibilities within the grasp of every follower of Our Lord. It is his pious belief, that God wrought such wonders in the case of St. Francis, that by deed, more than by word, He might attract all to the fruition of mystical bliss. Referring to St. Francis' experience on Mount Alvernia, he affirms: 'Positus est in exemplum perfectæ contemplationis, sicut prius fuerat actionis, tanquam alter Jacob et Israel, ut omnes viros vere spirituales Deus per eum invitaret ad huiusmodi transitum et mentis excessum magis exemplo quam verbo.'[25] Of itself, this passage would suffice to prove that the mystical experience is not regarded by Bonaventure as something

22. Sermo de Sabb. Sancto, ad. III, T. IX, p. 269.
23. Ibid., and cf. Sermo de SS. Apost., T. IX, p. 547.
24. Coll. in Hex., col. XXII, n. 39, T. V, p. 443.
25. Itin., cap. VII, n. 3, T. V, p. 312.

essentially extraordinary, and implying a special economy of grace, but as the perfect and fullest bloom of the life of grace, begun in the soul by its first acceptance.

Finally, to bring these preliminary remarks to a fitting conclusion, we must deal with the part played by desire. There are those who would declare, in the interests of a pure and safe Mysticism, that all desire of a religious experience exceeding the normal, should be absolutely banished. Such an attitude, apart from other considerations, is quite comprehensible, and it does not necessarily imply any Quietistic tendencies. Whereas the Quietists would banish desire simply because it is a disturbing factor, and even a barrier to that peculiar complacency beloved of Madame Guyon, other, and more orthodox writers, would reject it because of the psychological complications set up. It is so easy for desire to become mis-directed into ultra-normal channels. A few theologians distinguish, maintaining that desire of mystical graces is legitimate in the case of those who have already begun to experience them in a lower degree. A hint at least of the other distinction, between 'acquired' and 'infused' Contemplation, is given here.

An idea of the state of the problem may be gathered from the conclusion arrived at, by a recent student of Mysticism, P. Léonce de Grandmaison. He writes: 'On jugera que le désir d'une union croissante avec Dieu, n'a rien en lui-même, pourvu qu'il ne menace ni de déception, ni de rancœur, celui dans lequel il serait frustré, que de três legitime. Ce désir doit-il *exclure positivement* les hautes communications mystiques? On osera difficilement l'affirmer. Doit-il les *inclure implicitement?* Ceux-là même qui tiennent pour l'accessibilité maximale hésiteront, je pense, à le conseiller. Il semble que le mieux sera de s'en tenir a ce *désir général d'union la plus grande possible,* qu'aussi bien tout amour profond implique et inspire. Un tel désir ne precise ni n'exclut déterminément aucune des formes que l'union peut prendre içi-bas.' [26]

The writer indicates the many questions discussed concerning the point, and in the light of his conclusion, the Bonaventurian theory may be the better understood. Not only is desire of mystical experience quite lawful in the soul already possessed of grace, but those who wish to correspond fully with the workings of God upon the human soul, are bound in

---

26. Auct. cit., art. La religion personelle, L'élan mystique, in the Jesuit Études, 1913, pp. 332-3.

duty to have that desire. At once it must be understood, that the desire is not represented as extending to external phenomena, or to the exalted experiences attributed by tradition to Moses and to St. Paul. Bonaventure has the distinction between these, and the normal mystical experience in mind, when he writes: 'Hæc enim est (contemplatio), in qua mirabiliter inflammatur affectio, sicut eis patet, qui aliquoties consueverunt ad anagogicos elevari excessus. *Hunc modum cognoscendi arbitror cuilibet viro iusto in via ista esse quœrendum;* quodsi Deus aliquid ultra faciet, hoc privilegium est speciale, non legis communis.'[27] So too, in a passage already quoted, in which he deals with the various means to be adopted to attain to the mystical experience, he attaches the greatest importance to desire, using a symbolism supplied by Brother Giles: 'Intelligo, quod anima contemplativa, quæ exercet se, ut possit pervenire ad requiem, oportet, quod vias istas transeat, scilicet, ut primo ardeat per gladium flammeum atque versatilem, hoc est per ardentissimum desiderium amoris Dei et oblivionem sui, et gladio dividat se a terrenis. Hoc est principium diffusivum.'[28] This desire is made to cover all the preparation dwelt upon hitherto; in desiring the mystical union, the soul must likewise be willing to undergo the arduous task implied by asceticism. 'Vehemens desiderium porta est Sapientiæ'[29] he writes, and with equal precision: 'Ad hoc autem, quod anima recipiat illa lumina, requiritur vivacitas desiderii . . . Non enim est contemplativa anima sine desiderio vivaci. Qui hoc non habet, nihil de contemplatione habet, quia origo luminum est a supremis ad infima, non e converso.'[30] Quotations such as these might be multiplied. The whole of his *Itinerarium* is built upon the idea that the desire of mystical union is not merely a lawful tendency, but a necessary one, in the soul which is fully corresponding with the grace of God.[31]

Enough has been quoted, to show that Bonaventure is conceiving no unbalanced desire. Presumption is guarded against, not only by his constant reiteration of the truth that desire must equally extend to a life of self-denial and self-abnegation, but

27. II S. D. XXIII, art. II, q. III, ad 6, T. II, p. 546.
28. Sermo de Sabb. Sancto, T. IX, p. 269.
29. Coll. in Hex., col. II, n. 6, T. V, p. 337.
30. Ibid., col. XXII, n. 29, T. V, pp. 441-2; cf. also col. XX, n. 1, p. 425; Sermo II in Dom. III in Quadrag., T. IX, p. 229; Sermo IV in Epiph., ibid., p. 162; com. in Luc., cap. IX, n. 60-61, T. VII, pp. 235-6.
31. See Op. cit. 'Non enim dispositus est aliquo modo ad contemplationes divinas, quae ad mentales ducunt excessus, nisi cum Daniele sit vir desideriorum.' Prologus, n. 3, T. V, p. 296. And in the last chapter, where he dwells upon mystical union, he declares it to be a secret grace, known only to him who receives it, and received only by him who desires it. See ibid., cap VII, n. 4,—n. 6, T. V, pp. 312-313.

also by his frequent illustration of the disproportion existing between the highest merits possible to the human soul, on the one hand, and mystical union on the other. This is the theme of a whole chapter of his *Soliloquium*. The master, in the dialogue, has just spoken in eloquent language of the bliss of mystical union, and the soul cries out in longing for so sublime a state. The reply is full of reserve and discretion: 'O anima, magnum est quod desideras, inæstimabile donum est quod exoptas. Unde, ut æstimo, humano studio non potest obtineri, humano merito non potest promereri, sed a Deo humilibus precibus a digne dispositis, ex sola divinæ pietatis condescendentia vix poterit impetrari.' [32] The dialogue proceeds in the same cautious manner. Whilst the master explains how the soul is to prepare itself for mystic graces,[33] the soul expresses a longing to depart from the ascetic paths, to the enjoyment of the bliss of mystic union with God. Again comes the warning against presumption: 'O anima devota, loquar, salva reverentia; nimis es avara et utinam non præsumtuosa. Vires tuas perpende, merita considera, virtutes discute; et tunc, si placet, sufficiat tibi magis in odore divinorum unguentorum cum adolescentulis humiliter currere, quam præsumtuose super merita postulare.' [34]

There is no inconsistency between this, and what he has already said with regard to the need of desire. He is merely reminding the soul, that ascetical practices cannot be dispensed with, for, by way of concluding the chapter whence these quotations are taken, Bonaventure writes: 'Anima, magna es fides tua, valde fortis es in spe et confidentia. Et quamvis spes, quæ procedit ex meritis propriis et divinæ clementiæ confidentia, meritoria sit, laudabilis et sancta; consulo tamen sane, antequam ad quærendam ebrietatem supra te ascendas, prius per considerationem salubriter infra te descendas, ut discas tuum Sponsum reverenter timere, antequam incipias suum secretum cubiculum introire, quem non solum timere debes, cum irascitur, verum etiam, cum suavissime blanditur.'[35] Such directions as these surely make for a well balanced Mysticism.

These preliminary remarks, proper though they may seem to the science of the direction of souls, are necessary in view of the

32. Op. cit., cap. II, n. 14, T. VIII, p. 50.
33. See nn. 15-18, ibid., pp. 50-51.
34. Ibid.
35. Ibid., n. 20, p. 52.

important place given in most modern manuals of Mystical Theology to the problems around which they centre. In the quotations already given, may be found full justification for the assertion that the Seraphic Doctor has carefully studied the questions raised by those who have attempted to build up the science of Mysticism, as a distinct branch of Theology. There is scarcely a point contained in modern manuals, which he passes over in silence.

But the chief point of interest, and the most important in itself, is that regarding the nature of mystical Contemplation, or the mystical union to which reference has been made so often. Now it is of the utmost importance to note that Bonaventure presents as the mystic goal, not so much a single act, or a series of acts, in which God is mysteriously experienced, but a *life* of union with Him: a life in which no object other than Himself is desired, or, to express it still more truly, a life in which no object is desired, except in its relation to God. The mystic quest is for a form of life, in which the soul's attention and love will be so wholly absorbed in the Supreme Being, that it can neither think of, nor have any affection for, any creaturely object, except in its relationship to the Divine. This fact cannot be stressed too much. Yet, like all mystical writers, Bonaventure sometimes refers to, and attempts to explain the nature of certain special acts, special Divine favours, granted to the soul in this same state. These acts, we may say, are to the life of Union with God, what sudden intuitions of truth are to ordinary discursive meditation, be it in the spiritual or the non-spiritual realm. Moreover, as in the case of discursive meditation, or scientific concentration, such intuitions not infrequently become habitual, so, it would seem, does Bonaventure conceive of the possibility of the contemplative act becoming habitual in the 'Via Unitiva.' Hence the term 'Vita Contemplativa' is often used to cover the whole stage of spiritual growth, in which such acts are usually experienced. Frequent or rare, the act of Contemplation is but the consciousness of that will-union with God, absolute and true in every detail, that runs throughout the whole mystical life, giving it unity, and marking it out as the highest level of Christian attainment. Above, we made a qualification to the effect that it is in the 'Via Unitiva' that the contemplative act is usually experienced: usually, for as in the classical example of St. Augustine, it is sometimes given in the initial stages of the spiritual life.

Many in recent years have discussed the nature of the contemplative act, but we must not expect to find in Bonaventure's writings the same psychological treatment. The problem before us here is: What does he consider takes place in the act of Contemplation? The answer will again be the more clearly understood, if the solutions to the problem given by more descriptive writers be briefly recalled.

Père Poulain may once more be cited. His theory is that the constitutive element of the mystical act is the direct feeling of the presence of God: a theory based upon personal statements made by the best accredited mystics.[36] It is an intellectual and experimental knowledge of God. Père Poulain thus expresses his thesis: '(1) The mystic states which have God for their object attract attention at the outset by the impression of recollection and union which they cause us to experience. Hence the name of mystic union. (2) Their real point of difference from the recollection of ordinary prayer is this: that in the mystic state, God is not satisfied merely to help us to think of Him and to remind us of His Presence: He gives us an experimental, intellectual knowledge of this presence. In a word, He makes us feel that we really enter into communication with Him. (3) In the lower degrees, however (prayer of quiet), God only does this in a somewhat obscure manner. The manifestation increases in distinctness as the union becomes of a higher order.'

Another well known and authoritative writer, Lejeune, is no less explicit in his agreement with Père Poulain: 'L'élément constitutif de la contemplation mystique est donc le sentiment que l'ame éprouve de la présence de Dieu en elle, une sorte de perception, d'expérimentation de Dieu. Le trait qui appartient en propre à la contemplation mystique est içi nettement marqué.' [38]

When it comes to the question of explaining this, both writers have recourse to their peculiar doctrine concerning the 'spiritual senses.' The soul possesses intellectual 'spiritual senses' having some resemblance to the bodily senses, so that, in an analogous manner, and in diverse ways, it is able to perceive the presence of pure spirits, and the presence of God in particular.[39] Bonaventure knows of no faculties which can be described as they are in

36. See his Graces of Interior Prayer, chap. V, pp. 64-87.
37. Ibid., pp. 64-5.
38. Auct. cit., art. Contemplation, in Dict. de Théol. Cath., T. III, col. 1626.
39. See Poulain, op. cit., pp. 88-113.

modern treatises.[40] In whatever manner the experience called mystical is explained, it is God Himself, modern writers declare, and not a mere effect of Divine operation, that is conceived to be the direct Object.[41]

But the theory meets with the disapproval of M. Saudreau, who, though admitting that it is quite possible that God should sometimes make His Presence directly felt in mystical Contemplation, refuses to see in this, an essential, or even a characteristic element. For him, the fundamental element is the will-union with God.[42]

It is undoubtedly the fact, that in the minds of most men, Mysticism immediately implies some kind of direct communication with God in this life. It is only fair to the above-mentioned authors to state that they qualify their various theses. They are fully aware that God cannot possibly be present to the soul in mystical experience, in the same manner as in the after life: not even momentarily so. They therefore introduce with Père Poulain certain spiritual 'species impressæ,' representative of the Divinity, enabling the soul to behold its Object. Indeed, there has been built up a veritable 'système psychologique privilegié' to account for the whole, within the sphere of the supernatural.

The many explanations of the 'modus operandi' in connection with the mystical act, are not introduced here to be criticised, but to serve as a back-ground for what we believe to be, after careful examination of his works, Bonaventure's doctrine concerning the object of the mystical experience, and the manner in which the soul's longings for communion with God are satisfied. The first statement, for the sake of clarity, will be purely negative: one which may seem startling in view of the way in which the mystic claim is most often represented. It is this: whatever he understands by the expression 'the mystical communing of the soul with God,' he does not think that in it, there is vouchsafed a *direct* vision, or touch, or any other form of experience, of God Himself. It is always *indirectly* in this life, that the soul experiences God. This negative statement must be taken as applying to all the spiritual experiences falling below the essentially extraordi-

40. See supra, chap. II.
41. Thus Lejeune, op. cit. An opinion endorsed by A. B. Sharpe in Mysticism, its true nature and value, London, 1910, pp. 88-104: 'Mystical Contemplation is the sight of God. It canot be called anything else.' Also endorsed by F. Naval, Theologiae asceticae et mysticae cursus, Roma, 1920, p. 270.
42. See La vie d'union à Dieu, etc., pp. 7-27.

nary phenomena, attributed by many to Moses and to St. Paul, and to a few other exceptional cases.

The doctrine condensed here, has been gathered from Bonaventure's Commentary on the second book of Sentences, where he treats of the question in a manner that is speculative. He introduces the question: 'Utrum Adam in statu innocentiæ ita cognoverit Deum, sicut Deus in statu gloriæ cognoscitur?' [43] and, as might be expected, many of the purely speculative problems, which so largely occupied the mediaeval mind are dwelt upon. In spite of its complications, this portion of his work seems to be the best to choose from, to obtain his strictly theological teaching. Bonaventure interprets Hugo of St. Victor,[44] and others, as teaching that Adam before his fall, had a knowledge of God identical with that which is to constitute the joy of the soul in the next life. This he declares to be impossible; the Beatific Vision is the supreme reward of the human life, and the very fact that it constitutes man's supreme happiness demands its inamissibility. Yet Adam, he thinks, did enjoy a higher knowledge of God than that within the attainment of the ordinary Christian: 'Adam in statu innocentiæ non cognovit Deum immediate et in sua substantia, ut cognoscitur in gloria, sed per speculum, non autem in ænigmate.'[45]

It is not in accordance with Sacred Scripture, he argues, to adopt the extreme view, that God is never seen immediately, and as He is in Himself, not even by the Blessed in Heaven. St. Paul's 'Then shall I know, even as I am known' [46] as well as St. John's affirmation, 'We shall see Him, even as He is,' [47] refute this.

Another opinion upon which he passes judgment errs in the opposite direction, maintaining that God can be seen directly, and as He is in Himself, in the present state, by minds cleansed from all sin (a purgatissimis mentibus), even as He was seen by Adam in the state of innocence, and as He is seen in Heaven.[48] The Object seen is the same in all these states, the sole difference consisting in the degree of clarity, and the degree of clarity in vision is

43. II S. D. XXIII, a. II, q. III, p. 542.
44. Quoting his De Sacramentis, Lib. I, p. VI, cap. XIV. 'Cognovit ergo homo Creatorem suum, non ea cognitione quae foris ex auditu solo percipitur, sed ea quae potius intus per inspirationem ministratur. Non ea quidem qua Deus modo a credentibus absens fide quaeritur; sed ea qua tunc per praesentiam contemplationis scienti manifestius cernebatur.' P. L., T. CLXXVI, col. 271. But Hugo does admit some difference, for he adds: 'Excepto eo quod diximus quod per internam inspirationem visibiliter edoctus, nullatenus de ipso creatore suo dubitare potuit.' Ibid.
45. II S. D. XXIII, a. II, q. III, T. II, p. 543.
46. I Cor., 13, 12.
47. I John, 3, 2.
48. II S., Loc. cit., p. 544.

itself traced back to the relative freedom from the body and its needs.[49] St. Augustine is made responsible for this theory, and the works of the great Doctor of the West are quoted as teaching it.[50] Even though it is considered to emanate from so respected a source, it, too, meets with rejection. Bonaventure writes: 'Sed hæc positio, etsi non sit adeo veritati adversaria, sicut prima, nihilominus tamen, dictis Sanctorum non consonat.'[51]

He now mentions those by whom he prefers to be guided in the matter, and they are Pseudo-Dionysius and Gregory. These, and the majority of Christian writers, he affirms, had literally interpreted St. Paul's teaching, that whilst we are in the body, we are absent from the Lord, since we walk by faith and not by sight.[52] The general conclusion follows, and is made to cover the normal mystical experience: 'Unde si quæ auctoritates id dicere inveniantur, quod Deus in præsenti ab homine videtur et cernitur, non sunt intelligendæ quod videtur in sua essentia, sed quod in aliquo effectu interiori cognoscitur . . . nisi fortassis in his qui rapiuntur, sicut credimus fuisse in Paulo, qui specialitate privilegii statum viatorum supergrediuntur, nec ibi aliquid agunt, sed solum aguntur.'[53] The general thesis is therefore quite clear. The experience of St. Paul, and the few others, is altogether beyond the normal mystical union. It is in every sense extraordinary, whereas the normal mystical union is that to which grace, of its very nature, inclines the soul. Yet even when writers deal with this, the language most frequently used implies some direct communing with God: some direct, even if it be momentary vision, or touch of the Divine. Bonaventure here asserts that it is indirect, taking place as it does through the medium of some special interior effect.

Doubtless, he continues, returning to the classical instance of Adam, the first man, because of his other great gifts, also desired to behold the Divine Being in Himself, but this natural desire on his part, in no way forces us to accept the theory that in his case, it was fulfilled. In answer to the objection that if in Adam's case this desire had not been even momentarily fulfilled, he would have lacked something essential to true happiness, he replies:

---

49. Ibid.

50. Bonaventure quotes De Trinitate, Lib. VIII, cap. VIII, n. 12. See P. L., T. XLII, cols. 957-960; ibid., cap. II, n. 3, sqq. col. 948 sqq.

51. Loc. cit., p. 544.

52. See II Cor., 5, 6-7.

53. Loc. cit., p. 544. He refers to St. Paul's experience narrated in II Cor. 12, 2 sqq.—'I know a man in Christ above fourteen years ago (whether in the body, I know not, or out of the body, I know not; God knoweth), such a one caught up to the third heaven. And I know such a man . . . . that he was caught up into paradise, and heard secret words, which it is not granted to man to utter.'

'Verum est; sed sic desiderabat videre, quod aliquam cognitionem habebat, in qua reficiebatur, et aliquam expectabat in remunerationem et præmium. Et illa quam expectabat, erat cognitio patriæ; illa vero, quam habebat, erat contemplatio viæ, quæ erat visio per speculum—Et si tu quæras, utrum erat visio intellectualis, vel corporalis; dicendum, quod intellectualis; sed non ipsius divinæ essentiæ in se, sed alicujus gratiæ vel influentiæ; et illam in se per experientiam nosse et videre poterat, sicut sentit anima sancta, quando liquefit, cum Sponsus alloquitur eam.'[54]

There is one passage, which so thoroughly explains Bonaventure's attitude, that it may be quoted here in full, in spite of its length. It is an excellent summary of his theories concerning the nature of the various modes in which God is known of men: 'Nota, quod quadruplex est modus cognoscendi Deum, videlicet per fidem, per contemplationem, per apparitionem et per apertam visionem. Et primum est gratiæ communis, secundum est gratiæ excellentis, tertium gratiæ specialis et quartum gloriæ consummantis. Et sufficientia istorum modorum ita colligitur. Omne enim quod cognoscitur, cognoscitur per aliquid præsens; si igitur Deus cognoscitur, necesse est, quod per aliquid præsens intellectui cognoscatur; præsens autem voco hic, secundum quod Augustinus vocat, quod præsens est intellectui ad videndum. Aut igitur cognosco Deum per hoc quod est præsens mihi, aut per hoc quod est præsens alii. Si per hoc quod est præsens alii, sic est cognitio fidei. Quod enim Deus sit trinus et unus, hoc ego credo Dei Filio, qui hoc enarravit et prædicavit, et Spiritui sancto, qui hoc inspiravit . . . . Si autem cognosco Deum per hoc quod est præsens mihi, hoc potest esse tripliciter: aut per hoc quod est præsens mihi in effectu proprio; et tunc est contemplatio, quæ tanto est eminentior, quanto effectum divinæ gratiæ magis sentit in se homo, vel quanto etiam melius scit considerare Deum in exterioribus creaturis. Aut est præsens mihi in signo proprio; et sic est apparitio, sicut apparuit Deus Abrahæ in subiecta creatura, quæ ipsum Deum figurabat; et sicut Spiritus sanctus apparuit in columba. Aut est præsens Deus in lumine suo et in seipso; et sic est cognitio, qua videtur Deus in vultu suo, sive facie ad faciem; et sic est aperta visio, quæ tota dicitur merces omnium meritorum. Primum igitur et ultimum genus cognitionis statui innocentiæ non competebat . . . . Media vero duo, scilicet contemplationis et apparitionis, utrique statui communia esse potuerunt, maxime cognitio contemplationis, quæ

54. Loc. cit., n. 5, p. 546.

in utroque statu est. Ibi tamen potissime vigebat tum propter animæ puritatem, tum etiam propter carnis et inferiorum virium subjectionem; quibus duobus quia ut plurimum anima caret in statu naturæ lapsæ, ideo non potest ad illum gradum contemplationis attingere.'[55] On the authority of such a passage as this, which is so clear, and so easy to follow, it becomes impossible to count Bonaventure among the number of those who declare that the constitutive element of mystical Contemplation is a certain immediate intuition of God. M. J. Maréchal does so, however. Whilst acknowledging that Bonaventure 'est fort impressioné par les expressions négatives du Pseudo-Aréopagite, et par un texte de S. Grégoire,' and '(qu'il) recule devant le mot vision,'[56] he quotes him as defending the intuitionist theory. But the Seraphic Doctor makes his meaning clear when dealing with an admittedly mystical passage in the works of the Pseudo-Areopagite, for, when he comments upon the latter's application of the Psalmist's 'Deus posuit tenebras latibulum suum,' he adds: 'Vult (Dionysius) dicere, quod Deus non conspiciatur in via in claritate suæ essentiæ, sed quod conspiciatur in effectu gratiæ et experientia suavitatis suæ per ipsam anagogicam unitionem.'[57]

Considering Bonaventure's temperament, it was probably with greater reluctance that he dismissed the final difficulty presented. Love, it was objected, can find in God its direct Object; of its very nature it needs no medium. Why therefore is it not the same with the intellect? He responds: 'Amor enim, sicut vult Bernardus, multo plus se extendit quam visio . . . . Et ipse etiam dicit in libro de Amore Dei, quod ubi deficit intellectus, ibi proficit affectus. Et ratio huius est, quia visio est solummodo rei præsentis, sed dilectio non solummodo rei præsentis sed etiam absentis. Præterea, visio non dicit qualemcumque modum cognoscendi, sed modum cognoscendi completum; dilectio vero et perfecta potest esse et imperfecta: ideo quamvis immediata Dei dilectio sit in via, non tamen oportet, quod visio sive cognitio immediata.'[58]

An attempt has been made to give a correct and representative account of Bonaventure's ideas on this point, but others who

---

55. II S. D. XXIII, a. II, q. III, T. II, p. 545.
56. See his L'Intuition de Dieu dans la Mystique chrétienne in Recherches de Science religieuse, Paris, 1914, T. V, pp. 150-2.
57. III S. D. XXIV, dub. IV, T. III, p. 531; compare ibid., D. XXXV, dub. i, p. 787; coll. in Hex., col. XX, n. 9, T. V, pp. 426-7; coll. in Joan., cap. VIII, col. XXXIV, n. 2, T. VI, p. 574. In all these places he has an identical doctrine.
58. II S. D. XXIII, a. II, q. III, T. II, p. 545-6.. The work he quotes is not St. Bernard's, but the Tractatus de Contemplando Deo, cap. VIII, n. 17, P. L. T. CLXXXIV, col. 376. This work is now attributed to William of St. Thierry.

have attempted the same task have widely differed. For the difference there is a certain amount of justification. Scattered throughout his writings, there are many passages which at first sight seem to militate against the above, and to give weight to the intuitionist theory. There are, for example, his not infrequent references to a possibility in this life, of a direct experience of God, 'per simplicem contuitum.'[59] Moreover, and this still more seriously affects our case, he apparently admits, without reserve, in his Commentary on St. John's Gospel, that contemplative knowledge has God as its direct Object. He now says, as if in opposition to what he had taught in his theological work already quoted, that the sole difference between contemplative knowledge and the Beatific Vision is found, not in the direct object, but in the degree of clearness with which it is seen. He has discussed the vision of God 'per speculum,' and adds: 'Alio modo cognoscitur Deus in se; et hoc dupliciter: aut clare, et hoc modo a solo Filio et a Beatis; alio modo in caligine, sicut dicit beatus Dionysius, de Mystica Theologia, et sic vidit Moyses, et sublimiter contemplantes, in quorum aspectu nulla figitur imago creaturæ.'[60] Every created medium is certainly ruled out here.

With regard to the use of the word 'contuitus' or 'contuitio' for which he has so often been quoted as an Ontologist, it cannot, we venture to think, be accepted as synonymous with any direct intuition of God. The contexts prove this. Very often the term is used in reference to what can only be an indirect form of knowledge. Thus, in the *Itinerarium,* we find him expressing his ideas thus:—'Mens nostra contuita est Deum extra se per vestigia et in vestigiis, intra se per imaginem et in imagine, supra se per divinæ lucis similitudinem super nos relucentem et in ipsa luce.'[61] His theory of the origin of ideas is indicated here, and it is because of this same theory—one which he derived from St. Augustine — that he is frequently counted among the Intuitionists. It is to the effect that the mind comes to a knowledge of 'intelligibilia' by the aid of a special Divine Illumination.[62] Such a theory may sometimes mislead the reader, but it no more means that God Himself is seen when 'intelligibilia' are perceived in His Light, or in His Truth, than that the Sun itself is necessarily seen

59. See Itin., cap. IV, n. 2, T. V, p. 306; ibid., cap. VI, n. 1, p. 310; Sermo in Sabb. Sanct., T. IX, p. 269; De Plant. Parad., n. 3 and n. 10, T. V, p. 575 and p. 577.

60. Com. in Joan., cap. 1, n. 43, T. VI, p. 256.

61. Op. cit., cap. VII, n. 1, T. V, p. 312.

62. For a full synthetic account of his Ideology, see De humanae cognitionis ratione, etc., already quoted. Also, Gilson, E., La Philosophie de Saint Bonaventure, pp. 326, sqq.

when objects are viewed in its light. In at least one place, when he himself understands that St. Augustine has used the word 'contuitus' to mean a direct intuition of God, he rejects the idea entirely: 'Hæc positio . . . dictis Sanctorum non consonat.'[63]

More difficult of explanation, is the passage from the Commentary on St. John's Gospel. There is undoubted reference to a direct vision of God 'in Seipso;' every medium is ruled out: 'in quorum aspectu nulla figitur imago creaturæ.' Pseudo-Dionysius, hitherto quoted as an authority for the negative opinion, is now made to defend an opposite idea. To all this it may be answered that Bonaventure, in the passage quoted, is not propounding a principle applicable to every case of mystical union with God. He is referring to the experiences of Moses, and other 'sublimiter contemplantes,' which, as continually remarked, are always extraordinary. He is but voicing a belief shared by St. Thomas Aquinas, and the majority of the Schoolmen of the thirteenth century, and handed down to them from St. Augustine, that Moses and St. Paul, and a few others, were especially privileged by God, to enjoy a foretaste of the Beatific Vision: an experience differing from the Beatific Vision only in its transiency.[64] What happened to them in no way affects the other general principle, which he elsewhere makes to extend to the normal mystical experience. We are not forced back upon the teaching, that a transient visitation of the 'lumen gloriæ' is imparted by the very fact of the mystical union, so that, in the words of one who attempts to explain the problem on such a basis, 'the difference between the 'visio beatificans' of heaven, and the mystical vision of persons still living upon earth, is merely that the one is habitual and permanent, and the other transient and exceptional.'[65] On this basis, there is a great temptation to give a personal explanation of the process; but this is not a personal explanation. It is an attempt to represent Bonaventure's position faithfully. To his mind, the experiences of Moses and Paul are,

63. II S. D. XXIII, art. II, q. III, p. 544.

64. See next chapter for St. Augustine, and others. For St. Thomas' teaching, see his Secunda Secundae, Quaest. CLXXV, De Raptu, arts. III-IV (Leonine Edition), T. X, pp. 404-406; Quaest. CLXXX, De Vita Contemplativa, arts. II-IV, ibid., pp. 425-428; De Veritate, quaest. XIII, arts. II-IV, (ed. Parmae MDCCCLIX), T. X, pp. 219-225. St. Thomas' Commentary on 2 Cor. XII, 2-4, is valuable: 'Paulus vero dicitur raptus ad tertium coelum, quia sic fuit alienatus a sensibus et sublimatus ab omnibus corporalibus, ut videret intelligibilia nuda et pura eo modo quo vident angeli et anima separata; et quod plus est, etiam ipsum Deum per essentiam, ut Augustinus expresse dicit . . . . De Moyse autem, quod viderit Deum per essentiam, patet.' In Ep. II ad Cor. Lectio 1. S. Thomae Aquinatis in omnes Divi Pauli Epistolas . . . Expositio, Venetiis, 1541, f. CXLI b. This is the only copy of the Expositio available.

65. A. B. Sharpe, Mysticism, its true nature and value, p. 95.

in essence, rare and exceptional, whereas the mystical experience, though it may in fact be likewise of rare occurrence, is so simply because of man's unwillingness to undergo the rigorous self-training demanded as a preliminary. The most intense training could never lead, 'de jure' to the exalted heights of these two great figures, but, in his opinion, God has so willed it that it should lead to mystical union.

In some other way, therefore, must he explain the phenomenon. So far, we have discovered only what it is not, though here and there, among the foregoing negative statements, certain indications, of an affirmative nature have been given. From his description it appears, that the crowning act of the normal Christian life, possesses two constitutive elements, the one intellectual, and the other, of great importance, volitional. Often, in his rhapsodies on the delights of mystical union, Bonaventure dwells upon the one, almost to the exclusion of the other; again, though this is very rare indeed, there is no mention of intellect and will at all, but of the mysterious 'apex mentis' which the German mystics of the fourteenth century were to make so important.[66] But in ultimate analysis it is apparent that the mystical experience takes place through the agency of the natural powers, intellect and will, the supernatural factor being the gratuitous divine communication received by the agency of the gifts of the Holy Ghost. On the one hand, there is a higher knowledge received in the intellect, not by a direct intuition, but by grace, which, as an effect of divine activity, floods the soul as it were, with a deeper knowledge of God, and of things pertaining to Him; on the other, this same knowledge, by means of a similar Divine activity, becomes experimental, in the sense that the will is so inflamed with love for that concerning which the intellect has been enlightened, that by analogy, it may be said to 'taste,' to 'feel,' the Divine Presence.

If this needs further elucidation, the need may perhaps be met by showing briefly, what can, and what very often does take place on lower levels. By faith, and by reason, we know that among other things, the contemplation of Divine Beauty will constitute the ultimate happiness of the human soul. Meditation upon this

66. We can find out one definition of this 'apex mentis' in his works, and here it has none of the mysteriousness centring around it at a later date. It is not a 'spark of the Divine,' but the 'summum ipsius animae et quasi centrum, in quo recolliguntur omnes aliae vires.' Sermo IV in Epiph., T. IX, p. 162. For other definitions, see W. R. Inge, Christian Mysticism, Appendix C., pp. 359-60.

truth may surround the whole subject with a net-work of considerations and arguments, making the truth clearer to the intelligence. Affective resolutions may lead to the strenuous endeavour to obtain that cleanness of mind, and heart, without which, it is realized, we cannot make advance in the knowledge of God. Yet Divine Beauty is ever transcendent, and since it is transcendent, the knowledge of it admits of depths which ordinary meditation can never fathom. Now, it is Bonaventure's hypothesis, that, at a certain stage of spiritual progress, Divine grace comes to the aid of the devout soul. God, without showing Himself as He is, works upon the intellect, filling it with a deeper and truer knowledge of His Beauty than is possible in ordinary discursive meditation. Upon this insight into the transcendent Beauty of God, there follows an act of love in the will, which has also been inflamed by Grace: an act so intense that the will may be described as being in possession of the Beauty it desires so ardently. The will is said to 'taste,' to 'feel,' to 'possess' the Beauty of God, and since in God there is absolute unity, it possesses God Himself. In language such as this, the medium is sometimes lost sight of, but the theological background should always be remembered. It will be seen at once, that such an experience, whilst it is on a level higher than spiritual exaltation, which is so often unreasoned and purely emotional, cannot be strictly called a foretaste of the Beatific Vision. Many things enter into the mystical experience, making it quite incompatible with a veritable foretaste of the bliss of the after-life. There is faith for example; likewise there is the medium. These are always present; whereas, in the Beatific Vision, faith can have no part, and the 'lumen gloriæ' takes the place of every other Divine Gift.

The two elements, the intellectual and the volitional, are clearly expressed whenever Bonaventure attempts a positive explanation of the mystical union. They are found in this passage for example —'Est ibi inflammatio permaxima. Et in hoc est tota ratio contemplationis, quia nunquam venit in contemplatione radius splendens, quin etiam sit inflammans. Et ideo in Cantico loquitur Salomon per modum amoris et per modum cantici, quia ad illos fulgores non potest perveniri nisi per amorem.'[67] Repeatedly, he refers to the soul in Contemplation, as receiving illumination as to things Divine.[68] Again, he writes: 'Sicut sponsa desiderat

67. Coll. in Hex., col. XX, n. 12, T. V, p. 427.

68. See De plant. Parad., n. 3, T. V, p. 575; Coll. in Hex., col. II, n. 30, T. V, p. 341; Ibid., col. III, n. 30, pp. 347-8. De Trip. Via, cap. III, p. 17: Quaest, de Scientia Christi, q. VII, n. 21, T. V, pp. 42-43.

sponsum, et materia formam, et turpe pulchrum; ita anima appetit uniri per excessum contemplationis; et tunc, quando hemisphærium animæ totum luminibus plenum est, tunc homo exterius fit totus deformis, tunc homo fit sine loquela.'[69] His mystical interpretation of the sixteenth verse of the first chapter of Genesis, brings out the same conception: 'And God made two great lights, a greater light to rule the day; and a lesser light to rule the night.' Concerning this text, he writes: 'Hæc autem intelligentia per contemplationem suspensa datur intelligi per opus quartæ diei, in qua luminaria facta sunt. Anima autem illa sola per contemplationem suspensa est, quæ habet solem et lunam et stellas in firmamento suo. Considera, modo si non esset sol et luna et stellæ in firmamento, quid esset mundus? Non esset nisi quædam massa tenebrosa, quia etiam nox cum lumine siderum adhuc tenebrosa et horribilis est. Sic est de anima. Quæ enim non habet gratiam contemplationis est sicut firmamentum sine luminaribus; sed quæ habet est firmamentum ornatum luminibus. Et sicut differt cœlum non habens hæc luminaria a cœlo habente, sic anima non habens, ab anima disposita ad hoc; unde differt sicut Angelus a bestia. Bestialis est homo carens his et habens faciem inclinatam ad terram sicut animal; sed plenus luminibus est totus angelicus.'[70]

The object of such Divine Illumination is to fix the soul's attention upon God, and upon truths relating to Him. Its nature is such, that it results in a mysterious obscurity which, as Bonaventure often declares, can only be properly explained by him who has experienced it. It is higher illumination when compared with the knowledge attained by the soul in discursive meditation, but 'docta ignorantia,' 'nocturna et deliciosa illuminatio,' 'ascensus in caligine,' when compared with the 'Summa Veritas'—God Himself. How can such an obscurity be the effect of true illumination? He explains himself: 'Sed quid est, quod iste radius excæcat, cum potius deberet illuminare? Sed ista excæcatio est summa illuminatio, quia est in sublimitate mentis ultra humani intellectus investigationem. Ibi intellectus caligat, quia non potest investigare, quia transcendit omnem potentiam investigativam. Est ergo ibi caligo inaccessibilis, quæ tamen illuminat mentes, quæ perdiderunt investigationes curiosas. Et hoc est quod dixit Dominus, se habitare in nebula; et in Psalmo: Posuit tenebras latibulum suum.' [71]

69. Coll. in Hex., coll. XX, n. 19, T. V, p. 428.
70. Ibid., n. 2, p. 425.
71. Ibid., n. 11, p. 427. He refers to III Kings, 8, 12; Ps. 17, 12.

Further research throughout his *Opera,* for information regarding the nature of this 'night of the intelligence,' so familiar in subsequent mystical literature, is rewarded only by similar dogmatic statements. In his *Breviloquium,* he shows how the just man, in pursuit of a fuller knowledge of God, passes from the indirect knoweldge of His Being, obtained through the ministry of the senses, to the other form of knowledge, given in mystical Contemplation, adding in conclusion: 'Et in his gradibus consistit scala Jacob, cuius cacumen attingit cœlum; et thronus Salomonis, in quo residet Rex sapientissimus et vere pacificus et amorosus ut sponsus speciosissimus et desiderabilis totus; in quem desiderant Angeli prospicere, et ad quem suspirat desiderium sanctarum animarum, sicut cervus desiderat ad fontes aquarum. Quo quidem desiderio ferventissimo ad modum ignis spiritus noster non solum efficitur agilis ad ascensum, verum etiam quadam ignorantia docta supra se ipsum rapitur in caliginem et excessum, ut non solum cum sponsa dicat: In odorem unguentorum tuorum curremus, verum etiam cum Propheta psallat: Et nox illuminatio mea in deliciis meis. Quam nocturnam et deliciosam illuminationem nemo novit nisi qui probat, nemo autem probat nisi per gratiam divinitus datam, nemini datur, nisi ei qui se exercet ad illam.'[72]

Yet it is not in this mystical illumination, but rather in the outbursts of love, that Bonaventure finds the consummation of the mystical act, so that it is not unfrequently described simply by reference to this inflaming of the will: 'Hæc enim est (contemplatio) in qua mirabiliter inflammatur affectio.'[73] Furthermore, to show how little is the part played by the intellect, in comparison with the volitional activity, he sometimes makes extreme negative statements. 'Ibi non intrat intellectus, sed affectus,'[74] is typical. In the *Itinerarium* there is a passage which condenses the opinion common to most of the later Franciscan theologians, Matthew of Acquasparta, John Peter Olivi, Raymond Lull, to mention only a few.[75]

---

72. Op. cit., pars. V, cap. VI, T. V, p. 260: The Scriptural refs. are to Gen. 28, 12; III Kings 10, 18; Cant. 5, 16; I Peter 1, 12; Ps. 41, 1; Cant. 1, 3; Ps. 138, 11; and compare, Itin., cap. VII, n. 5-6, ibid., p. 313; II S. D. XXIII, a. II, q. III, T. II, p. 546.

73. II S. D. XXIII, a. II, q. III, n. 6, T. II, p. 546; compare III, S. D. XXIV, dub. IV, T. III, p. 531; Sermo in Quadrag., T. IX, p. 219; Sermo de S. Domin., ibid., p. 564.

74. Coll. in Hex., col. II, n. 32, T. V, p. 342.

75. For Matthew of Acquasparta, see Quaestiones Disputatae, q. IX, Quarrachi, 1903, pp. 399-340. 'Propterea dico indubitanter quod raptus prout provenit ex vehementia devotionis, non tantum pertinet ad intellectum sed potius et principalius et perfectius ad affectum, non solum per casum aut per concomitantiam aut redundantiam, sed per essentiam.' John Peter Olivi, see

It is precisely towards the arousing of this act of love, in which the will is described as being in possession by grace, of its Object, that the intellectual illumination is directed as a subordinate factor, so subordinate, that unless the act of love follow, the illumination, no matter how intense, is worthless where the need of the soul is concerned. Only a union of love between God and itself will satisfy that need: 'Hæc est suprema unitio per amorem.'[76] To St. Paul is traced the doctrine that the act of the will is supreme. The Apostle of the Gentiles had written: 'I bow my knees to the Father of Our Lord Jesus Christ . . . . . that He would grant you, according to the riches of His glory, to be strengthened by His Spirit with might into the inward man, that Christ may dwell by faith in your hearts; that being rooted and founded in charity, you may be able to comprehend with all the saints what is the breadth, the length and height and depth: to know also the charity of Christ which surpasseth all knowledge, that you may be filled unto all the fullness of God.'[77] On the Apostle's authority therefore, Bonaventure declares that love transcends all knowledge in the mystical act: 'iste amor transcendit omnem intellectum et scientiam,'[78] for it is principally towards the 'charity of Christ' that the Apostle's hopes are directed. The fact remains, that the mystical experience is, as often as not, referred to by the term 'contemplatio.' Contemplation primarily implies a reception of knowledge. If the most important element in the experience, be an act of love, how is this term to be justified? To St. Paul he again makes appeal. Knowledge is received, but it is a knowledge of an order higher than that attainable by the intellect, however illuminated it may be; in a word, it is 'experimental knowledge,' perfected in the will, and infused by 'Him, Who is able to do all things more abundantly than we desire or understand.'[79]

Bonaventure proceeds to explain, that when the soul is united to God in this sublime act of love, it may, at one and the same time, be described as 'sleeping' yet 'watchful:' 'sleeping,' since the intellect has failed to fathom the infinite depths of the knowledge of God, even when aided by special illuminations from on

---

his An contemplatio principalius sit intellectu et in actu eius? ed. by Ehrle, in Archiv. für Lit. und Kirchengeschichte, Bd. III, p. 503. Raymond Lull, see Probst, Caractère et origine des idées du B. Raymond Lulle, Toulouse, 1912, pp. 102-112; pp. 285-288.

76. Coll. in Hex., col II, n. 30, T. V, p. 341.

77. Eph. 3, 14-19; quoted in loc. cit.

78. Coll. in Hex., col. II, n. 30, T. V, p. 341.

79. Eph. 3, 20.

high: 'watchful,' because the will, reäcting upon that very inability, finds but further impetus in its act of love.[80] For a further reason is the intellect to be described as 'sleeping;' the experience Bonaventure has in mind is ineffable: 'Unde cum exprimi non possit nisi quod concipitur, nec concipitur nisi quod intelligitur, et intellectus silet; sequitur, quod quasi nihil possit loqui et explicare.'[81] Finally, in the adjectives he applies to this mystical act of Divine love, he indicates the effects which he considers it has upon the soul. The mystical love of God is 'sequestrativus, soporativus, sursumactivus.' His own words best explain his idea: 'Sequestrat enim ab omni affectu alio propter sponsi affectum unicum; soporat et quietat omnes potentias et silentium imponit; sursum agit, quia ducit in Deum. Et sic est homo quasi mortuus; et ideo dicitur, fortis ut mors dilectio, quia separat ab omnibus. Oportet enim, hominem mori per illum amorem, ut sursum agatur.'[82]

In view of the above, we are not surprised to find him recommending, in the last stage of the spiritual life, the Pseudo-Areopagite's 'Via Negativa' as the best mode of approach to God. Nor does this contradict what was said in the previous chapter, with regard to the *Itinerarium*. In Pseudo-Dionysian Mysticism, the 'Via Negativa' apears as the initial step. For Bonaventure, it is the better step, only after a genuine intellectual search for traces of his God. True love will adopt the negative process after the intellect has performed its task. He gives us what is probably the neatest explanation of the twofold approach to God to be found in mediaeval literature: 'Iste autem ascensus fit per affirmationem et ablationem; per affirmationem, a summo usque ad infimum; per ablationem, ab infimo usque ad summum; et iste modus est conveniens magis, ut: non est hoc, non est illud; nec privo ego a Deo quod suum est, vel in ipso est, sed attribuo meliori modo et altiori, quam ego intelligo.—Ablationem sequitur amor semper. Unde Moyses primo a senioribus sequestratur, secundo ascendit in montem, tertio intrat caliginem. Alium exemplum: qui sculpit figuram nihil ponit, immo removet et in ipso lapide relinquit formam nobilem et pulchram. Sic notitia Divinitatis per oblationem relinquit in nobis nobilissimam dispositionem.'[83] The last word is all important. There is no question of creating

80. 'Unde cum mens in illa unione coniuncta est Deo, dormit quodam modo, et quodam modo vigilat: Ego dormio, et cor meum vigilat. Sola affectiva vigilat et silentium omnibus aliis potentiis imponit.' Coll. in Hex., col. II, n. 30, T. V, p. 341; the Scriptural reference is to Cant. 5, 2.

81. Ibid.

82. Ibid.

83. Ibid., n. 33, p. 342.

in the mind a blank which God is expected to fill. The 'Via Negativa,' as adopted by Bonaventure, undoubtedly aims at producing the recognition that God transcends all the knowledge acquired concerning Him. Even in its negations, therefore, it is positive, and it is to the transcendent God that love stretches forth.

With two minor details this attempted synthesis may be concluded.

It has been said, that in the mystical act, the intellect and will are employed, but that they are supernaturalized by Divine grace. The language used by the Franciscan Doctor will be the better understood, it it be remembered that the effective principle of the mystical experience is the purely gratuitous and special action of the Holy Ghost upon the soul's faculties. To the operation of the Holy Ghost, the mystical union is nearly always attributed, explicitly or implicitly. 'Iste ascensus fit per vigorem et commotionem fortissimam Spiritus Sancti; sicut dicitur de Elia: Ecce, spiritus subvertens montes et conterens petras. Hunc ignem non est in potestate nostra habere; sed si Deus dat desuper, sacerdotis est nutrire et ligna subiicere per orationem.'[84] More definitely still, the action of the Holy Ghost is explained by the special use of the gifts of Understanding and Wisdom. These become the proximate supernatural principles of mystical Contemplation. The illumination already described is attributed to the gift of Understanding. By faith, the soul accepts as true, and as directive of life, various revealed mysteries concerning God; but, by the gift of Understanding, without comprehending them, it obtains a deeper insight into their import: 'Ad donum intellectus spectat contemplatio clarior et excellentior, quam sit cognitio fidei.'[85] Far from clashing with faith, it is founded thereon: 'Super assensum fidei fundatur,'[86] and it prepares the soul for the other supernatural operation—the use of the gift of Wisdom, wherein the mystical act is consummated: 'Hæc (cognitio) est doni intellectus, quæ quidem viam præbet ad usum doni sapientiæ; quæ ideo gratuita est, quoniam super assensum fidei fundatur et ulterius ordinat ad sapientiæ gustum.'[87]

---

84. Coll. in Hex., col. II, n. 32, T. V, p. 342; The Scriptural references are to III Kings, 19, 11; Levit. 6, 12. Compare Itin., cap. VII, n. 6, T. V, p. 313; De Plant. Paradisi, n. 4, T. V, p. 575; Sermo II de S. Agnete, T. IX, p. 509; Sermo in Pentecost., T. IX, pp. 345-6; etc. etc.

85. III S. D. XXXV, a. 1, q. III, ad IVum, T. III, p. 779.

86. Ibid., ad IIIum.

87. Ibid. True we find him attributing something like mystical joy and love even to the gift of Understanding, but he makes it perfectly clear, that it is not here that we may find the perfection of the mystical experi-

The gift of Wisdom brings with it the experimental knowledge of God of which we spoke. Wisdom has many meanings, but the perfection of Wisdom is obtained only in mystical union: 'Dicitur sapientia magis proprie, et sic nominat cognitionem Dei experimentalem; et hoc modo est unum de septem donis Spiritus sancti, cuius actus consistit in degustando divinam suavitatem.'[88] Since such an act necessarily presupposes some understanding of what is experienced it follows, that even the gift of Wisdom is in part intellectual, and in part volitional, the intellectual element however, being again subordinated to the volitional: 'Et quoniam ad gustum interiorem, in quo est delectatio, necessario requiritur actus affectionis ad coniungendum et actus cognitionis ad apprehendendum, hinc est, quod actus doni sapientiæ partim est cognitivus, et partim est affectivus: ita quod in cognitione inchoatur et in affectione consummatur, secundum quod ipse gustus vel saporatio est experimentalis boni et dulcis cognitio.'[89] Primacy of place is thus once more given to the volitional element, both the gift of Understanding, and the intellectual element in the gift of Wisdom itself, being of a purely dispositive value: so dispositive and subordinate, that the perfection of the mystical act does not, in its essence, depend upon the satisfying of the intellect. Again the extreme statements are made: 'actus doni sapientiæ omnino se teneat ex parte affectionis et nullatenus ex parte cognitionis,'[91] and the general tendency of Franciscan thought is marked when he writes: 'Optimus enim modus cognoscendi Deum est per experimentum dulcedinis; multo etiam excellentior et nobilior et delectabilior est quam per argumentum inquisitionis.'[91] The gift of Wisdom becomes the true and essential principle of mystic union. Wisdom it is that gives a knowledge of God which cannot deceive the soul. It is such that of its very nature its Divine origin is appreciated, without the need of further argument. By a process known only to him who has experienced it, the soul is fully persuaded that, though it be only indirectly, the Object of its love is God Himself.

With brief reference to the question of bodily phenomena exhibited in mystical experience, this synthesis of Bonaventurian theology may be concluded. Such phenomena all too often form

ence: 'Nihilominus tamen in ipso actu intellectus est quaedam delectatio, sed longe inferior quam in dono sapientiae. Delectatur enim quis in cognitione veritatis, sed non sic, sicut in gustu summae suavitatis.' Ibid.

88. III S., D. XXXV, a. 1, q. 1, T. III, p. 774.
89. Ibid.
90. Ibid., fund. Vum, p. 773.
91. Ibid., ad. Vum, p. 775.

the central subject of interest in Treatises of this kind, but we think it need not be the case here. Bonaventure's mystical union is essentially internal; it concerns God and the soul. Rarely is he led into a mode of expression which would betray the idea that the experience is manifested outwardly. When he does so, we are reminded more of an interior preöccupation, an intentness of the soul in communion with God, a peaceful rest, unbroken and undisturbed by distractions of bodily origin, than of the lifelessness, the total suspension of bodily faculties, the hearing of material words, the elevation of the body above the ground, and the other multitudinous forms, which mystical phenomena usually take. We do not go so far as to say that he denies the possibility of such phenomena; we merely assert that they do not enter into the essence of the mystical union he describes. There is of course the 'raptus' attributed to Moses and Paul, and this undoubtedly implies for him a momentary separation of body and soul; but the 'raptus' is not the mystical union which constitutes the fulness of the Christian life. Some may regard our interpretation of his doctrine as a watering down of the chief subject of interest: while the terms used to express the mystical experience seem to imply far more than has been admitted—'excessus mentis,' 'stupor mentis,' 'elevatio mentis,' 'mors,' 'ebrietas,' and the apparently conclusive 'ecstasis.' [92] Into the experience which can be called 'ecstasis,' it is said, a bodily phenomenon surely enters. But an examination of the contexts in which all these terms occur only leads back to the conclusions already arrived at. The 'excessus mentis' of most frequent occurrence in Bonaventure's writings, as in those of St. Bernard and Richard of St. Victor,[93] seems to be based upon the Vulgate rendering of a text in St. Paul's second Epistle to the Corinthians: 'Sive enim mente excedimus, Deo: sive sobrii sumus, vobis.'[94] It would be beyond the scope of the present task, to examine the scriptural use of the terms of which 'excessus' is a derivative, but as used by Bonaventure, it implies no external phenomenon: no momentary separation of body and soul. The justification for the use of such a term is found in this, that in the mystical experience the intellect is the subject of the subordinate illumination, and is 'carried out of itself' in the sense that it grasps truths, not in their own light, nor

92. For his description of 'ecstasis,' see Sermo I, in Sabb. Sanct., T. IX, p. 269. It may be admitted that Bonaventure is not perfectly consistent with regard to the use of the term 'ecstasis,' but generally speaking it is not made to denote the same phenomenon as 'raptus.'

93. See next chapter.

94. Chap. 5, verse 13.

yet in the ordinary supernatural light of faith, but in the light of the higher gift of Understanding. 'Stupor mentis' finds a similar explanation. 'Mors' implies nothing beyond the fact that in mystical union with God, the soul banishes all affection for, and thought of anything not related to Him. Bonaventure's 'ecstasis,' generally speaking, is not the ecstasy of the later mystical manuals, but simply the exalted will-union of the soul with God: the absorption of the will in the Beloved of the mystical quest: an absorption effected by the gift of Wisdom. Examination of the foregoing quotations, will, we think, sufficiently prove the truth of these last statements.

For the present, it is not intended to criticise from any point of view the material now at hand. It is enough to have given what we consider to be a faithful presentation of Bonaventure's doctrines concerning the mystical experience. Other interpretations have been made, but generally speaking, many of the important major works of Bonaventure have been neglected. Such interpretations have differed from one another, and, in turn, the foregoing differs in various details from all.[95] Hence, Bonaventure has, as far as possible, been allowed to speak for himself, at the risk of a wearisome multiplication of quotations. If, however, this part of our task has resulted in a coördination of his most important ideas, it will have attained the purpose for which it was begun.

95. Étienne Gilson writes: 'La mystique bonaventurienne distingue au moins deux états contemplatifs nettement différents. Dans le raptus, état extraordinaire dont ont joui Moise et saint Paul, l'âme, momentanément separée du corps, est élevée pour quelques instants au sejour des bienheureux: elle voit donc Dieu face à face et redescend ensuite içi-bas sans pouvoir redire ce qu'elle a vu. Dans l'extase, état beaucoup plus fréquent, l'âme purifiée par l'ascèse et entrainé par une méditation appropriée, peut, avec le secours de la grace, éprouver la présence de Dieu par la joie de l'amour, mais sans le voir par l'intellect.' Art., La Conclusion de la Divine Comédie et la mystique Franciscaine., in Revue d'histoire Franciscaine, T. I, p. 57. Elsewhere (p. 63), we find "extase franciscaine, sommet ardu, mais accessible à tous, de la vie chrétienne, et qui couronne normalement cette vie.' Gilson's conclusions seem to be in perfect agreement with those arrived at in the present chapter.

CHAPTER VI.

Sources of Bonaventure's doctrine of Contemplation.—No attempt to give a full account of the teaching of any writer mentioned. — Pseudo-Dionysius.—St. Augustine.—St. Gregory.—St. Bernard.—The Victorines, Hugo and Richard.—St. Francis of Assisi and his reticence with regard to personal spiritual experience. — Bonaventure's doctrine criticised. — His directive principles.—The encouraging of desire for Contemplation does not lead to an unbalanced Mysticism.—The teaching that Contemplation is open to all, independently of special vocation, not repudiated by Sacred Scripture. — The value of Bonaventure's teaching to explain what is generally understood to take place in mystic experience.—Grace and its connexion with mystic experience.—Limits to Bonaventure's explanation. The objectivity of mystical states.—Utility of presenting the contemplative life as the goal of Christian endeavour.

The mystical union has been set forth as an experience equally accessible to all who are willing to undertake the arduous task of preparing for it, with the aid of grace: an experience, not identical with the raptures attributed to Moses and St. Paul, which is explained by a Divinely-given illumination of the intellect, and a special inflaming of the will in relation to God. Apart altogether from the doctrine synthesized in the previous chapter, Bonaventure's method of presenting that doctrine has perhaps been made sufficiently clear, so as to need no further lengthy comment. His teaching is not professedly built upon personal experience, but is always referred back to Sacred Scriptures, to the writings of the Fathers, and to those of his immediate predecessors. Wherever he has used the Scriptures to illustrate his ideas, the fact has already been noted. In this chapter, Patristic and other influence is investigated.

Bonaventure is unquestionably indebted to others for the teaching he hands down in his *Opera*. He scarcely gives expression to a single thought, without having recourse to authority. In striving to ascertain details concerning his indebtedness, there is a great temptation to concentrate entirely, where the question of Contemplation is concerned, upon the writings of Richard of St. Victor, for again and again he reproduces Richard's ideas, often in the very same language. However, it is patent that he himself, in his own studies of the various problems connected with Mystical Theology, went back beyond Richard, to the same direct sources whence the Victorine drew much of his teaching. Because of his manifest respect for the weighty authority of the Pseudo-Areopagite, for St. Augustine, St. Gregory and St. Bernard, whose writings he constantly quotes, some mention of these writers, however brief, must be made.

No pretence is made of giving anything approaching a complete survey of the teaching on Contemplation of any single one of the writers mentioned. They have various points of view, their use of terms familiar to the student of Mysticism is not identical, and their final conception, both of the route to be followed in the quest for mystical union with God, and of what takes place when that same quest is brought to a successful issue, is certainly not fully expounded here. For a full exposition, a series of historical studies dealing with one great figure at a time is required. Only with the aid of such a series could each be given with exactness the position due to him in relation to the Mystical Theology of the thirteenth century. Of necessity, the present aim is far more modest. If the writers mentioned seem to be dismissed all too summarily, it is not because their importance in the history of mystical thought is unrecognized, but because it would be impossible within the scope of this work to treat of them at greater length. The problem before us is: with what great figures in the realm of Christian thought must Bonaventure's teaching on mystical Contemplation be linked? Guided most often by the expressed predilection of the Seraphic Doctor, and by his copious quotations from various sources, we have turned back to the literature with which he was obviously most familiar. The conclusion is this: that no matter how much Pseudo-Dionysius may differ in thought from SS. Augustine, Gregory and Bernard, and these in turn from the Victorines, Hugo and Richard, Bonaventure has been guided in the expression of his own doctrine by their fundamental theories. He has done little beyond reproducing the authoritative statements of authors whom he respected. There are divergencies, of course, but the traditions concerning the main beliefs form the warp and woof of his teaching. In addition to this, as St. Francis is for him what St. Benedict was for Gregory and Bernard—the classic type of the true mystic—we have looked to the life of the 'Poverello,' to discover whether there is traceable any influence coming from this source.

As far as possible, the danger attending the isolation of passages from their context has been avoided. There is always the danger, greater still when each writer is not completely represented, of changing the meaning of passages, and of neglecting the emphasis to be put upon certain points. Only when there is full evidence for the belief that the writers mentioned have in mind a religious experience similar to that described by the Franciscan: only when it is considered on the authority of the works quoted, that they are occupied with the fulness of the Christian life, have their words been reproduced. The objection may be raised, that frequently they refer only to the form of Contemplation now known as 'acquired.'[1] Bonaventure does not know the distinction here implied. Beyond the mystical union he describes, and which he attributes to the agency of the gifts, Understanding and Wisdom, there is no other state which he regards as the fulness of the Christian life. Were it not for the fact that even the most enthusiastic exponents of the distinction admit that the passage from the lower to the higher form of Contemplation is itself mysteriously graded, so that it is well-nigh impossible to draw with certainty a line of demarcation at a particular point, we should have to examine the Patristic texts singly, to see whether they actually do refer to one or other of the modes. Since full evidence is not yet forth-coming for the belief that writers prior to Bonaventure were acquainted with the distinction, such a course does not seem necessary.

Perhaps we may pardonably begin with the influence of Pseudo-Dionysius, giving him at once, by courtesy, the priority of place he assumed when he identified himself with the disciple of Paul, and the historical position he would naturally have in the mind of Bonaventure, who betrays no suspicion as to the authenticity of the *Dionysiaca*. Pseudo-Dionysius, through the translations of Scotus Eriugena, undoubtedly influenced his conception of the ultimate attainment in the Christian life. Yet the God with whom Bonaventure finally becomes united in the mystic act, is wholly and clearly a God of love: and the love is as between two personalities. He is still unknown in the depths of His Being, to the finite intelligence, and the greater the depth unfathomed, the greater the love. The Franciscan speedily recognizes with Pseudo-Dionysius the incapacity of the human intellect; but whereas the one is content quietly to accept the fact of

1. Thus, Dom C. Butler, in his Western Mysticism, whilst admitting that there is a tendency among quite recent authors to reäct against the two kinds of Contemplation, as unused by, and unknown to, the older writers on Mystical Theology (p. 282), declares that it is of acquired, active and ordinary Contemplation that we must understand the early writers to be speaking, when they say that Contemplation is the natural and normal issue of the spiritual life, p. 283.

the Divine Incomprehensibility, without labouring the point, the other presses forward by way of endless, bewildering negations, in the pursuit of the great 'Nameless Being,' until we wonder what is left as the object of the love described in the *De Divinis Nominibus*. For here it is stated, that it is in ecstatic love for this mysterious 'Anonymous,' that the mystical union is consummated.[2] It has already been shown, that Bonaventure has adopted a more human and more comprehensible form of the 'Via Negativa' made famous in the Pseudo-Areopagite's works. The resultant 'Docta Ignorantia' and the 'Divina Obscuritas' met with before, come from the same source. A word may be added to what has already been said with regard to the interpretation of the 'Via Negativa.' The knowledge of God by negation, whatever it has been made to mean at various times, amounts with Bonaventure to nothing more than this: that we must, in order to know God, deny in a certain sense all we think and all we say of Him. This is not because our assertions, based as they often are upon Sacred Scripture, are false, but because they are in themselves ill-proportioned to, and scarcely befitting the transcendent perfection of the Divine Being. No matter how intense the effort to know Him may have been, no matter how sublime the resultant conception, even in the highest stages of contemplative illumination, we must always deny that the result, both of effort and illumination, can be in any way commensurate with His high and impenetrable Majesty.

In his attempts to arouse the intense desire for mystical experience, which he makes an indispensable element in the spiritual process, Bonaventure frequently reproduces Eriugena's version of the prayer, with which Pseudo-Dionysius commences his *Mystica Theologia:* 'Trinitas superessentialis, et superdeus, et superoptime Christianorum inspector theosophiæ, dirige nos in mysticorum eloquiorum superincognitum et superlucentem et sublimissimum verticem, ubi nova et absoluta et inconversibilia theologiæ mysteria, secundum superlucentem absconduntur occulte docentis silentii caliginem, in obscurissimo, quod est supermanifestissimum, supersplendentem, et in qua omne relucet, et invisibilium superbonorum splendoribus superimplentem invisibiles intellectus.'[3] This becomes his typical prayer of desire. Moreover, the Pseudo-Areopagite's exhortation to Timothy, to give

2. See infra.

3. Scotus Eriugena, Versio Operum S. Dionysii, Mystica Theologia, cap. I, P. L., T. CXXII, cols. 1171-2.

himself up diligently to mystical Contemplation, by abandoning the senses, and the operations of the intellect, in order to rise to union with Him Who is above all being and all knowledge,[4] becomes the guarantee of the accessibility of such an experience. 'Beatus Dionysius,' as Bonaventure calls him, had urged Timothy forward, had encouraged him to pray for, and strive after, the mystic union; hence it is lawful to desire it; hence too, must the experience be within man's attainment, independently of any special vocation. To the 'uninitiated' alone is it refused, Pseudo-Dionysius had declared; but this assertion in no way touched upon the question of the accessibility of mystical union to all Christians, seeing that the 'uninitiated' were not those who did not possess a special call to the mystic life, but those who lacked faith in the existence of the Supreme Being.[5] Upon the authority of the same 'Beatus Dionysius,' Bonaventure states his general principle, that in mystical Contemplation there can be no face to face vision of God, however momentary, in one place interpreting Dionysius' words to mean, that even Moses, in his rapture, did not see God. In the *Mystica Theologia*, it is written, that though on a certain occasion, Moses was privileged, when raised up in rapture, to behold many lamps flashing manifold pure beams, and though he had attained to the height of the Divine Ascent, he nevertheless did not come to the presence of God Himself, since He cannot be looked upon.[6] Bonaventure personally credits Moses with something more than this,[7] but the negative statement of Pseudo-Dionysius does influence his conception of the normal mystic experience. In this he teaches that God is only experienced indirectly, 'in effectu proprio'—a conception traceable to Pseudo-Dionysius' positive statement: 'Et si quis videns Deum intellexit quod vidit, non ipsum contemplatus est, sed quid eorum ab ipso existentium et cognitorum.'[8]

In the same writings, he had learnt that whilst even the knowledge of God gained in mystical Contemplation, being so ill-proportioned to the Divinity, could only be described as 'Ignorantia,'

---

4. 'Tu autem, o amice Timothee,' etc., ibid., col. 1173.
5. 'His autem, vide, quomodo nemo indoctorum auscultet. Indoctos autem dico, in his, quae sunt, conformatos, et nihil super existentia superessentialiter esse imaginantes.' Ibid.
6. 'Etenim non simpliciter divinus ipse Moyses primus mundari jubetur, et iterum ab his, qui tales non sunt, segregari . . . . et videt luminaria multa aperte fulgurantia . . . Deinde . . . et cum electis sacerdotibus in summitatem divinarum ascensionum praecurrit: et si eis sic manentibus fit Deo, contemplatur vero non ipsum, invisibilis enim, sed locum ubi stetit.' Ibid.
7. It will be remembered that in one place he even uses the Pseudo-Areopagite's authority for his statement that Moses saw God directly. See supra, chap. V.
8. Ep. ad Caium, ibid., col. 1177.

it was truly 'Docta Ignorantia,' since in that very obscurity, the fact of the Divine Incomprehensibility was grasped more fully, and Divinely given illumination aided the intellect in its apprehension of the mysteries enveloping the God-head. 'Est eis,' translates Eriugena, 'intellectualis operatio clara, et incontaminata puritate splendida, sciens et conspiciens divinarum intelligentiarum impartibiles et immateriales.' [9] Lastly, however, wanting in power of attraction, the final union with the 'Nameless One' described by Pseudo-Dionysius may generally seem, there is, in the *De Divinis Nominibus,* the clear statement, that it is in a union of ecstatic love between God and the soul that the Christian life, here below, finds its completion: a statement to which Bonaventure firmly clings.[10] The rhapsodies of the *De Divinis Nominibus* become compressed, in Bonaventurian language, in such beautiful expressions as: 'Puto, anima mea, quod verius es, ubi amas, quam ubi animas.' [11] With the author of the *Hierarchies,* therefore, must Bonaventure's teaching be connected; not that Bonaventure ever reached the sublimity of philosophical thought or expression of that mysterious personality, but substantially, his conception of what takes place in the mystic communing between God and the human soul is identical with that of Dionysius.

Nor could he whom Vaughan has so aptly called the 'large-souled Augustine' [12] fail to have a profound influence upon Bonaventure's thought. In St. Augustine he saw one who united in himself the two constitutive elements of the mystical life, namely, a most penetrating intellectual vision into things Divine, and a love of God that could rightly be called a consuming passion. It might seem, that Pseudo-Dionysian and Augustinian influence could scarcely meet in one and the same person.[13] Yet the two streams of thought do meet in Bonaventure. Pseudo-Dionysius may find a greater philosophical interest in repeated negations, whilst the intellectual vigour of St. Augustine may speed him on in his race through creatures to something more positive—to the Light, the Beauty, the Goodness of the God of Whom he has

---

9. De Divinis Nominibus, cap. VII, ibid., col. 1153, and compare Coelest. Hierarchia, cap. III, ibid. col. 1045.

10. See Op. cit., cap. IV, P. L., T. CXXII, cols. 1128—1146 especially. In Col. 1136 we find: 'Est autem et ecstaticus divinus amor, non sinens seipsos esse amantes, sed amandorum . . . Proinde et Paulus magnus in excellentia divini factus amoris, et mente excedentem suam virtutem assumens, divino ore: Vivo ego, ait, jam non, vivit autem in me Christus.'

11. Soliloquium, cap. II, n. 12, T. VIII, p. 49.

12. Hours with the Mystics, p. 131.

13. It is not, of course, assumed that the sources of Augustinian and Pseudo-Dionysian thought are diverse. We refer to the Areopagite's marked anxiety to pass beyond creatures, in contrast to St. Augustine's delight in seeking traces of God in all things.

caught glimpses in his passage: Pseudo-Dionysius may press still further the thought of Divine Incomprehensibility, whilst Augustine meditates upon the possibility of acquiring a yet higher knowledge than that gained in response to the 'quære supra nos' of creatures — all this may be true, but both ultimately come to rest in an ecstatic union with God, which they believe to constitute the fulness of the Christian life.[14]

It is upon the union they describe that Bonaventure concentrates his attention. He was well acquainted with all the then known works of Saint Augustine, and with others which critical research has since proved spurious, and in the genuine *Enarrationes in Psalmos,* he could find full authority for the importance he attaches to desire, in relation to the mystic union. St. Augustine, commenting on the forty-first Psalm, fully encourages desire of the mystical experience, with its wondrous, ineffable illuminations of the mind, and its power to satisfy the soul's longing for God: 'Curre ad fontes, desidera aquarum fontes. Apud Deum est fons vitæ et insiccabilis fons: in illius luce lumen inobscurabile. Lumen hoc desidera . . . . . . Curre ad fontem, desidera fontem . . . . impigre curre, inpigre desidera fontem.'[15] The same desire for union with God finds expression in the *Liber de Videndo Deo.*[16]

Intellectualism prevails in the works of Saint Augustine, and probably only the well-disciplined mind could follow him in his path, but he teaches that the highest point in Christian attainment is not the privilege of the more gifted. It is open to all who steadfastly hold to the course commanded by God; hence to the 'little ones' who can follow Christ Crucified, as well as to those possessed of superior intellectual powers. He writes in his *De Quantitate Animæ:* 'Illud plane ego nunc audeo tibi dicere, nos si cursum quem nobis Deus imperat, et quem tenendum suscepimus, constantissime tenuerimus, perventuros per Virtutem Dei atque Sapientiam ad summam illam causam, vel summum auctorem, vel summum principium rerum omnium, vel si quo alio modo res tanta congruentius appellari potest: quo intellecto, vere videbimus quam sint omnia

14. As illustrating the differences of thought, compare Pseudo-Dionysius' interpretation of the vision of Moses, with St. Augustine's ready admission that St. John, whilst still 'in via' had been privileged to contemplate the Eternal Light, with steady gaze, (fixis oculis). In Joan. Evangel. Tract. CXXIV, Tract. XXXVI, cap. VIII, P. L., T. XX, cap. V, col. 1666. 'Restat aquila: ipse est Joannes, sublimium praedicator, et lucis internae atque aeternae fixis oculis contemplator.'

15. Op. cit., P. L., T. XXXVI, col. 465.

16. Or, Epistola CXLVII, P. L., T. XXXIII, cols. 596 sqq.

sub sole vanitas vanitatum.'[17] That he is here referring to an experience of God in this life may be gathered from the opening words of the section in which the passage quoted occurs. He declares that certain choice souls have enjoyed such an experience, and have tried in some measure to describe it.[18] Elsewhere[19] he declares that the reception of the highest spiritual privileges depends upon one's being faithful to the Divine commands, and though he seems prepared to grant to all a more exalted experience than that described by Bonaventure, he stresses the idea of its accessibility to others, besides the more intellectually gifted: 'Nam quidam etiam minimi, et tamen in via fidei perseverantissime gradientes, ad illam beatissimam contemplationem perveniunt: quidam vero quid sit natura invisibilis, incommutabilis, incorporea, utcumque jam scientes, et viam quæ ducit ad tantæ beatitudinis mansionem, quoniam stulta illis videtur, quod est Christus crucifixus, tenere recusantes, ad quietis ipsius penetrale, cujus jam luce mens eorum velut in longinqua radiante perstringitur, pervenire non possunt.'[20] Such an idea as this could not fail to influence Bonaventure, to whom the following by faith of Christ-Crucified is all important, and to whom all knowledge is worthless, unless it aids the soul to know Christ better.

It would seem, that in the *Epistola* just quoted, St. Augustine is prepared to admit the accessibility to all of an experience similar to that of St. Paul; the strict road of faith leads 'ad summitatem contemplationis, quam dicit Apostolus, facie ad faciem.' However, in his concession that the request of Moses to see God face to face met with a favourable response, he gives at least a hint of the extraordinary nature of so great a privilege, and a general principle covering all mystic experience is entirely absent: 'Quamquam et illi fidelissimo antiquo famulo Dei Moysi, mirum nisi in hac terra laboraturo, populumque illum adhuc recturo, concessum est quod petivit, ut claritatem Domini videret, qui

17. Op. cit., cap. XXXIII, n. 76, P. L., T. XXXII, col. 1076.

18. 'Jamvero in ipsa visione atque contemplatione veritatis, qui septimus atque ultimus animae gradus est; neque jam gradus, sed quaedam mansio, quo illis gradibus pervenitur; quae sint gaudia, quae perfructio summi et veri boni, cujus serenitatis atque aeternitatis afflatus, quid ego dicam? Dixerunt haec quantum dicenda esse judicaverunt, magnae quaedam et incomparabiles animae, quas etiam vidisse ac videre ista credimus.' Ibid.

19. 'Jam ergo si fideles sumus, ad fidei viam pervenimus, quam si non dimiserimus, non solum ad tantam intelligentiam rerum incorporearum et incommutabilium, quanta in hac vita capi non ab omnibus potest, verum etiam ad summitatem contemplationis, quam dicit Apostolus, facie ad faciem (1 Cor. XIII, 12), sine dubitatione perveniemus.' Epistola CXX, n. 4, P. L., T. XXXIII, col 454.

20. Ibid.

dixerat: Si inveni gratiam ante te, ostende mihi temetipsum manifeste. Accepit enim in præsentia congruum responsum, quod faciem Dei videre non posset, quam nemo videret, et viveret; hoc modo significante Deo alterius potioris vitæ illam esse visionem. . . Quod autem dicere institueram, desiderio ejus etiam illum quod petierat, fuisse concessum, in libro Numerorum postea demonstratum est; ubi Dominus arguit contumaciam sororis ipsius, et dicit aliis Prophetis in visione se apparere et in somno, Moysi autem per speciem, non per ænigmata: ubi etiam addidit dicens: Et gloriam Domini vidit. (Num. XII, 6-8).' [21]

There is no evidence for the belief that anything approaching this enters into the normal mystical experience, according to Saint Augustine's idea. He admits he is dealing with an exception: 'Quid ergo est quod eum sic fecit exceptum . . . . ?' [22] The normal mystical experience, when received, seems to bring with it the intellectual enlightenment, and the rapturous sense of union with God, dwelt upon by Bonaventure, although generally speaking, in Augustinian writings, passages in which it is described only in terms of intellectual illumination, prevail. The characteristic description of the Christian experience, after which St. Augustine strives, sets it forth as a beholding with the mind's eye something unchangeable[23] which, we venture to think, is only Bonaventure's deeper insight into Divine truths by the agency of the gift of Understanding. The same applies when he makes it the attainment of the end of a quest, itself understood as a search for some unchangeable truth.[24] When St. Augustine's ideology is recalled, it will be admitted that such statements as these need not necessarily imply any direct vision of God. Even though it is true that his favourite mode of describing the highest point in Christian attainment is by dwelling upon the Light received in the intellect, he does not fail to mention the joys and the spiritual sweetness to which the illumination gives rise. Both the *Enarrationes* and the *Libri Confessionum* can vie with any later works as the expression of intellectual attainment, but even these contain passages of rare and exquisite beauty, descriptive of that love-union between God and the soul, which is an integral element of the mystic experience. In the one,

---

21. Epistola CXLVII, cap. XIII, n. 32, P. L., T. XXXIII, cols. 610-611.
22. Ibid.
23. 'Ecce acie mentis aliquid incommutabile, etsi, perstrictim et raptim, perspicere potuimus.' Enarrat. in Ps. XLI, n. 10, P. L., T. XXXVI, col. 471. N. B. To this he prefixes the statement: 'Ecce jam quadam interiore dulcedine laetati sumus.' Ibid.
24. 'Aliquam quaerit incommutabilem veritatem,' ibid., n. 7, col. 469.

he dwells again and again, upon the indescribable sweetness of which the mystic is the recipient,[25] whilst in the other, his tone becomes still more personal, when dealing with its unwonted and ineffable nature: 'Et aliquando intromittis me in affectum multum inusitatum introrsus ad nescio quam dulcedinem, quæ si perficiatur in me, nescio quid erit quod vita ista non erit.'[26] When this love within the soul reaches the height of perfection, the result is a life of intimate and habitual union with God. For love, of its very nature, tends towards such perfect union. 'Quid amor omnis?' asks Augustine, and he continues: 'Nonne unum vult fieri cum eo quod amat, et si ei contingat, unum cum eo fit?'[27] This general principle, we think, extends primarily to the love of the soul for God. Ideas such as these, though they by no means represent Augustinian thought completely, constitute the basis of the assertion that Bonaventure's name in the sphere of Mystical Theology must be linked with that of the great Doctor of the West.

It must also be connected with the name of St. Gregory, in whom we find to some extent a reversion to the type of Mysticism associated with the works of Pseudo-Dionysius: not that this reversion has been proved to be due to a study of those works.[28] Unlike St. Augustine, all that Gregory can find in creatures is but a mass of cares and worries, to be laboriously forced aside. He demonstrates the voluntaristic attitude towards the great problem of sanctifying grace, and with him, the mystical experience becomes a gratuitious gift of God indeed, yet the reward bestowed by Him, after strenuous efforts in the exercise of virtue. When he maps out the various degrees in the actual ascent to Christian perfection, Contemplation becomes the normal term of spiritual activity,[29] and an experience by no means the privilege of a few. This last is sufficiently proved by the fact that his most exhaustive explanations of Contemplation and of all that is necessary thereto, appear in exhortations and public sermons

25. 'Tamen dum miratur membra tabernaculi, ita perductus est ad domum Dei, quamdam dulcedinem sequendo, interiorem nescio quam et occultam voluptatem, tanquam de domo Dei sonaret suaviter aliquod organum: et cum ille ambularet in tabernaculo, audito quodam interiore sono, ductus dulcedine, sequens quod sonabat, abstrahens se ab omni strepitu carnis et sanguinis, pervenit usque ad domum Dei.' Enarrat. in Ps. XLI, n. 9, ibid., col. 470.

26. Confess. S. Aug., Lib. X, cap. XL, T. XXXII, col. 807.

27. De Ordine, Lib. II, cap. XVII, n. 48, T. XXXII, col. 1017.

28. Gregory in one place refers to 'Dionysius Areopagita, antiquus videlicet et venerabilis Pater,' and quotes the Heavenly Hierarchy indirectly. See Hom. in Evangel., Lib. II, Hom. XXXIV, P. L., T. LXXVI, col. 1254. But we do not find any extensive use of the Dionysiaca.

29. See his Moral., Lib. XXII, cap. XX, P. L., T. LXXVI, cols. 240-244.

delivered in the Lateran Basilica, not merely to monks, but to very mixed congregations. Is Gregory referring to something below the true mystic union, when he so positively declares that no condition or state of life can justly be debarred from the realization of a loving communion with God? The context makes him at least appear to have in view the highest point of Christian attainment when he writes: 'Non enim contemplationis gratia summis datur et minimis non datur, sed sæpe hanc summi, sæpe minimi, sæpius remoti, aliquando etiam conjugati percipiunt.'[30] Beneath this, there is plainly the idea that a retired life, for example the monastic life, is more conducive to the enjoyment of mystic communing with God, but there is no question of a special vocation. It is possible of attainment, even amid the distracting cares of service of others. He treats it as an acknowledged fact that many, whilst busily engaged with external affairs, have been led by grace to higher levels of the spiritual life.[31]

Bonaventure presented his doctrine that in the act of Contemplation the soul is vouchsafed no vision or direct experience of God, on the authority of Gregory as well as of Pseudo-Dionysius. Nor does he seem to have misrepresented Gregory's teaching. Gregory repeatedly asserts that God cannot be known or seen as He is in this life by man; whatever man sees, is not, and cannot be, God Himself, but only a similitude of the glory that is Divine.[32] Nothing more explicit than the following statement could be found. He writes: 'Deum hic nonnisi de longe prospicimus. Quantumlibet enim in hac vita positus quisque profecerit, necdum Deum per speciem, sed per ænigma et speculum videt. E vicino autem cum respicimus, verius cernimus: cum vero longius aciem tendimus, sub incerto visu caligamus. Quia igitur sancti viri in altam se contemplationem erigunt, et tamen Deum, sicut est, videre non possunt, bene de hac aquila dicitur: Oculi eius de longe prospiciunt. Ac si diceret: Intentionis aciem fortiter tendunt, sed

30. Hom. in Ezech., Lib. II, Hom. V, n. 19, P. L., T. LXXVI, col. 996.

31. 'Quod quotidie in sancta Ecclesia cernimus, quia plerique dum bene ministrant exteriora quae accipiunt, per adjunctam gratiam ad intellectum quoque mysticum perducuntur, ut etiam de interna intelligentia polleant qui exteriora fideliter administrant.' Hom. XL in Evangel., Lib. I, Hom. IX, n. 5, T. LXXVI, col. 1108.

32. 'Quid enim in universo mundo sancti Spiritus gratia agat aspiciens, ait: Hic erat aspectus splendoris per gyrum. Quae vero interius ejusdem sancti Spiritus gloriae maneat, considerare volens, sed sicut erat non valens, subjungit: Et haec visio similitudinis gloriae Domini. Non enim ait: Visio glorae, sed similitudinis gloriae, ut videlicet ostendatur quia quantalibet se intentione mens humana tetenderit, etiamsi jam phantasias imaginum corporalium a cogitatione compescat . . . ' etc., Hom. in Ezech., Lib. I, Hom. VIII, n. 30, T. LXXVI, col. 868.

necdum propinquum aspiciunt, cujus claritatis magnitudinem penetrare nequaquam possunt. A luce enim incorruptibili caligo nos nostræ corruptionis obscurat.'[33] It is easy to see how Bonaventure has been impressed by this, and by a similar dogmatic utterance: 'Mens cum in contemplationis sublimitate suspenditur, quidquid perfecte conspicere prævalet, Deus non est.'[34]

In spite of his uncompromising attitude with regard to the vision of God, Gregory admits that a supernatural illumination is an element in the act of Contemplation: an illumination which he calls the 'chink of Contemplation.' The soul cannot directly gaze upon the Infinite Light, but just as a sunbeam passing through a chink in a darkened room is seen, so too, may a ray of the Divine Light penetrate into the depths of the soul.[35] By its radiance ,is the soul enabled to apprehend more clearly the 'profunda Dei.' Again, the full contemplative act is not experienced, till there is a subtle mysterious 'tasting' of the sweetnesss of boundless Truth: 'Quasi enim sibilum tenuis auræ percipimus, cum saporem incircumcriptæ veritatis contemplatione subita subtiliter degustamus.'[36] A theory like Bonaventure's, that the illumination received in Contemplation is dispositive with regard to the love which perfects the mystic union, seems to underlie the further statement, that the food of love is received from the pastures of this contemplated truth: 'Sicque fit ut ipsis bonis actibus adjuta, ad superiora rursus in contemplationem surgat, et amoris pastum de pabulo contemplatæ veritatis accipiat.'[37] The soul has sought after the unencompassed Light; it has been permitted to see its ray, and beholding that ray, it attains to the essential and perfecting element in the mystical act—the 'tasting' of that which it has sought: 'Miro modo hoc ipsum quod accipere quærit, degustat.'[38] Gregory has come to the end of his theorizing concerning the mystical state when he writes: 'Cumque internam dulcedinem degustat, amore æstuat.'[39] Mystic love is there undoubtedly, but in Gregory's

33. Moral., Lib. XXXI, cap. LI, n. 101, T. LXXVI, cols. 628-9. Compare ibid., Lib. IV, cap. XXIV, n. 45, T. LXXV, col. 659: 'Sancti igitur viri videre verum mane appetunt, et, si concedatur, etiam cum corpore illud attingere lucis intimae secretum volunt. Sed quantolibet ardore intentionis exsiliant, adhuc antiqua nox gravat, et corruptibilis hujus carnis oculos, quos hostis callidus ad concupiscientiam aperuit, judex justus a contuitu interni sui fulgoris premit.'

34. Ibid., Lib. V, cap. XXXVI, n. 66, T. LXXV, col. 716.

35. Ibid., cap. XXIX, n. 52, cols. 706-7; also see Hom. in Ezech., Lib. II, Hom. V, n. 16—n. 18, T. LXXVI, cols. 994-5.

36. Moral., Lib. V, cap. XXXVI, n. 66, T. LXXV, col. 716.

37. Hom. in Ezech., Lib. I, Hom. V, n. 12, T. LXXVI, col. 826.

38. Moral., Lib. XV, cap. XLVII, n. 53, T. LXXV, col. 1108.

39. Ibid., Lib. V, cap. XXXIII, n. 58, col. 711.

case, we are struck by the almost impersonal character given to its Object; the greater warmth of Bonaventurian writings is painfully absent. The religious thought which finds expression in these, is personal in a new way, and because it is personal, it has greater powers of attraction to the devout soul. For the personal aspect of his religion, the Franciscan is largely indebted, together with his contemporaries, not only to St. Francis with his vitalizing Christ-love, but also to St. Anselm and St. Bernard.

Bernard's is a name which will always be given an important place in the full history of mystical thought. In him we find the dividing line between the Patristic and the Middle Ages. Not the 'Anonymous,' nor 'That which is,' nor yet 'The Unencompassed Light,' but Jesus, the Word, conceived as the Spouse of the Soul, with lips to kiss, and hands and feet, is the Object of Bernard's love. The truth that desire of mystic joys is an indispensable preliminary to their actual attainment becomes a veritable commonplace in his eighty-six Sermons on the *Canticle of Canticles;* to be mystically united to Jesus is the reward only of the 'man of desires.'[40]

The fact that Bernard addressed these Sermons to monks, to encourage them to give themselves up to the contemplative life, to which they were bound by their vocation, in some measure tends to make his Mysticism the privilege of a special class. Now and again, is it viewed as within the grasp of all. In one place, he declares that there is no single individual among the faithful members of Christ's Church, with respect to whom His mystical promise may not be fulfilled;[41] and in another, there is the confession of the belief, that if there is anyone who feels it good to draw near to God: any one in such a way a man of desire, that he longs to be dissolved and to be with Christ, such a one, whoever he may be, will assuredly receive the Word, in mystic communion.[42] But it would seem that Bernard, in his love of

40. See Sermo III, n. 5, P. L., T. CLXXXIII, col. 796; Sermo IX, n. 3, col. 816; Sermo XXXII, n. 2, col. 946.

41. That is, Christ's promise to abide within His faithful servant. Commenting on this, Bernard writes: 'Quid singulus quisque nostrum? putamusne in nobis quempiam esse, cui aptari queat quod dicitur? Quid dixi, in nobis? Ego autem et de quovis intra Ecclesiam constituto si quis hoc quaerat, non omnino reprehendendum censuerim . . . Denique non propter animam unam, sed propter multas in unam Ecclesiam colligendas, in unicam astringendas sponsam, Deus tam multa et fecit et pertulit, cum operatus est salutem in medio terrae.' Sermo LXVIII, n. 4, col. 1110.

42. 'Ergo si cui nostrum cum sancto Propheta adhaerere Deo bonum est, et, ut loquar manifestius, si quis in nobis est ita desiderii vir, ut cupiat dissolvi et cum Christo esse, cupiat autem vehementer, ardenter sitiat, assidue meditetur; is profecto non secus quam in forma sponsi suscipiet verbum in tempore visitationis, hora videlicet qua se astringi intus quibusdam brachiis sapientiae, atque inde sibi infundi senserit sancti suavitatem amoris.' Sermo XXXII, n. 2, col. 946.

the monastic life, and in his conviction that herein alone could Christian perfection be found, makes such statements with a reluctance unknown to Bonaventure. When Bernard explains the nature of the mystical act, he is as explicit as Gregory in excluding the idea of an experience to be judged as a foretaste of the Beatific Vision. 'Talis visio,' he writes, after giving a glowing account of its beauties, 'non est vitæ præsentis, sed in novissimis reservatur.' [43] The most ardent defender of the thesis that the mystical experience is in some way a foretaste of the Beatific Vision, might, however, be the author of this utterance, understanding it to mean that in its fulness the Beatific Vision is reserved for the next life. Bernard means more than this, for in the same Sermon he declares: 'Et nunc quidem apparet quibus vult; sed sicuti vult, non sicuti est. Non sapiens, non sanctus, non propheta videre illum, sicuti est, potest, aut potuit in corpore hoc mortali.' [44] Moses, to whom Augustine granted the vision of God Himself is, to Bernard, but one who presumes upon favours already received; his request to see God face to face was indeed rewarded, but not in the manner desired: 'Accepit autem pro ea visionem longe inferiorem, ex qua tamen ad ipsam quam volebat, posset aliquando pervenire.' [45] What he will not admit in the case of Moses, he readily grants in favour of his Holy Father St. Benedict, who was, though only 'ad modicum,' he declares, snatched up to that vision of God which constitutes the Blessedness of the Elect.[46]

The practical identity of St. Bernard's and Bonaventure's thought is manifested in descriptions of the normal term of the spiritual life. It is most frequently, with Bernard, the love-union between the soul and its Beloved, though he does not entirely neglect the intellectual aspect of Contemplation. When all stains of sin and the rust of vices have been consumed by the fire of love: when the conscience has been purified and calmed: 'Sequatur subita quædam atque insolita latitudo mentis, et infusio luminis illuminantis intellectum vel ad scientiam Scripturarum, vel ad mysteriorum notitiam.' [47] This illumination, ascribed by Bonaventure to the gifts of the Holy Ghost, is, according to Bernard, effected in the soul by the suggestions of Holy Angels:[48] a thought

43. Sermo XXXI, n. 2, col. 941.
44. Ibid.
45. Sermo XXXIV, n. 1, col. 960.
46. See his Sermones de Diversis, Sermo IX, n. 1, P. L., T. CLXXXIII, col. 565.
47. Sermones in Cant., Sermo LVII, n. 8, col. 1053.
48. Sermo XLI, n. 3, col. 986. He describes how in ecstasy something from God momentarily sheds its ray upon the mind, and there present themselves certain imaginary likenesses of lower things, suited to the meanings

on a lower level, no doubt, but sufficiently developed to prove continuity. There is little need to expand the argument, that Bernard's highest point in the mystical life is a state of love: of a resting of the will in an undisturbed possession of its Object. From Bernard, especially, does Bonaventure borrow the finest passages in the *Soliloquium,* to express the truth that love is the great reality: the only one among all the movements, feelings, and affections of the soul in which creatures are able to respond, adequately, to the advances of the Creator.[49]

Hugo of St. Victor need not, in this connection, receive lengthy treatment. Most of his mystical ideas have been continued in the works of his disciple Richard, for whom he was the 'præcipuus theologus nostri temporis.'[50] No one can read Hugo's *De laude charitatis,*[51] or his *De Amore Sponsi ad Sponsam,*[52] without realizing that the contemplative act, bringing with it the Divine Illuminations of which Bonaventure speaks, is perfected in love. In the fact that Hugo rendered, as Vaughan has noted,[53] the Pseudo-Areopagite's *Heavenly Hierarchy* more scriptural, more spiritual, and far more human, is his principal influence upon Bonaventure to be found. It is not too much to say that by this work he showed the Franciscan how the other ponderous translations of Scotus Eriugena were to be interpreted.

Richard's is a spirit kindred in many ways to that of Bonaventure. Not only are they both led to seek inspiration for their ideas on Mystical Theology in practically the same sources, but they seem to be moved to dwell upon the benefits of the contemplative life, by the degenerate state of religion in their respective spheres. Richard, even in his most profound expositions of the highest forms of the religious life, laments the evils he finds, not only abroad, but at home, where the finest fruits of devotion might be expected,[54] and, as we have already seen, Bonaventure is saddened when he compares the lives of the friars and companions of

---

which have been infused from above, and by means of which the most brilliant ray of truth is in a manner shaded. 'Existimo tamen ipsas formari in nobis sanctorum suggestionibus angelorum.'

49. Sermo LXXXIII is especially quoted: 'Qualiter anima, quantumcunque vitiis corrupta, adhuc per amorem castum et sanctum potest redire ad similitudinem Sponsi, id est Christi.' Cols. 1181-84.

50. Benjamin Major, Lib. I, cap. IV, P. L., T. CXCVI, col. 67.

51. Contained in P. L., T. CLXXVI, cols. 969 sqq.

52. Ibid., cols. 987 sqq.

53. Hours with the Mystics, Bk. V, c. 2, p. 155.

54. The history of the once holy Abbey of St. Victor bears witness to the truth of Richard's complainings: 'Heu in quam inferiori saeculo dilapsi sumus! Heu in quos fines, imo, faeces saeculorum homines devenerunt! cum (ut de saeculi hominibus taceamus quos excaecavit ambitio) ipsa religionis electio nostra miserabili tempore tanta divisione spargatur, ut vix unus alteri conveniat in unum, nisi forte adversus Dominum et adversus

St. Francis with those of his own contemporaries. They write in the hope of raising the standard of devotion among the Canons of St. Augustine, and the Franciscan Friars respectively. Again, like the later Theologian, Richard was no less renowned for his learning than for his piety and zeal for reform. Keeping closely to the path made by Hugo, he adds still more of the products of Scholasticism, but, curiously enough, beneath his endless subdivisions and distinctions in which the Scholastics delighted, there is a Mystical Theology representing an advance rather than a retrogression. It becomes more definite. In his *De Gradibus Charitatis,* Mystical Theology, understanding by this the religious experience itself is not the privilege of a few, but, as he writes: 'Offertur omni, aufertur nulli, ut nullus nisi suo vitio illa careat.'[55] Such a declaration may be made, because, like Bonaventure in his *Itinerarium,* he emphasizes the truth that in the attainment of this sublime grace compunction of heart avails more than profound investigations; sighs avail more than arguments.[56]

We are more fortunate now, in being able to find exact definitions of terms used, though it must be confessed that Richard has the mediaeval weakness for departing from definitions on the slightest pretext. In the *Benjamin Major,* he defines Contemplation as the 'libera mentis perspicacia in sapientiæ spectacula cum admiratione suspensa,'[57] a definition as incomplete as Hugo's which he rejects, unless 'cum admiratione suspensa' denotes the ecstatic love, which he afterwards makes the essential element in the mystical act. Though it has been prepared for by compunction of heart, and the various spiritual exercises already mentioned, in itself it is made possible only by a gratuitous Divine working upon the soul. When it is experienced, Contemplation costs the soul no effort.[58] In it, though not always with the same

---

Christum ejus. Ubique apparent scissurae civitatis David, et intantum jam hiant, ut vicinam ruinam omnino minentur. Servatur sub tunica una et veste simili cor varium et omnino dissimile, ita ut de religione antiqua vix signa serventur, et venientibus ad sepulchrum Domini quod claustrum est, Christum quaerentibus sola linteamina pateant, id est, habitus forma . . . . Fateor, taedet hic esse.' De Gradibus Charitatis, cap. IV, P. L., T. CXCVI, col. 1204.

55. Ibid., cap. col. 1205.

56. Benjamin Major, Lib. IV, cap. VI, col. 139. 'Puto ergo quia opus est in hoc opere intima potius compunctione, quam profunda investigatione, suspiriis quam argumentis, crebris potius gemitibus quam copiosis argumentationibus. Scimus autem quia cordis intima nil adeo purgat, mentisque munditiam nil adeo reparat; nihil sic ambiguitatis nebulas detergit, cordisque serenitatem nil melius, nil citius adducit, quam vera animi contritio, quam profunda et intima animae compunctio.'

57. Op. cit., Lib. I, cap. IV, T. CXCVI, col. 67; compare ibid., Lib. V, cap. XIX, col. 193.

58. Ibid., cap. III, cols. 66-7 'Contemplatio permanet sine labore cum fructu.'

intensity—Contemplation admitting of many degrees[59]—the soul is ravished by the wonders of the object contemplated.[60]

What is this object? Richard refers to the 'spectacula sapientiæ' which could be rendered 'the wonders of Divine Wisdom,' and thus be made to denote a deeper insight into the hidden truths concerning the Godhead. Yet both Vaughan,[61] and Maréchal claim to have discovered in his writings evidence for something far more exalted than this, the latter going so far as to declare, expressly, that Richard admits the possibility of a vision of the Divine Essence in the act of Contemplation.[62] Whilst this claim cannot be summarily dismissed, there is much ground for the statement that, like Bonaventure, he rules out such a possibility, and explains the act of Contemplation in some other way. The following, taken from his *Adnotationes Mysticæ in Psalmos,* is sufficiently explicit. 'Eumdem tamen in cœlis esse, et in cœlis videri non dubitamus. Sciendum tamen est quod aliter videtur per fidem, aliter autem per contemplationem, aliter vero cernitur per speciem. Quod est inter cœlum et terram, hoc interest inter fidelem et infidelem, et possumus quemlibet perfectum dicere cœlum propter fidem. Huic tamen cœlo supereminet alium cœlum, dignitas scilicet spiritualium virorum, cui tamen superfertur tertium sublimitas, videlicet angelorum. In primo itaque videtur per solam utique fidem; in secundo autem videtur etiam per contemplationem; in tertio vero cernitur facie ad faciem. Per fidem eum videmus, quando illa quæ de eo scripta sunt firmiter credimus. Per contemplationem autem eum cernit, qui in eo quod de illo prius credidit, ex inspiratione divina intelligentiæ oculos figit. Per speciem vero videtur, quando in propria substantia, sicuti est facie ad faciem cernitur. Verumtamen quocumque modo videatur, non tamen videtur nisi in cœlo.'[63]

A sharp distinction is thus drawn between the threefold way in which God may be seen, and it is made sufficiently clear that the Object of Contemplation is not God Himself. So too, in another scriptural commentary, this negation is equally stressed. The soul on fire with love for Christ knows its Beloved indeed, but cannot yet behold His Head: the head of Christ being

59. See for these degrees: Ibid., Lib. I, cap. V, cols. 68 sqq.

60. Ibid., cap. IV, col. 68. 'Nam veritatem quidem diu quaesitam tandemque inventam mens solet cum aviditate suscipere, mirari cum exultatione, ejusque admirationi diutius inhaerere.'

61. Hours with the Mystics, bk. V, c. 2, pp. 162-3, and note to p. 163 given on p. 172. Vaughan is evidently impressed by the quotation: 'Egressus autem quasi facie ad faciem intuetur,' etc. See infra.

62. L'intuition de Dieu dans la mystique chrétienne, in Recherches de Science religieuse, T. V, 1914, pp. 147 sqq.

63. Op. cit., P. L., T. CXCVI, col. 270-1.

for Richard the symbol of His Divinity: 'Caput ejus divinitas ejus est, quia caput Christi Deus est. Quod caput aurum optimum est, quia divinitatis bonitas omnibus quæ ab ea facta sunt antecellit, hoc est aurum terræ viventium, et aurum terræ illius optimum est. Nam fulgens ut humanis oculis, et a viventibus in carne videri non possit. Non enim videbit Deum homo, et vivet. Ideo ergo dilectus meus, quia hoc caput ejus, hoc principale ejus, hoc sublime quod videri non potest.' [64]

These quotations would suffice to prove that Bonaventure continues Richard's doctrine, were it not for Richard's frequent descriptions of contemplatives as those to whom it is given to see God face to face: 'Per contemplativos debemus illos intelligere, quibus datum est facie ad faciem videre;' [65] or whose privilege is a direct communing with God: 'Habet (contemplativus) in oratione cum Deo familiare colloquium . . . facie ad faciem cum Deo loquens.' [66] Passages such as these, it is admitted, present serious difficulties, but they should not be interpreted too literally. A religious enthusiasm, and an intense appreciation of the wonders of mystic union with God, sometimes carry Richard, as well as other writers, beyond the strict theological bounds so carefully marked in more critical moods. When he so freely speaks of a face to face vision of God, there are serious reasons for supposing that he has, for a while, departed from theological language, for he elsewhere qualifies his statements: 'Nihil itaque aliud est montes in modum arietum exsultare, nisi viros contemplativos per mentis excessum summam veritatem nuda et aperta visione attingere, et quasi facie ad faciem videre.' [67] Prior to his other utterance, he writes: 'Homines quamvis boni, quamvis sancti, vident tamen in nocte, id est in obscuritate, ... etiam hi qui lucent virtutibus et vitæ sanctitate, obscurantur tenebris humanæ cæcitatis.'[68] This is a return to the thought of Bonaventure.

'Visio Dei quasi facie ad faciem' may, in spite of its being a qualified statement, present certain difficulties, but Richard uses the expressions merely to show forth the superiority of contemplative knowledge over that of faith. In the mystic, as in the ascetic states, the soul has concepts of God, concepts of His Being, and of truths connected with Him, but whereas

64. Explic. in Cant. Cantic., cap. XXXVI, col. 509.
65. Adnot. Mysticae in Psalmos, adnot. in Ps. CXIII, col. 337.
66. Explicat. in Cant. Cantic., cap. V, col. 420.
67. Adnot. Mysticae in Psalmos, cols. 341-2.
68. Explicit. in Cant. Cantic., cap. V, col. 419.

the ascetic, even after strenuous efforts, has only a weak apprehension of things Divine, the mystic, without effort, penetrates more deeply into various religious truths: 'Per contemplationem autem eum (i. e. Deum) cernit, qui in eo quod de illo prius credidit, ex inspiratione divina intelligentiæ oculos figit.'[69] The Victorine's teaching, that the supernatural enlightenment received in mystic communion with God is based upon, and inseparable from, the knowledge of faith, became, not only for Bonaventure, but for future generations of mystical theologians, one of the chief tests for the discriminating between true and false Mysticism.[70] Because of its exalted nature, therefore, mystical illumination can be called the 'visio Dei, quasi facie ad faciem;' not, however, because it implies a direct, however momentary, experience of God.

There is no need to dwell at greater length upon the truth that Richard makes a supernatural illumination one of the integral elements of mystical Contemplation. It is in love that the contemplative experiences its fulness: 'In hoc statu, dum mens a seipsa alienatur, dum in illud divini arcani secretarium rapitur, dum ab illo divini amoris incendio undique circumdatur, intime penetratur, usquequaque inflammatur, seipsam penitus exuit, divinum quemdam affectum induit, et inspectæ pulchritudini configurata tota in aliam gloriam transit. . . . Cum enim ferrum in ignem projicitur, tam frigidum quam nigrum procul dubio primo videtur. Sed dum in ignis incendio moram facit, paulatim incalescit, paulatim nigredinem deponit, sensimque incandescens, paulatim in se ignis similitudinem trahit, donec tandem totum liquefiat, et a seipso plene deficiat, et in aliam penitus qualitatem transeat. Sic itaque, sic anima divini ardoris rogo intimique amoris incendio absorpta, æternorumque desideriorum globis undique circumsepta, primo incalescit, postea incandescit, tandem autem tota liquescit, et a priori statu penitus deficit.'[71]

A word may be said concerning his use of the term 'excessus mentis' which occurs at frequent intervals, denoting the mystical act of union with God.[72] It seems

69. Adnot. Mysticae in Psalmos, adnot. in Ps. II, col. 271.

70. 'Sed si jam te existimas ascendisse ad cor altum, et apprehendisse montem illum excelsum et magnum, si jam te credis Christum videre transfiguratum, quidquid in illo videas, quiquid ab illo audias non ei facile credas, nisi occurrant ei Moyses et Elias . . . Suspecta est mihi omnis veritas quam non confirmat Scripturarum auctoritas nec Christum in sua clarificatione recipio, si non assistant ei Moyses et Elias.' Benjamin Minor, cap. LXXXI, col. 57; compare ibid., caps. LXXVIII-LXXX, cols. 55-57.

71. De Quattuor Gradibus Violentae Charitatis, col. 1221.

72. See Benjamin Minor, cap. LXXIV, col. 53; Benjamin Major, Lib. IV, cap. XXIII, col. 167.

to imply nothing more than this, that the soul is so engrossed in things Divine that it can give no attention to other matters. It implies likewise, that the knowledge acquired, and the love enkindled within the soul, are deeper and more intense than the knowledge and the love experienced in the ordinary Christian life. What has already been said regarding Bonaventure's use of 'excessus mentis,' and even 'ecstasis,' applies with equal truth in the case of the Victorine.

Richard it is who develops the presentation of mystical problems, carried still further by Bonaventure, which is based upon the 'given' of Scripture. The Holy Ghost, the Source of all power and strength, revealed in Scripture as working within the soul of man to effect reunion with God, is the effective cause of the mystical experience: 'Hæc omnia operatur unus atque idem Spiritus'[73] he writes, after describing the illumination received by the contemplative, and the resultant ecstatic act of love. Again, 'Ecce tot hominum mentes tot modis informat, et omnium voluntates ad voluntatis suæ arbitrium sine aliqua coactione inclinat, ipso revelante, veritas agnoscitur, ipso inspirante, bonitas amatur.'[74] In this passage, the intellectual and the volitional elements constituting the mystical act of Contemplation are both attributed to the operation of the Holy Ghost. He has not developed to the same extent, the theology of the 'Dona Spiritus Sancti,' found in the Franciscan's works, but he certainly realizes the part played by the gifts, in relation to the mystical life. That the gifts, like the virtues, are general principles of spiritual activity, he admits in his *Benjamin Major,*[75] but in the *Commentary on the Apocalypse,* he has the following, which intimately connects them with the mystical experience: 'Agnus ergo, id est Christus, septem cornua, et septem oculos qui sunt septem spiritus Dei missi in omnem terram habet, quia per septiformem Spiritus sancti gratiam quibus vult regni spiritualis sublimitatem, et suæ veritatis agnitionem præbet. Quos vult ad regnandum exaltat, quos vult ad contemplandum fontem boni spiritualium bonorum radiis illustrat. Missi in omnem terram, ut de omni terra aliquos ad spiritualis regni celsitudinem exaltent, et ad spiritualium bonorum

73. Benjamin Major, Lib. III, cap. XXIV, col. 134.
74. Ibid., col. 133.
75. Op. cit., Lib. III, cap. XXIV, col 134. 'Toties namque servitutis nostrae debitum divina benignitas augescit, et sibi nos magis obnoxios reddit, quoties in nobis scientiae et sapientiae dona accrescit. Haec itaque et quaelibet ejusmodi in augmentum sunt debiti potius quam meriti,' etc.

contemplationem illuminent.'[76] Bonaventure's theology of the gifts is only the further development of this.

The quotations adduced do not, we repeat, fully represent any single one of Bonaventure's predecessors. Later theologians, by recourse to the same works, have built up entirely different theses. It is readily conceded that a closer examination, a more competent comparison of texts, a more scholarly acquaintance with Patristic Theology, may set Pseudo-Dionysius, Augustine, Gregory and the rest, in a different light: may prove ultimately that any or all of them granted the mystic a more exalted experience than that which Bonaventure is prepared to admit. But the fact remains that it is upon their authority that he himself hands down his teaching. He is persuaded that he has read their works aright, and that his doctrine is not his own, but one constructed by the master-minds of the Church, and inspired by Sacred Scripture. Does he interpret them correctly? On the authority of the foregoing attempt to pass with Bonaventure through his sources, we think he does.

St. Francis of Assisi, as we have said, stands for the Seraphic Doctor as a perfect type of the true mystic: a follower of Christ: a Saint who derived his strength in frequent communings with Him: one whose insight into Divine mysteries was wondrous indeed, but as nothing when compared with the love that absorbed him. All this is true, but from the point of view of written or spoken doctrine, with regard to the precise nature of mystical Contemplation, he seems to owe little or nothing to the 'Poverello.'[77] Francis is the example of the true man of mystic desire;[78] he is the example brought forward to show that God calls all, irrespective of any special vocation, to the mystical life;[79] he is the example of the perfect lover of the Crucified,[80] and doubtless his conception of the life led by the Founder of his Order did much to vitalize what we may call the 'Science of Sanctity' which he derived from tradition.

To give an example of what we mean — the doctrine that the highest mystical state is open to all who ardently desire it, and are willing to undertake the difficult task

---

76. Op. cit., Lib. II, cap. III, col. 757.

77. There is the little treatise on the contemplative life, but this contains nothing on the nature of Contemplation; it is a guide to those who wish to give themselves up to Contemplation. See The Writings of St. Francis of Assisi, trans. and edit. by P. Robinson, pp. 89-90.

78. See Legenda, cap. IX, pp. 530-3.

79. See Itin., cap. VII, n. 3, T. V, p. 312.

80. Ibid., Prologus, p. 295.

of preparing for it, was, until the advent of Francis, a theory at best. It seems to have been generally accepted that the true saint was the inhabitant of the cloister or convent, that there were heights of sanctity to be attained only after assuming the habit of the monk or nun. This general acceptance could doubtless have been proved false by the writings originating in the monasteries themselves. Nevertheless, the tendency seems to have been in the direction of making sanctity, and Contemplation, accessible only in seclusion. Francis appears as the religious democrat, breaking down, in deed and word, the barriers supposed to exist between class and class, in the sphere of the service of Christ: proving in his own life, and by his own example, the truth of the doctrine, enunciated centuries before by St. Augustine, that the 'minimi,' the 'little ones' who follow Christ Crucified, possess the same powers, in relation to fellowship with Him, as the more gifted. An ease in clothing one's religious thought in terms of philosophy or scientific theology is helpful, Francis would admit; so too, the inheritance of a traditional rule of life, aquired within the cloisters of the great Monastic Orders. But they are not essential. Those who follow Christ, possessing neither philosophy nor theology, nor yet again a traditional rule of life, may, by love and devotion, attain to equal heights of holiness. This was Francis' message to the world, and we consider that it is only by realizing the spirit in which it was delivered, that the other problem, concerning his attitude towards scientific study, can ever be rightly settled. That message could not fail to influence Bonaventure. It did not find set theological expression, it is true, but in Francis he saw one who did, in reality, come to the enjoyment of mystical communing with God, by the use of means which all possess. St. Francis became for him the concrete proof that Contemplation is accessible to all.

Whilst it is perfectly true that Bonaventure's Scholasticism would naturally incline him towards an impersonal and an objective presentation of his Mystical Theology, there can be little doubt that his knowledge of St. Francis' life served as a newer motive for reticence with regard to his own experiences in the religious life. It is acknowledged that Francis' reputation for sanctity depended upon the testimony of witnesses, rather than upon self-revelation. For Francis was markedly silent, not only with regard to the relatively unimportant secondary phenomena of Mysticism, but also where the more important love-union between his soul and God was concerned. Only now and again, when he realized that revealing of certain Divine communications would be of positive benefit to his brethren, did he break his wonted silence. On one occasion, he is said to have received in prayer a sure knowledge of the future glory of his Order, which knowledge he communicated to the Friars, excusing himself on the ground that charity constrained him to do so.[81] At another time, after his final exaltation on Mount Alvernia, when he went out into the world with the 'Stigmata' upon his body, he was constantly at pains to hide them, not only from the general public, but also from the Friars themselves. Imparted knowledge of future things, as well as the 'Stigmata,' were unimportant when compared with the delights experienced within his soul when mystically united to God. If he was unwilling to have the former known, he was even more silent where the all-important interior experience was concerned. He keenly felt the folly of publishing abroad the details of consolation received in mystic union, appreciating deeply the beauty of silence in such things. However holy his Friars might be, his will was that they should maintain a like silence: 'Blessed is the servant who treasures up in Heaven the good things which the Lord shows him, and who does not wish to manifest them to men through the hope of reward, for the Most High will Himself manifest His works to whomsoever He may please. Blessed is the servant who keeps the secrets of the Lord in his heart.' [82] Bonaventure has appreciated the sacredness of Francis' injunction. He calls others therefore to a mode of life which, he is convinced, is the highest offered by Christ to the devout soul; upon the relationship of his doctrine to the Gospel, not upon a personal proof of its worth, does he rely for its attractiveness and acceptance. It is the method dictated by faith—'habitus quo intellectus noster voluntarie captivatur in obsequium Christi.' [83]

* * *

The points of view from which we might attempt a criticism of the foregoing doctrines are obviously numerous. With the modern authors of manuals of Mystical Theology, we could dwell at length upon the question: Is Bonaventure sound in his directive principles, teaching as he does that mystical union with God is to be ardently desired, and that it is within the reach of all, independently of any special vocation? Again, when he explains the

81. See Celano, Legenda Prima, cap. XI (ed. Alencon), pp. 28-30.
82. Writings of St. Francis, trans. and edit. by P. Robinson, p. 19.
83. II S. D. XXIII, a. 1, q. 1, T. III, p. 471.

nature of the experience, unanimously associated with the mystics, as a supernatural enlightenment of the intellect, and an inflaming of the will through the agency of the Gifts of the Holy Ghost, rather than by some direct experience of God Himself, what value does his theory possess? Indeed, in view of the results of most recent psychological research, it has been questioned whether an explanation of Mysticism necessarily demands the introduction of grace in any form. Further questions can easily be multiplied, to include that which seeks definite proof of the objectivity of the experience claimed by the mystics, and described by Bonaventure, as well as the other, demanding proof of its utility in the religious or social spheres. Questions such as these, though by no means exhausting the number possible, and even reasonable, seem to be the most important. Now, even though we confine ourselves to those mentioned, it cannot be hoped that any fully conclusive arguments will be given. The difficulties surrounding the whole subject are too numerous, and too great, to admit of final dismissal in the little remaining space at our disposal. The primary end of this treatise has been to give Bonaventure his due place among those who have treated of the many problems of Mystical Theology. Since his day, other discoveries have been made, other channels of thought have been opened up, and we can scarcely hope that on his authority every problem will be solved, or that we shall find him prepared to meet the newly-framed objections. The best we can hope to do at present is to advance certain opinions, always where possible with special reference to the Franciscan's teaching, which may make for a clearer understanding of the situation.

Firstly, we may treat of Bonaventure's directive principles. We can discover no weighty reason for rejecting them as unsound, no matter how much they may be opposed to the teaching of certain schools of thought. When rightly understood, they in no way open up the path for any of the evils, to prevent which the more rigid directive principles were formulated. It is conceivable that the suppression of desire, and the presenting of the true mystical experience as a grace which God is willing to bestow only on a few chosen souls, would be more effective in checking a religious emotionalism altogether divorced from a willingness to tread the difficult ascetic way. Insistence upon these two ideas would likewise check the tendency to find in the mystical union merely a way of escape from the many disquieting elements in human life. Knowing that the mystical union may not be desired, knowing, too, that it is a gift which God bestows upon but few chosen souls, the vast majority would not be too eager to disregard all social obligations, in the endeavour to cultivate the more interior spirit. The desire, however, upon which Bonaventure dwells, is well balanced in itself and in its effects. We have already seen that, extending as it does to all the asceticism which forms the subject of the first part of this work, it is not likely to lead to spiritual presumption. If Mysticism were once admitted to be the outcome of a weariness of spirit, of a disgust with the evils of human life, or the result of an unwillingness to comply with social obligations, the encouraging of desire would be indeed regretted. It is hard to conceive of such disquiet or disgust, as in themselves, and apart from any other consideration, excusing the desire of 'resting with Christ.' Desire built upon such weariness of spirit is, for Bonaventure, a sign of imperfection, and not of perfection: 'Desiderium quiescendi cum Christo, potest venire ex duplici causa: vel propter tædium malorum præsentium, vel propter contemptum malorum et abundantiam prægustationum cœlestium. Primo modo est signum imperfectionis, non perfectionis, quia sic recusat laborare.' [84] Undoubtedly, in relation to God, the mystics must despise earthly things; they must deny to themselves many of the comforts coming from social existence, but this does not imply necessarily a downright disgust for the natural order of things. From his communings with God, the mystic, in Bonaventurian theology at least, must return to the service of others in a continued imitation of the Christ-life. The idea of benefiting others must be implicit in the desire of attaining to mystical union. It has already been shown that it is their strong hope of benefiting their fellow men that sustains the mystics, even in their absolute renunciation of the world.[85] Understood thus, the encouraging of desire does not seem to be in any way harmful.

Furthermore, admitting for the moment the truth of Bonaventure's other principle, that the mystical experience is open to all who will seriously labour for it, it is only natural that he should be so emphatic as he is with regard to desire. The two principles are perfectly logical. For the mystic quest needs the greatest strength of purpose; various difficulties must be overcome; the whole character must be rigidly trained, and it is only a strong

84. III S. D. XXIX, dub. VI, T. III, p. 654. This is his answer to the objection: 'Ad perfectam caritatem non pertineat dicere: Cupio dissolvi et esse cum Christo, sed magis: cupio laborare pro Christo.'

85. See Supra, chap. III.

desire that will ensure progress. Desire it is that gives vitality to all effort. Desire is the very key to conquest and success in every sphere of life. It is desire, moreover, that underlies the unwavering fixity of purpose which has characterized the victors of battles, external as well as internal. If all this be true, then, when the mystic's progress is viewed, with Bonaventure, as a continued struggle with the lower self, or with St. John of the Cross, as one that inevitably leads through the 'Dark Night of the Soul,' there must be, within the mystic, an ardent desire, which the increasing severity of the struggle only serves to intensify.

All these arguments, however, fall to the ground, once it is proved that the mystical union is 'de jure divino' given only to a few chosen souls. On this hypothesis, it would be as dangerous to encourage a desire for mystical union as it is to encourage the desire for miracle-working, or prophecy. But the hypothesis has not much to recommend it. As a matter of fact, theologians will never know definitely either way. God's ways of dealing with men are themselves incomprehensible. All we can say is, that Sacred Scripture does not anywhere repudiate Bonaventure's teaching that the mystical union is open to all, independently of any special vocation. On the contrary, Holy Scripture seems to form the basis of that teaching, for it presents to us a Christ delivering to all, without any special reservation either as to class or as to degree of perfection, the promise to abide within the faithful soul: 'If any one love me, he will keep my word, and my Father will love him, and we will come unto him, and will make our abode with him.' [86] And the mystical experience is but the fullest realization of this promise. On the other hand, it must not be inferred from Bonaventure's teaching that the mystical experience is offered to all without any reservation, that therefore those who do not attain to the heights of sanctity are blameworthy. He is well aware of the fact that the mystics are in the truest sense heroes of sanctity, and that not all men are prepared to make the stern uncompromising sacrifices which are the preliminaries to heroism. His positive attitude is that all the wealth of Christ's Love is open to those who will make the necessary sacrifice: to those who will be heroes. The answer he would give to the objection that it seems strange, that to all appearance only few attain to so high a level, would be in perfect accord with the response of the later author of the *Imitation of Christ:* 'This is

86. John, XIV, 23.

the reason why there are found so few contemplative persons, because few know how to separate themselves wholly from created and perishing things.' [87] All this seems to be more in accord with the universality of Christ's Love, than the other opinion which would make the fulness of His Charity, 'de jure,' the privilege of the few and the specially chosen.

Undoubtedly, we are often led by Sacred Scripture to think of God as calling souls to Himself by the interspersion among the many of men of extraordinary gifts and abilities. Moses and Paul are types. Among those who admit the mystic's claim to be valid, and who see in the mystic the veritable religious genius, there are those who would put him in the same category. The mystic's privilege is similar to those other privileges, of which St. Paul speaks: 'To one indeed, by the Spirit, is given the word of wisdom: and to another, the word of knowledge, according to the same Spirit; . . . . to another, the working of miracles; to another prophecy; to another the discerning of spirits; to another, diverse kinds of tongues; to another, interpretation of speeches.' [88] St. Paul refers to special gifts divided by the Spirit, 'according as He will,' and for the spiritual edification of the whole Church. But the mystical experience is none of these things; it is the fulness of the charity of Christ, and it is of that same charity that the Apostle of the Gentiles speaks, when he writes: 'If I speak with the tongues of men, and of angels, and have not charity, I am become as sounding brass, or a tinkling cymbal. And if I should have prophecy and should know all mysteries, and all knowledge, and if I should have all faith, so that I could remove mountains, and have not charity, I am nothing.' [89] Common sense dictates that the extraordinary gifts referred to by St. Paul are not within the reach of all men. The prophet cannot call all to a share in his power of prophecy; nor can the worker of miracles call all to a reception of a like gift; but the perfect lover of Christ can bid all to follow him in his path, with an equal hope of final union with God. It is only a persistence in finding in the unessential phenomena, which are sometimes concomitants of the mystical experience, something more than the purely subordinate and the unnecessary, that has led, we think, to any confusion on these points.

However, these points are of relative unimportance. The question is far more important which asks the value Bonaventure's

---

87. Op. cit., Bk. III, chap. 31.
88. I Cor., XIII, 8-10.
89. Ibid., XIII, 1-2.

theory possesses as an explanation of the mystical union itself. It has been seen that he views the mystical union as an objective fact, and explains it by a supernatural enlightenment, and an inflaming of the will. The fact that he introduces supernatural agencies marks him off from others who have treated of the problem from a non-theological point of view, but in stressing these two characteristics of the mystical state, he is really at one with practically all who have examined the problem.

William James is probably to be accepted as voicing the universal belief among psychologists, when he singles out the noetic quality, as one of the marks characterizing genuine mystical states. He writes: 'Although so similar to states of feeling, mystical states seem to those who experience them to be also states of knowledge. They are states of insight into depths of truth unplumbed by the discursive intellect. They are illuminations, revelations, full of significance and importance, all inarticulate though they remain; and as a rule they carry with them a curious sense of authority for after-time.' [90] But the first of the marks by which he attempts to classify any state as mystical is that of ineffability, in which peculiarity, he declares: 'Mystical states are more like states of feeling than like states of intellect.'[91] He continues: 'No one can make clear to another who has never had a certain feeling, in what the quality or worth of it consists. One must have musical ears to know the value of a symphony; one must have been in love one's self to understand a lover's state of mind.' [92] Here he touches upon the precise cause of the ineffability of the mystic states. They are ineffable, because they are states of love, of will-union with God. Dr. Moberly, who, though not a Catholic, has a sound appreciation of the mystic union, has also singled out light and love as the characteristics of the experience the mystic strives to realize: 'It is an inward light which makes itself manifest as character; a direct communion of love which is also, to the fullest extent, wholly rational at once and wholly practical; it is as much knowledge as love, and love as knowledge.' [93]

These two characteristics, which seem to be universally accepted, Bonaventure traces to supernatural agencies, as we have said. There are those who would declare that he has not

90. The Varieties of Religious Experience, London, 1902, pp. 380-1. This is valuable as coming from a dispassionate witness.
91. Ibid., p. 380.
92. Ibid.
93. Atonement and Personality, London, 1901, p. 314. No one, we venture to think, will quarrel with this.

gone far enough in this direction; that the mystical experience is only explicable on the hypothesis of some direct experience of God Himself. On the other hand, there are many who wish to rule out the doctrine of grace altogether. Bonaventure does not in any way limit the possibilities of Divine activity, when the soul is concerned. That God could grant some direct experience of Himself in this life, he is prepared to admit, but his position is, that He grants the mystic joys through the medium of certain interior effects. It is doubtful whether, in ultimate analysis, the best accredited mystics have described their experiences otherwise than by the introduction of some such medium. St. John of the Cross, we are told, though not a scholar, was intimately acquainted with the *Summa* of St. Thomas Aquinas,[94] and he nowhere contradicts the categorical statement made by that Doctor: 'In contemplatione Deus videtur per medium, quod est lumen sapientiæ, mentem elevans ad cernenda divina; non autem ut ipsa divina essentia immediate videatur.'[95] The question, however, naturally arises: Does love, whose immediacy Bonaventure acknowledges, need a medium whereby it may be united to the Object, which is God? If there be no momentary intuition of God on the part of the intellect, the medium does seem to be necessary, to arouse in the will an act of love more or less proportioned to its Object. To the finite intelligence, God is still hidden in the depths of His Being, and the intensity of the soul's love is more explicable on the ground of some such medium as the gift of Wisdom.

But need the supernatural element be brought to bear upon the problem at all?[96] Are there not experiences in the lives of people other than the Christian saints, akin in nature to that which these claim for themselves, yet in connection with which it would be futile to introduce the supernatural? These supernatural agencies of Bonaventure admirably explain the mark of passivity characterizing mystic states. William James has once more expressed a conclusion arrived at by most psychologists who have been interested in Mysticism, when he writes: 'Although the oncoming of mystical states may be facilitated by preliminary voluntary operations, as by fixing the attention, or going through

---

94. See The Ascent of Mount Carmel, trans. by D. Lewis, London, 1906, Introduction by B. Zimmerman, p. 13, and p. 17.

95. De Veritate, q. XVIII, a. 1, ad 4 (ed. Parmae), T. X, p. 275.

96. To present possible misunderstanding we may here assert that we do not even consider the possibility of a true Mysticism without the Supernatural: without Grace. Here the question is asked and discussed merely because non-Catholic writers frequently regard Supernatural Mysticism as a species of Mysticism. To us it is the only kind.

certain bodily performances, or in any other ways which manuals of mysticism prescribe; yet when the characteristic sort of consciousness once has set in, the mystic feels as if his own will were in abeyance, and indeed sometimes as if he were grasped and held by a superior power.' [97] God, working on the soul through the instrumentality of the gifts, will, as we say, explain the mark of passivity. In mystic states, as Bonaventure frequently declares, the soul is to be regarded as acted upon, rather than as itself acting. Where we feel Bonaventure's theology to be especially weak is in this, that he does not set forth the mystic experience in the light of the possibilities of unaided intellect or will. His psychology does not extend to those intuitions into truth, those states akin to religious ecstasy, which appear in lives not professedly religious, or in lives which are even vigorously anti-religious. His attitude, it is true, is uncompromising enough. His only genuine mystical experience is essentially the full development of grace; it is moreover specifically Christian: 'Omnes alii a Christianis sunt sicci ab ista gratia.' [98] Had his psychology been as advanced as is the psychology of the present, he would probably have attempted to show that in the genuine mystical experience, which is inseparable from grace, there is an element differentiating it from every other. Unfortunately, he is silent.

That such states exist, akin in nature to the mystical state he describes, there can be no question. Instances will be found in practically every treatise on religion written from a psychological point of view.[99] They are very frequently personal accounts, and they point to experiences, similar to those which Bonaventure declares to be so essentially the effect of grace. Others, besides the Saints, have spoken of themselves as the subjects of certain exaltations of mind, without abnormal physical concomitants, resulting in the delights attributed by theologians to the will-union of the soul with God. Often it is non-religious in the means of its production, and non-religious, or only vaguely religious, in its content. Sometimes such experiences are produced by drugs.[100] The more the possibilities of the unaided intellect and will are established and multiplied by psychological research, so much the

---

97. The Varieties of Religious Experience, p. 381. Yes! And the power is the power of God.

98. Sermo de Sabbato Sancto, Sermo 1, T. IX, p. 269.

99. Thus, see The Varieties of Religious Experience, pp. 383 sqq. The author quotes many instances.

100. William James declares that nitrous oxide and ether, especially nitrous oxide, when sufficiently diluted with air, stimulate the mystical consciousness in an extraordinary degree. See his Varieties, etc., p. 387. De Quincey's opium reveries will also be recalled.

more tempted do writers become, to see in the exaltation of the poet, the intuition of the metaphysician, and in the experience of the Christian mystic, but various forms of one and the same phenomenon. We must, consequently, it is argued, cease to assign to grace a necessary part in the mystical experience. The differences discovered can be traced to purely natural origins: to varieties of temperament, and varieties of previous training. Thus, the mind already attuned to metaphysics, will be the subject of experiences of which the primary character is metaphysical; to a mind attuned to religion by years of discursive meditation on matters religious, the experience will assume a definitely religious character.

The task before those who wish to establish the essential connection between grace and the mystical union resolves itself into this—they must prove that there is in that act in which their Theology centres an element which is not present in the act of which the poet or the metaphysician speaks. The favourite mode of differentiating the genuine religious state from the non-religious is by the application of the pragmatic test. Within the Church it amounts to this: that by its *fruits,* in the religious or social spheres, we shall be able to distinguish the genuine from the spurious. Only the genuine variety will be attributed to grace. For example, the genuine mystical experience has not been enjoyed, if it results in the embracing of religious truths directly opposed to the accepted Rule of Faith. Mystical experience will not be genuine, if it causes the subject to enter into competition with the *Magisterium* of the Church: if it leaves its sphere of the personal and the experimental, and becomes didactic in opposition to already defined dogmas. Bonaventure knows this test which was formulated by Richard of St. Victor, but he applies it, like the Victorine, not with special reference to purely psychological posibilities, but rather to show that those who base heretical dogmas upon supposed Divine illuminations, are charlatans; to him, the claims of such people have absolutely no objective value. In like manner, the genuine mystic, after his experience, must still be subject to the general laws of morality. If he fails in these, and in similar tests, which easily suggest themselves when it is remembered that the mystic is a member of Society, whose beliefs and laws are already established, his claim is absolutely rejected.

Now, we are far from denying that these tests possess a certain value. But are they sufficient of themselves, so that, after applying them, we can, with certainty, say that this or that is the genuine mystical experience: it appears as the consummation of the life of grace—can we say therefore, that true Mysticism and grace are inseparable? Such a conclusion seems to take too much for granted, and it neglects the truth that even those who have been bound to God by the closest ties can fall from grace. Presumably, two men might be the subjects of an identical experience. The one, when he begins to translate his experience into thought and activity might, on the authority of his intuition, found a new religion, or become the greatest enemy of law and order. His free will, of which he is not deprived by union with God, can be responsible for all kinds of deviations from truth and rectitude. The other might return from his experiences with a firmer grasp of tenets already accepted by the majority as true, and might appear as a more vigorous champion of the moral code. After-behaviour, to which the tests are applied, might easily be traced therefore, in both cases, to something other than the mystical experience itself. This being so, we feel that we must look further, for some intrinsic difference, if we are to establish the relationship claimed to exist between Mysticism and grace.

Bonaventure is weak here, in that he does not explicitly help us. Implicitly, however, he does do so, for, to establish the diversity of the experiences claimed by the Saints on the one hand and by these who are strangers to sanctity on the other, we can look to the general directive principles he sets forth. It is more reasonable to suppose that different modes of life will culminate in different results. What we have already said of Bonaventure's asceticism shows sufficiently that the would-be mystic must not merely attune his mind by meditation to religious truths: he must lead a practical life of heroic devotion; he must enter into the life of Christ, by the practice of His virtues. Involving, as it does, not a continuous change of thought, but an entire change of life, it is only reasonable to suppose, we repeat, that this preliminary asceticism will lead to an experience, differing in nature from that which is the culmination of ideas, imaginings and other things, which have not their root in action—in genuine change of life. It is impossible to suppose that the drug-taker, with no thought of moral values, or—if we may be pardoned for mentioning the drug-taker and the metaphysician in the same connection — the metaphysician, whose sphere is that of pure thought, will attain to precisely the same experience as the supernatural mystic who, by heroic, unceasing toil, has substituted virtue for vice, sacrifice for ease and comfort: who has transmuted thought itself into prayer, by relating it directly to the Transcendent God-head.

It is readily admitted that even this is not fully conclusive. The result is at best a probability, but the probability seems to be of a higher degree than that obtained by the application of the above mentioned tests. It does not meet the case of the poet, for example, who, however explicit in his rejection of all religious values, may find his true inward life in the continued contemplation of beauty: or of the metaphysician, who discovers his in prolonged concentration of thought. To the poet or the metaphysician, beauty and thought may mean all that the cultivation of virtue, or the constant denial of the self, mean to the Christian ascetic. However, these remarks are offered, not in the hope of settling the problems raised. For the Christian, the path is an easy and a true one; it is that of *faith*. We believe by faith that they who wish to enjoy in fulness the delights of communion with God must, in some way, be conjoined with Him. It is grace alone that effects the radical union between God and the soul; it will therefore be through grace alone that we can come to the perfection of that union with Him in this life which is the goal of the Mystic Quest.

Intimately connected with the above problem, though differing from it in many respects, is the next question, which asks whether all these states, be their origins in the supernatural or in the natural, possess any objective value: whether the subject has derived his experience from a genuine trans-subjective source. When the mystics relate their experiences, are they merely relating the results of pure imaginings, are they victims of certain diseases, or are they merely conscious of a store of past experiences accumulated during a long period of time? In determining this, the impressions of truthfulness, sanity and reality, left by the reading of the reports of the great Christian mystics, will be of the greatest importance. Here especially, we are inclined to regret Bonaventure's impersonal method of expression. Personal testimony, coming from a man of his temperament, from one fully developed intellectually, robust in his physical constitution, little given to vain imaginings, inclined to distrust the psycho-physical concomitants of Mysticism, or at least insistent upon the fact that they are unessential—from such a one, personal testimony would have been of the greatest worth. Dogmatically, of course, his mystical experience is trans-subjective: it has its origin outside the mind, in the activity of God upon the soul. According to him, the soul knows, and is convinced, that it has received something which it did not possess before.

There are few who are inclined to doubt the good faith of the greater mystics, but their good faith alone, their conviction that these experiences have a trans-subjective origin, does not prove sufficient. Fortunately, in these latter days, there is no need to dwell at length upon the once popular method of making certain diseases, especially mental diseases, responsible for the experiences claimed. A St. Teresa is no longer seriously regarded as a hysterical patient, nor a St. Francis as a victim of any other form of nervous disorder. Even the discovery that the majority of the mystics have been physically weak, or even neurotic, does not serve to establish the relationship of cause and effect between disease and mystical experience. As Báron Von Hügel has pointed out, practically every manifestation of genius is accompanied by certain psycho-physical phenomena which point to diseases of some kind or other: 'In such cases as Kant and Beethoven, a classifier of humanity according to its psycho-physical phenomena alone, would put these great discoverers and creators, without hesitation, among hopeless and useless hypochondriacs.'[101] Yet, as he so rightly continues: 'The truth of their ideas, and the work of their lives have to be measured by quite other things than by this, their neural concomitance and cost.'[102] The mystic is, in the sense explained, the *religious genius.* He has been dominated by one central idea, and has worked towards a definite end and object. It is more likely that whatever abnormalities he betrays, instead of being the cause, are but the inevitable consequences of the continual subordination of the flesh to the spirit.[103] Disease in the case of the great Christian mystics, as in the case of the genius in spheres other than religious, is incapable of sustained effort; it is incapable 'per se' of the prolonged subordination of all interests to the attainment of one ideal. From this particular quarter it would seem there is little fear that anything definite will come to disprove the trans-subjective value of the mystical experience.

The theory which centres upon the subconscious self, that psychic state whose powerful operations and rich content are being revealed by the latest psychological research, produces far more potent arguments. It is the content of the subconscious self that the mystic experiences, in his wonderful communings,

---

101. The Mystical Element of Religion, vol. II, p. 42.
102. Ibid.
103. We cannot reasonably hope to find a man who spends years in self-denial in the same state of bodily health as one who never dreams of bodily asceticism.

so we are told. There is little doubt that psychology can become a good friend to religion. This examination of the subconscious self will do much to eliminate the true from the false, the results of subjective imaginings from genuine illuminations. It will probably, if rightly directed, serve to remove the many misconceptions surrounding the subject of Mysticism. But it must not suppose too much. It cannot be denied that very often so-called visions, locutions, and other secondary phenomena of Mysticism, are ultimately traceable to past experiences, long since forgotten by the subject. So too, it is possible that when he who has received a genuine mystical experience tries to translate it into human language, many ideas, or facts, stored away in the subconscious mind, spring up and are spontaneously pressed into service. Will all this, however true it may be, prove satisfactorily that the will-union of the soul with God, which lies beneath all these things, is itself to be explained as purely subjective—with no relation to anything outside the mind? We have seen Bonaventure, with other dogmatic mystics, declaring emphatically that to attain to mystical union, the soul must transcend itself; it must rise above all sense and intellectual knowledge, or at the most, it must use such knowledge as a stepping stone to something higher. On the volitional side, it must dismiss all affection for creaturely objects. Indeed, it would be difficult to discover language more forcible than theirs, to express the truth that it is in a communing with an essentially extra-mental Object that the mystical quest is brought to a successful issue. This is always represented as an experience of an Absolute Being, beyond the limits of the self, attained only after the reduction of the self to a state of sheer instrumentality in relation to the transcendent Godhead. Before tracing this ineffable experience to a purely subjective source, we must surely examine our right to do so. They — the mystics — alone have experienced that of which they speak, and they declare it has objective value. True, the mystical life has already been described as the attempt to realize the inherent possibilities of that which is within: of grace and its supernatural concomitants. But grace is not co-natural; it is the mysterious means whereby God communicates Himself to the human soul. From that God, through the use of the graces bestowed, Bonaventure declares, the mystic receives his illuminations; with that God, through a like means, the mystic feels united.

To us it would seem that we do not possess sufficient data to warrant a denial of the objectivity of the experience itself. If the mystics cannot fully persuade us that they really have consciously communed with God Himself, our only logical position would be the admission that it is still an open question. This is the least that seems demanded by sound reasoning. For it is nearly always admitted in the case of those forms of genius, whose intuitions into things are at times akin to the mystic experience itself, that they are intuitions of objective worth, although they are beyond the normal reach. Art, for example, in its highest forms, is rightly regarded, not as a subjective figment, without objective reference, but as an apprehension, however subjective in its medium, of a trans-subjective beauty, existent outside the artist. The question naturally arises: Is Mysticism to be the only sphere in which value is divorced from all objective existence? Can we readily attach the stigma of self-hallucination to the mystic, when he emphatically asserts that his experience is not only sought after, but attained, in a manner only explicable on the hypothesis of objective worth? The stronger position seems to be held by the religious genius himself.

We come now to the last point. This has reference to the utility of setting forth, as Bonaventure does, such a secret, hidden, and ineffable union with God as the goal of the Christian life. That it has its dangers he is quite willing to admit. Even love can be disordered. But the dangers of the mystical life are not necessary concomitants. Most of us, Catholic and non-Catholic, are prepared to admit with Dr. Moberly that Our Divine Lord appears as the Example of the true Mystic, that He alone, albeit in a transcendent manner, has realized *all* that Mysticism and mystics have aimed at, that in Him, moreover, that perfect realization evidently means a harmony, a sanity, a fitly proportioned completeness.[104] In those who strive to imitate Him, there will be a certain amount of disproportion no doubt, and from the disproportion will spring the dangerous elements. The mystic who has left the world for example, not out of disgust, but with the sound enough idea of gaining, in solitude, that which he cannot reach amid the cares and worries of the world, may begin, after success in his efforts, to despise all social activity. Here is a want of true proportion.

Of course our appreciation of the value of the mystical experience will depend entirely upon our attitude towards religion as a whole, as well as upon our pre-conceived notions of what it is.

---

104. Atonement and Personality, p. 314. In other words: Our Divine Lord is the Supreme and Perfect Exemplar of all that we are to strive after.

As described by Bonaventure, the supreme delights of the experience for the mystic himself cannot be denied. Nor can we deny the utility of all the preparation Bonaventure deems absolutely necessary. In the stern fight for the supremacy of the spirit over the flesh, in the rigid asceticism, demanding so much energy and patience, unsuspected depths of character are revealed. The discipline the individual mystic voluntarily imposes upon himself, cannot but benefit him.

But were his religion of a type that is wholly passive, we should have good reason for questioning its utility, from the point of view of the community. To accept it as useful from this point of view, we must show that in its best forms it somehow reacts in favour of the many. Nor is this difficult. The number of the mystics and their rôle in the life of Christian Society, prove that it is from them that Christianity has derived much of its vitality. They have stood firmly by the great realities of religion, and have done their best to communicate their convictions to others. Within the Church they have championed the great truth, frequently forgotten in times of prosperity, that the religious life is primarily from within. At times, when the outward splendour of the Church was at its highest point of magnificence, they have preached that the breath of Divine Life was absent, and that that absence was due to the lack of interior prayer. History is indeed kind to Mysticism in its best forms, and it bears witness to its utility. It shows us a St. Francis returning from his mystic communings with God, to preach with wonderful results to a fast-degenerating people: a St. Teresa, even in her seclusion, holding a leading position in the religious life of the Spain of her day. Francis and Teresa are but two out of many.[105]

With special reference to Bonaventure, we cannot help remarking, before we conclude, that he champions this genuine and inward spirituality, he makes it the basis of his greater dogmatic works, precisely because he realized, that if his Order was to be of any utility to the World, it must draw its life from this source. He knew well that when this inward communing with God, with all that it implies, is held up as the goal of Christian endeavour, all hypocrisy and deceit must disappear. He knew that the very

105. For evidence as to the social service rendered by the mystics, see Royce, J., The World and the Individual, New York, 1900, vol. I, pp. 85-7; Jones, R. M., Studies Mystical Religion, London, 1909, pp. 30-31. Underhill, E., Mysticism, London, 1911, pp. 209 sqq., 512 sqq. This evidence is the stronger since it comes from non-Catholic sources. Within the Church the value of the true mystic has always been recognized.

evils, which he so bitterly lamented, and which threatened the Order's existence from within and without, were due to the absence of this spirituality: that the Franciscan ideal, mystical in its origin, demands a mystical approach. And the history of the Order bears testimony to the truth of his conviction. In the absence, or universal neglect, of this inward spirituality, it has sunk to its lowest depths. When this spirituality has been present, there has been a return to the primitive ideal, and it has produced men after the pattern of St. Francis of Assisi. The world cannot but benefit by the multiplication of such types. For the secret of the wonderful influence of the 'Poverello' lies in this, that he teaches men how to interpret Christ. In a personal interpretation of Christ, or in the adoption of so genuine an interpretation as that of Francis, the possibilities, in the purely religious or in the social sphere are endless. It is Mysticism that has revealed and proved those possibilities.

CONCLUSIONS

On the authority of the foregoing, we now feel in a position to make a few general statements, covering the work already done. These statements have been grouped together under the following headings, viz:—

(1) The principles of Bonaventure's Mystical Theology.

(2) The sources of his teaching, (*a*) General, and (*b*) Particular.

(3) The chief characteristics of his doctrine.

(1) *The Principles of St. Bonaventure's Mystical Theology*:—

The opinion that Bonaventure is a mystical writer of great importance seems to possess a solid foundation, whilst the suggestion that he has made but rare references to the subject of Mysticism can only be accounted for, by the very ill-defined nature of the subject itself. If Mysticism deal with the possibilities of Divine Love in relation to the human soul, the amount of material to be gathered from his works is extensive. It is quite true that unlike his admirer of a later date, Gerson, he has not been the author of a work which may strictly be called a *Compendium* of Mystical Theology, but he has expressed definite ideas with regard to the many problems confronting every writer on matters mystical. The fact that his teaching is so scattered did not prevent it from exercising, as we hope to show in a continuation of the present work, a great influence upon subsequent mystical thought.[1]

1. A little has already been done on this point, but, as has been noted, many works, now proved to be of different authorship, are introduced. Any treatise on his influence upon subsequent mystical thought should, we think, make the edition of his Opera, published at Quarrachi, the starting point. Bonaventure's dogmatic works were displaced by those of Duns Scotus, but his Opuscula Mystica were always popular within the Franciscan Order. Indeed, they formed the models of many beautiful treatises, which, in turn, exercised a great influence. Bonaventure determined the direction taken by later spiritual writings, emanating from Franciscan sources. These writings, are, almost without exception, Christocentric and affective in character. They exhibit the specifically Franciscan love of Our Lord's Humanity, and the devotion to His Passion. We may mention a few of the better known works:—There is Peccam's beautiful lyric, Philomena, undoubtedly inspired by Bonaventurian thought. (Printed in the Opera of St. Bonaventure, T. VIII. pp. 669 sqq) .The Septem Itineribus Aeternitatis, and the Stimulus Amoris, are also well known, and they contain whole passages taken verbally from the genuine works of the Seraphic Doctor. (They will be found in the Vatican Edition of the Opera). The Meditationes Vitae Christi, (also contained in the Vatican Edition, and frequently translated into various European languages), had a widespread influence throughout Europe. (See Oliger, L., Le Meditationes Vitae Christi del Pseudo-

The Seraphic Doctor has viewed the whole spiritual life of man objectively, and he sees in the exalted experience of the Christian mystic the culmination of the life begun within every soul acknowledging Christ's dominion, by the first outpouring of Sanctifying Grace. Grace and its concomitants, the Virtues and the Gifts, make the soul capable of responding to the advances of Divine Love, and Bonaventure's Mysticism is based upon the conception that in such a response the soul is subject to a vital development in relationship to the Divine. It is first cleansed from sin and its consequences; then it is illumined; finally it enters into a secret union with the only Object conceived of as capable of satisfying its cravings after happiness.

As a preliminary to the mystical life stands an asceticism demanding genuine labour and continued effort: an asceticism, which views the grace of God as working in, and through man indeed, but not in such a way as to render conative activity in any degree the less necessary. Consequently, Bonaventure's Mystical Theology offers no short road to a fuller communion of the Christian soul with God. This lies beyond the arduous paths of Purgation and Illumination.

The Supreme Guide presented by the Franciscan's Mysticism is Jesus Christ in His twofold Nature, Divine and Human. Our Lord is the Guide in word and deed. Only by imitating the many virtues of which Christ in His Human Nature is the Exemplar, only by attempting to re-live His Life in some fashion, can the soul enter into communion with the Divinity. An imitation of Christ, determined as to details by diversities of vocation, is the *Via Illuminativa* which constitutes what may be called the 'bridge' between the purgative life and the more developed life of the Christian Saints.

Bonaventure's Mysticism proceeds by way of Meditation and Prayer. Meditation is not the mere intellectual satisfaction derived from the reflection upon truths, even though these truths be

---

Bonaventure, Arezzo, 1922). Ubertino da Casale, in his Arbor Vitae made great use of Bonaventure's Lignum Vitae (see Callaey, F. Étude sur Ubertin de Casale), and it would be interesting to discover any indebtedness on the part of the other 'Spiritual,' Jacopone da Todi, whose beautiful Laude are well known. Lastly, there are the Visiones et Consolationes of Angela of Foligno. (See B. Angelae Fulginatis, Vita et Opuscula, Fulginiae, MDCCXIV). Through many of the works first mentioned, Bonaventure influenced some of our own English mystical writers, e. g. Rolle and Hilton. It has likewise been asserted that he inspired the author of the Imitation of Christ to a large extent. (See Symphorien, P., L'Influence spirituelle de S. Bonaventure et l'Imitation de Jésus-Christ, Paris, 1923). More documentary evidence is needed, however, to prove this conclusively. It is hoped that in a further and more popular study new facts with regard to Bonaventure's influence upon mystical writings will be brought forward.

of a specifically religious and devotional order. The Meditation conceived as leading up to Contemplation should be called a life: an endeavour to live in strict accord with truth. The basic principle of Bonaventure's teaching on Meditation is, that holiness in the will, and in action, must be the fruit of truth in thought, if that truth is to be of any benefit in the spiritual life. This being so, he can offer as material for Meditation, not only the Scriptures, and the specifically religious dogmas with their multitudinous consequences which go to make up the science of Theology, but also the more philosophical search after traces of God in Nature. His doctrine of Prayer springs from a sense of God's Love, and Mercy, and Omnipresence on the one hand, and from a realization of human frailty and shortcomings on the other.

The Seraphic Doctor has likewise well-defined ideas as to what takes place in the mystical experience itself, and the proximate dispositions required for its enjoyment. The mystical experience in his Theology is represented as the reward which Divine Love bestows upon all who have been willing to respond fully to the graces working in and through them: the reward offered to all who are animated by an ardent desire of a fuller communion with the Divine, and are prepared to undergo the rigorous self-training implied in that desire. His theological system acknowledges no clear-cut distinction between the mystic and the non-mystic, on the basis of special predestination or vocation. In theory, it admits that the highest experiences of the Saints are open to all, though it grants that in practice few do attain to such experiences, because of the great difficulty of the work demanded in preparation. Bonaventure has analyzed the act of Contemplation, and finds it impossible to subscribe to the opinion that the mystical phenomenon is to be explained by any form of *direct* experience of God Himself. It is not, in a real sense, a foretaste of the Beatific Vision. To explain what takes place, he has recourse to the potentialities of the many Graces coming from God. The illumination claimed by the Christian mystics is traced to the Gift of Understanding. This endows the soul with a more penetrating knowledge of truths already received by faith: a knowledge which is never divorced from faith. The element in the mystical experience which makes it ineffable is traced to the Divine working upon the will, through the agency of the Gift of Wisdom. The use of the gift of Wisdom results in a mysterious experimental knowledge of the truths contemplated. Moreover, it enables the will to send forth its love in all intensity to the God

Who is still hidden in the depths of His Being from the finite intelligence, even though this intelligence be the recipient of special illuminations. Without seeing God, the soul enjoys a fuller union with Him than is possible in lower levels of the spiritual life. Bonaventure is willing to acknowledge more than this in the instances of Moses and St. Paul, on account of the exalted position they held with regard to the Old and New Dispensations, but the normal experience of the Christian Mystics is believed to be such as he describes. It implies no Pantheistic merging of the being of the human soul into the Being of God; nor does it necessarily imply any wonderful psycho-physical phenomena. From such a mysterious union with God the mystic derives his strength to fulfil his special vocation in life.

(2) *Sources of his Teaching.*

(*a*) *General.*

The doctrine Bonaventure offers is one which he believes will reveal itself to him who makes a devout study of Holy Writ. It centres upon the promise made by Christ to abide within the faithful soul, and the mystic union is but the highest fulfilment in this life of that promise. In an especial manner, he has favoured the teaching of the Synoptic Gospels, finding in them the authority for the importance attached to the imitation of Christ's earthly life, and to the attempt to discover traces of God in the created world. His Mystical Theology is illustrated by the vast amount of literature bequeathed to the Christian Church by his predecessors. Common Tradition guides him when he dwells upon the value of Asceticism in his understanding of the term, and when he develops his doctrine of Mediate Contemplation. It also guides him, when he insists upon the need of desire in relation to mystical union with God, and when he emphatically asserts that such a union is not reserved to any particular class of men, but is open to all. Finally, Tradition has guided him in his description of the twofold element in the mystical act, the intellectual and the volitional.

(*b*) *Particular.*

In this exposition, however, there are distinct traces of individual influences. The writings of Pseudo-Dionysius, to whom priority of place has been given throughout, for reasons already stated, cause him to declare with especial insistence that the God with Whom the mystic in some mysterious fashion finally enters into union, is infinitely raised above all knowledge received of Him. These writings stand as valued authority for the statement, that God Himself is not directly seen in the act of Contemplation. From Pseudo-Dionysius, he has borrowed the terminology under which he describes the three ways of Purgation, Illumination, and Union.

Saint Augustine's influence, without doubt, saves his Mystical Theology from the extreme interpretation given to the Pseudo-Dionysian 'Docta Ignorantia' at a later date.[2] With this great Doctor of the Western Church, Bonaventure regards the things of sense as pledges of spiritual realities, and the acquisition of all forms of knowledge as a valuable preliminary to a final emptying of the self. Augustinian Theology and Philosophy form the background of his mystical thought.

In Gregory, the Franciscan theologian has found a forcible exponent of the voluntarism he champions: using the term voluntarism to denote the doctrine which emphasizes the need of conative activity, in relation to Grace. With Pseudo-Dionysius, Gregory is another authority for the statement that in Mystical Contemplation the direct Object seen, is not God Himself.

SS. Anselm and Bernard are responsible to no little degree for the personal warmth of his religious thought, and for his championship of the devotion to the Humanity of Christ. They have taught him to unite speculative thought with most affective piety.

Hugo of St. Victor has continued Augustinian tradition, whilst his interpretation of Pseudo-Dionysian theology has influenced Bonaventure's own understanding of that same theology.

From Hugo's disciple, Richard, Bonaventure has inherited the tendency to schematization, and the insistence that the Gifts of the Holy Ghost play an important part in the act of mystical Contemplation.

The whole of Bonaventure's Mystical Theology is coloured by the spiritual traditions set up by the Founder of his Order, Francis of Assisi. He has continued Francis' moderate teaching with regard to bodily penances. Needless to say, Francis' conception of Poverty is the primary element in Bonaventure's Asceticism. He exhibits Francis' personal love of Christ, the Saviour of the World, and retains much of that definitely Franciscan philosophy,

2. See Vansteenberghe, E., Autour de la docte ignorance. Une controverse sur la Théologie Mystique au XVe siècle, Münster i. W., 1915. This controversy will find its place in the proposed continuation of this work.

which refuses to see in creaturely objects so many barriers in the mystic path. With Francis of Assisi, Bonaventure, the Mystical Theologian, directs the soul into wide spiritual channels, counselling, not only the withdrawal into the self in order to come into communion with God, but also the loving meditation upon every existing relationship between God and the outside World. Bonaventure is the Scholastic exponent of that belief in the preëminence of love, which characterized every deed of the 'Poverello.'

(3) *Characteristics of his Doctrine.*

We do not therefore claim for the Seraphic Doctor any great originality. Nor do we affirm that his Mysticism has attained to the heights of Augustinian thought. In the sphere of Mysticism, he is what he professes to be in the sphere of Dogma—an exponent of received traditions. Yet we can and do assert that he has given to the religious world a teaching unspoilt by the vagaries and abuses which have brought the subject of Mysticism into disrepute: a teaching which will be admitted to be at once sane, and sound, and powerful in its practical possibilities.

Whilst it must be called a Supernatural Mysticism, it is not a debased form of Supernaturalism, since it safeguards the truth that even in relation to the most inward activities, the human soul never surrenders its co-natural capacities. It receives indeed great graces from God, but the reception of such graces in no way destroys its freedom as to after-behaviour. On the external side it is free from what has been called by non-Catholic writers a debased Supernaturalism, inasmuch as Bonaventure's Mystical Theology is far from being merely the sum total of those extraordinary phenomena which seem, at times, to be unworthy of the sacred relationship existing between the Supreme Being and human nature in general.

In so far as Quietism is to be identified with the tendency to destroy the efficacy of human effort, and to neglect the lessons taught by Christ in His life upon earth, his teaching is definitely anti-Quietistic. It is Christocentric, presenting Our Lord as the 'Bridge' uniting in Himself the Human with the Divine: the Leader, bringing men by His own example into fuller communion with the Father.

It is a Mystical Theology characterized by an optimistic view of the World, and of the destiny of the human race. For it does not withdraw men from the world, in the belief that Christian Perfection is attainable only in strictest retirement, but it upholds the idea, that a wider life can be conducive to higher spiritual realities. Because of this optimism, the world of sense offers no stumbling block to the mystic in his path: neither does a life spent in the service of others.

It is non-Pantheistic, for it insists that even in the most exalted states of union the soul loses nothing of its own being.

Whilst we admit that Bonaventure's teaching possesses certain limitations—it does not, for example, examine the mystical problem from a psychological point of view—we claim that he has handed down a teaching which should not fail to find an honourable place in the history of mystical thought. His is a Mysticism which is simple and practical, being in ultimate analysis, nothing more than the dedication of life to the service of God: making for the best interests, not only of the individual mystic, but also of the whole community of men.

BIBLIOGRAPHY

Allen, E. H.
Authorship of the Prick of Conscience, Boston, etc., 1910.

Amoni, L.
Fioretti di S. Francesco d'Assisi, Roma, 1889.

Angela of Foligno.
B. Angelae Fulginatis, vita et opuscula, Fulginiae, MDCCXIV.

Anselm, S.
Opera Omnia, Migne, P. L. T. CLVIII-CLIX.

Augustine, S.
Opera Omnia, Migne, P. L. T. XXXII-XLVII.

Bardenhewer, O.
Patrology, Freiburg im B., 1908.

Bernard, S.
Opera Omnia, Migne, P. L., T. CLXXXII-CLXXXV.

Berthaumier, A.
Histoire de S. Bonaventure, Paris, 1858.

Besse, L. de.
La Science de la Prière, Paris, 1924.

Bonaventura, S.
Opera Omnia, Quarrachi, 1882-1902.
do. (Another edition, containing spurious works), Romae, 1588-96.

Bossuet, J. B.
Instruction sur les États d'Oraison (Seconde Traité), Paris, 1897.

Bozitkovic, G.
S. Bonaventurae doctrina de gratia et libero arbitrio, Balneis Marianis, 1919.

Bremond, H.
Histoire Littéraire du sentiment religieux en France, Paris, 1916-21.

Butler, C.
Benedictine Monachism, London, 1919.
do. Western Mysticism, London, 1922.

Callaey, F.
Étude sur Ubertin de Casale, Louvain, 1911.

Carvahlo, L. de.
Saint Bonaventure, Le Docteur Franciscain, Paris, 1923.

Clop, E.
Saint Bonaventure, Paris, 1922.

Comper, F. M.
The Fire of Love or Melody of Love and the Mending of Life of Richard Rolle, London, 1914.

Coulton, G. G.
Mediaeval Studies (First Series), London, 1915.
do. Christ, St. Francis and to-day, Cambridge, 1919.

Cuthbert, F.
St. Francis of Assisi, London, 1921.
do. The Romanticism of St. Francis, London, 1915.

Deanesly, M.
The Incendium Amoris of Richard Rolle of Hampole, Manchester, 1915.

Delacroix, H.
Essai sur le mysticisme spéculatif en Allemgne au quatuorzième siècle. (Thèse) Paris, 1899.
do. Note sur Christianisme et Mysticisme, Paris, 1909.

Delaporte, P. A.
Étude sur l'Itineraire de l'âme à Dieu de de Saint Bonaventure, Paris, 1863.

Denifle, H.
Chartularium Universitatis Parisiensis, Parisiis, MDCCCLXXXIX.

Devine, A.
A Manual of Mystical Theology, London, 1903.

Dionysius the Areopatite.
Opera Omnia, Migne, P. G. T. III-IV.

Eriugena, J. Scotus.
Versio Op. S. Dionysii, Migne, P. L. T. CXXII.

Evangelista, P.
Sanctus Bonaventura Scholae Franciscanae magister praecellens, Paris, 1888.
Facin, D.
S. Bonaventura Doctor Seraphicus Discipulorum S. Augustini alter princeps, Venetiis, 1904.
Fanna, F.
Ratio novae collectionis operum omnium S. Bonaventurae etc. Taurini, 1874.
do. De Humanae Cognitionis Ratione. Anecdota quaedam Seraphici D. S. Bonaventurae et nonnullorum ipsius discipulorum, Quarrachi, 1883.
Felder, H.
Histoire des Études dans l'Ordre de Saint-François, Paris, 1908.
Ferrers-Howell, A. G.
S. Bernardino of Siena, London, 1903.
Fleming, W. K.
Mysticism in Christianity, London, 1913.
Fournier, P.
Études sur Joachim de Flora, Paris, 1909.
Francis of Assisi, S.
Opera Omnia, ed. in. Medii Aevi Bibliotheca Patristica, T. VI, Parisiis, 1880.
do. Opuscula S. Patris Francisci Assisiensis. Quarrachi, 1904. (See Robinson).
Gardner, E.
Joachim of Flora and the Everlasting Gospel, in Franciscan Essays (Extra Series), Aberdeen, 1912.
do. Dante and the Mystics, London, 1913.
Gaspare de Monte Santo.
Gesta e dottrina del serafico dottore S. Bonaventura, Macerata, 1793.
Gerson, J.
Opera Omnia, Parisiis, MDCVI.
Ghellinck, J. de.
Le Mouvement Théologique du XIIe siècle, Paris, 1914.
Gilson, E.
Études de Philosophie médiévale, Strasburg, 1921.
do. La Philosophie de Saint Bonaventure, Paris, 1924.
Gregory, S.
Opera Omnia, Migne, P. L., T. LXXV-LXXIX.
Haskins, C. H.
Studies in the History of Mediaeval Science, Cambridge (U. S. A.) 1924.
Hauréau, B.
Histoire de la Philosophie, Paris, 1880.
Herrmann, W.
The Communion of the Christian with God. (Trans. by R. W. Stewart), London, 1906.
Hilton, W.
See Underhill.
Horstman, C.
Richard Rolle of Hampole, London, 1895.
Hügel, Baron Von.
The mystical element of religion as studied in St. Catherine of Genoa and her friends (2nd Ed.), London, 1923.
do. Essays and addresses on the philosophy of religion, London, 1921.
Hugo of St. Victor.
Opera Omnia, Migne, P. L., T. CLXXV-CLXXVII.
Inge, W. R.
Christian Mysticism, London, 1899.
do. Studies of English Mystics, London, 1906.
James, W.
The Varieties of Religious Experience, London, 1902.
Jeiler, I.
S. Bonaventurae principia de concursu Dei generali ad actiones causarum secundarum etc. Quarrachi, 1897.
John of the Cross, S.
The Ascent of Mount Carmel (trans. by D. Lewis), London, 1906.
do. A Spiritual Canticle of the Soul (trans. by D. Lewis), London, 1909.
Joly, H.
The Psychology of the Saints, London, 1898.
Jones, R. M.
Studies in Mystical Religion, London, 1909.

Jörgensen, J.
Saint Francis of Assisi (trans. from the Danish, by T. O'Conor Sloane), London, 1912.

Jourdain, C.
La Philosophie de Saint Thomas d'Aquin, Paris, 1858.
do. Recherches sur les anciennes traductions latines d'Aristote, Paris, 1843.

Keble, J.
On the Mysticism of the early Fathers of the Church, Oxford, 1868.

Lecoy de la Marche, A.
La chaire Française au moyen âge, Paris, 1868.

Lemmens, L.
S. Bonaventura, Milano, 1921.

Love, N.
See Powell.

Mandonnet, P.
Siger de Brabant et l'Averroisme Latin au XIIIe siècle, Fribourg, 1899.

Maria d'Agreda.
La mistica ciudad de Dios, Madrid, 1670.

Margerie, A. de.
Essai sur la philosophie de Saint Bonaventure, Paris, 1855.

Martigné P. de.
La scolastique et les traditions Franciscains, Paris, 1888.

McNabb, V.
The Mysticism of St. Thomas Aquinas, Oxford, 1924.

Mignon, A.
Les origines de la scolastique et Hugues de St.-Victor, Paris, 1895.

Montmorency, J. de.
Thomas a Kempis, his age and book (2nd ed.), London, 1907.

Naval, F.
Theologiae Asceticae et Mysticae Cursus, Romae, 1920.

Oliger, P. L.
Le Meditationes Vitae Christi del Pseudo-Bonaventura, Arezzo, 1922.

Origen,
Opera Omnia, Migne, P. G., T. XI-XVII.

Ozanam, A. F.
Les poëtes franciscains en Italie au XIIIe scècle, Paris, 1882.

Palhoriès, G.
Saint Bonaventure, Paris, 1913.

Picavet, F.
La Place de Roger Bacon parmi les Philosophes du XIIIe siècle, in Roger Bacon Essays (ed. by A. G. Little), Oxford, 1914.

Poulain, A.
The Graces of Interior Prayer (authorized English trans.), London, 1921.

Pourrat, P.
La Spiritualité Chrétienne, Paris, 1921.

Probst, A.
Caractère et origine des idées du B. R. Lulle, Toulouse, 1912.

Powell, L. F.
The Mirrour of the Blessed Lyf of Jesus Christ, Oxford, MCVII.

Richard of St. Victor.
Opera Omnia, Migne, P. L., T. CXCVI.

Richard, J.
Étude sur le mysticisme spéculatif de Saint Bonaventure, Heidleburg, 1869.

Robinson, P.
The writings of St. Francis of Assisi, Philadelphia, 1906.

Rolle, R.
See Comper, Deanesly and Horstman.

Rousselot, P.
Pour l'Histoire du Problème de l'amour au Moyen Âge, Münster, 1908.

Royce, J.
The World and the Individual, New York, 1900.

Sabatier, P.
Vie de S. François d'Assise, Paris, 1894.
do. Speculum Perfectionis seu S. Francisci Assisiensis Legenda Antiquissima auctore F. Leone, Paris, 1898.

Salimbene.
Cronica F. Salimbene de Adam, Ordinis Minorum,
Catalogus Generalium Ministrorum Ord. F. Min., ed. in
Monumenta Germaniae Historica, T. xxxii, Hannoverae et Leipsiae, MDCCCCV-MDCCCCXIII.

Saudreau, L'Abbé.
La Vie d'union à Dieu, etc., Paris, 1921.

Sbaralea, J. H.
Supplementum et Castigatio ad Scriptores trium Ordinum S. Francisci a Waddingo aliisve descriptos, Romae, MDCCCVI.

Scotus, J. Duns.
Opera Omnia, Parisiis, apud Vivès, MDCCCXCIV.

Sharpe, A. B.
Mysticism, its true nature and value, London, 1910.

Storr, R.
Concordance de Imitatione Christi, Oxford, 1910.

Suso, B. H.
Autobiography (trans. by T. F. Knox), London, 1865.

Symphorien, P.
L'Influence spirituelle de S. Bonaventure et l'imitation de Jésus-Christ de Thomas à Kempis, Paris, 1923.

Taylor, H.
The Mediaeval Mind, London, 1914.

Tempesti.
Mistica teologia secondo lo spirito e le sentenze di S. Bonaventura, Venezia, 1748.

Teresa, S.
Interior Castle (Stanbrook ed. and trans.), 1906.
do. Autobiography (trans. by D. Lewis), London, 1904.

Theologia Germanica.
See Winkworth.

Thomas Aquinas, S.
Opera Omnia, Leonine Edition, Romae, 1882.—(This Edition used where possible).
do. De Veritate (Parma Edition), MDCCCLIX.
do. In omnes Divi Pauli Epistolas Expositio, Venetiis, 1541.

Thomas of Vallgonera.
Mysticae Theologiae D. Thomae, Turin, 1890.

Thorold, A.
An Essay in aid of the better appreciation of Catholic Mysticism. London, 1900.

Tyrrell, G.
The Faith of the Millions (First Series), London, 1901.

Ubertino da Casale.
Arbor Vitae, etc., Venetiis, 1485.

Underhill, E.
Mysticism, London, 1911.
do. The Scale of Perfection by W. Hilton, London, 1923.

Vaughan, R. A.
Hours with the Mystics (2nd Edit.), London, 1860.

Vansteenberghe, E.
Autour de la docte ignorance. Une controverse sur la Théologie Mystique au XVe siècle, Münster, 1915.

Wadding, L.
Annales Minorum, Romae MDCCXXXI.

Watkin, E.
The Philosophy of Mysticism, London, 1920.

Webb, C. C. J.
The Devotions of St. Anselm, London, 1903.

Winkworth, S.
The Theologia Germanica (trans. from the German), London, 1874.

For articles on St. Bonaventure, Mysticism, Contemplation, etc., etc., and for editions of minor mediaeval MSS., I am also indebted to the following:—

Acta Ordinis Minorum, Romae, 1890.
Analecta Bollandiana, Bruxellis, 1903 etc.
Analecta Franciscana, Quarrachi, 1885 etc.
Archiv für Litteratur-und Kirchengeschichte des Mittelalters, Berlin, 1895, etc.

Archivum Franciscanum Historicum, Quarrachi, 1922 etc.
Catholic Encyclopedia, New York, 1907 etc.
Dictionnaire de Théologie Catholique (Vacant, Paris, 1905 etc.
Dublin Review, London, 1914 etc
Encyclopedia of Religion and Ethics (Hastings), Edinburgh, 1910.
Études Carmélitaines, Paris, 1920.
Études Religieuses, Historiques et Littéraires, Paris, 1913.
Franziskanische Studien, Münster, 1921.
Récherches de Science Religieuse, Paris, 1914.
Revue d'Histoire Franciscaine, Paris, 1924.
Revue néo-scolastique, Louvain, 1903 etc.

To the above must be added the Report of the Eighth Annual Meeting of the Franciscan Educational Conference, Washington, D. C., 1926, which appeared after this work was completed.